The Outrage Industry

STUDIES IN POSTWAR AMERICAN POLITICAL DEVELOPMENT

The Delegated Welfare State: Medicare, Markets, and the Governance of Social Policy
Kimberly J. Morgan and Andrea Louise Campbell

Rule and Ruin: The Downfall of Moderation and the Destruction of the Republican Party, From Eisenhower to the Tea Party
Geoffrey Kabaservice

Engines of Change: Party Factions in American Politics, 1868–2010
Daniel DiSalvo

Follow the Money: How Foundation Dollars Change Public School Politics
Sarah Reckhow

The Allure of Order: High Hopes, Dashed Expectations, and the Troubled Quest to Remake American Schooling
Jal Mehta

Rich People's Movements: Grassroots Campaigns to Untax the One Percent
Isaac William Martin

The Outrage Industry: Political Opinion Media and the New Incivility
Jeffrey M. Berry and Sarah Sobieraj

The Outrage Industry

*Political Opinion Media
and the New Incivility*

Jeffrey M. Berry
and
Sarah Sobieraj

OXFORD
UNIVERSITY PRESS

OXFORD
UNIVERSITY PRESS

Oxford University Press is a department of the University of Oxford.
It furthers the University's objective of excellence in research, scholarship,
and education by publishing worldwide.

Oxford   New York
Auckland   Cape Town   Dar es Salaam   Hong Kong   Karachi
Kuala Lumpur   Madrid   Melbourne   Mexico City   Nairobi
New Delhi   Shanghai   Taipei   Toronto

With offices in
Argentina   Austria   Brazil   Chile   Czech Republic   France   Greece
Guatemala   Hungary   Italy   Japan   Poland   Portugal   Singapore
South Korea   Switzerland   Thailand   Turkey   Ukraine   Vietnam

Oxford is a registered trade mark of Oxford University Press
in the UK and certain other countries.

Published in the United States of America by
Oxford University Press
198 Madison Avenue, New York, NY 10016

© Oxford University Press 2014

First issued as an Oxford University Press paperback, 2016

CIP data is on file at the Library of Congress

ISBN: 978-0-19-992897-2 (hardcover); 978-0-19-049846-7 (paperback)

Jeff dedicates this book to Willa and Eli

Sarah dedicates this book to her parents,
who taught her first about politics and opinions

CONTENTS

ACKNOWLEDGMENTS

Since its inception, this book has benefited from the support of many. We would not have thought to collaborate without the encouragement of our colleague Vickie Sullivan and the largesse provided by Leonard Bernstein and Jane Holmes Bernstein through the Bernstein Faculty Fellows program at Tufts. This fellowship, designed to promote interdisciplinary collaboration between junior and senior faculty, brought us together to discuss our overlapping interests and provided the financial support and course release time we needed to launch our research. We hope they recognize how deeply we appreciate their generosity.

Tufts' Faculty Research Awards program, the Summer Scholars Program, the Faculty Fellows Program at Tisch College, and the Provost's Office have also supported the project, primarily by allowing us to bring on outstanding undergraduate research assistants. Some of these young scholars—Miriam Umaña, Kevin Lownds, Suzanne Schlossberg, and Dan Rosenblum—were deeply involved in the design and data collection portions of the research. Their sharp eyes and insightful questions made our work stronger and undoubtedly more pleasant. The work of summer scholar Amy Connors contributed significantly to Chapter 5, of which she is a third author. We also appreciate having had an opportunity to work briefly with Kathryn Bond, Thomas Calahan, Yuanzhi Gao, Alex Leipziger, and Griffin Pepper. And we are grateful that the pilot interviews conducted by Amy Connors, Sara DeForest, Matt McGrath, Brittany Robbins, and Charlotte Steinway provided us with the groundwork and inspiration to conduct many more.

A village of discipline-spanning colleagues proved enormously valuable in helping us think through our ideas as the project evolved. Very early, Ron Shaiko invited us to speak at the Rockefeller Center's Going to Extremes Conference at Dartmouth College; we are grateful to him for this invitation and to Deborah Jordan Brooks and Robert Boatright for their feedback while we were there. We also benefited from sharing pieces of this work at Colby College, the University of North Carolina at Chapel Hill, Johns Hopkins University, and our professional conferences. Thank you to Frank Baumgartner,

Sandy Maisel, Michael MacKuen, Steven Teles, and Bill Roy for creating those spaces and making the experiences rewarding. Parts of this work have appeared in print elsewhere. A portion of Chapter 2 appeared in *Political Communication*, an earlier version of Chapter 5 appeared in *Poetics*, and a small segment of Chapter 3 appeared in *PS: Political Science & Politics*. We are grateful to the anonymous reviewers and editors who shared their insights and strengthened those pieces, and the project as a whole. Thank you also to those who offered advice or feedback in other contexts, including John Conklin, E. J. Dionne, Tina Fetner, Jessica Fields, Ron Jacobs, Paul Joseph, David Kimball, Heather Laube, Peter Levine, Frinde Maher, Helen Marrow, Natalie Masuoka, Susan Ostrander, Kent Portney, Anna Sandoval, Debbie Schildkraut, Richard Skinner, and Kristen Wallingford. We also wish to thank Chris Uggen for allowing us to use his figure in Chapter 3.

Not all ideas prove fruitful, but we are grateful to have had an opportunity to explore them. We thank Melanie Hulbert, Vincent Munoz, Brian Shelly, and Earl Smith for working with us to pilot test a multi-campus experiment that we ultimately decided to leave by the wayside. Their gracious willingness to work with us on that endeavor is something we will not soon forget.

A special thanks to Rob Davis, Heath Podvesker, and Len Berry who (respectively) tutored us in the fields of cable television, advertising, and marketing. Not only did they spend a great deal of time with us but they were also kind enough to provide introductions to leading figures in their fields who, in turn, sat for interviews. We also appreciate the time and energy of the many fans, tea party leaders, industry experts, and advocacy group leaders who shared their experiences, strategies, affinities, and aversions with us. Their personal accounts provided the richest data we were able to obtain.

We wish also to thank series editor, Steven Teles, for his interest and support, and David McBride at Oxford University Press for shepherding the manuscript into print.

Last, we thank our wonderful families and friends for letting us share our tales from the field and for reminding us that not all opinions are outrageous.

The Outrage Industry

CHAPTER 1

✣

Outrage

Sandra Fluke's statement on behalf of Georgetown Law Students for Reproductive Justice during a House Democratic Steering and Policy Committee in February 2012 placed her in the center of a firestorm. Her public advocacy for insurance coverage of contraceptives resulted in an extended series of personal attacks from radio personality Rush Limbaugh. Limbaugh's three-day tirade began on February 29, when he offered demeaning characterizations of Fluke, including that she "wants to be paid to have sex. She's having so much sex she can't afford the contraception. She wants you and me and the taxpayers to pay her to have sex. What does that make us? We're the pimps." Although this suggests that Fluke proposed that tax revenues be used to pay for contraceptives, her actual position was that contraception should be covered by the student-funded health insurance in place, which was not subsidized by the (Catholic) university or the government.[1]

The next day Limbaugh was even more aggressive, revisiting his prostitution analogy and adding new fuel to the fire remarking, "Ms. Fluke, have you ever heard of *not* having sex? Have you ever heard of not having sex so *often*?" Over the course of the broadcast he said that Fluke was having so much sex that it was "amazing" that she could still walk, questioned her morality, suggested that her life had no purpose, commented that she had no self-control or personal responsibility, and said he would have stayed away from someone like her when he was in school because they might carry sexually transmitted diseases. He also pretended to *be* Fluke, using a crybaby voice to suggest she was an entitled whiner. Perhaps most crudely, he suggested, "So, Ms. Fluke and the rest of you feminazis, here's the deal: If we are going to pay for your contraceptives, and thus pay for you to have sex, we want something for it. And I'll tell you what it is. We want you to post the videos online so we can all watch...if we're going to have a part in this, then we want something in return, Ms. Fluke, and that would be the videos of all this sex posted online so we can see what we are getting for our money." On the March 2 show, Limbaugh repeated variations on the statement that she was having "so much sex that she can't afford it" at roughly 10 separate points in the broadcast, erroneously indicating more than once that this information came from Fluke's testimony in front of the committee, although Fluke did not comment on her sex life in her statement.[2]

Limbaugh's commentary about Fluke produced the most dramatic outcry against the show in its 25-year history.[3] Criticism came from all quarters: Liberal media watchdog group Media Matters organized a social media campaign lobbying Limbaugh advertisers to drop his program. Advocacy groups, particularly women's rights organizations, also took action. The National Organization for Women called for Clear Channel Communications, the corporate parent of the *Rush Limbaugh Show*, to drop the program. Seventy-five Democratic members of Congress signed a letter to House Speaker John Boehner urging him to condemn Limbaugh's behavior, and President Barack Obama called Fluke to express his personal support. Republican leaders who were asked to comment chose their remarks gingerly; presidential candidate Mitt Romney said merely, "it's not the language I would have used."

Under pressure from advertisers who were dropping the show, Limbaugh made a half-hearted apology to Fluke on his March 6 broadcast, expressing regret over his use of "those two words to describe her" (presumably slut and prostitute), but he also continued to offer criticism of Fluke and of the contraception policy she endorsed. The apology did not stem the tide; in a little more than a week Limbaugh lost more than 50 advertisers. He publicly claimed the loss was not hurting business, "That's like losing a couple of french fries in the container when it's delivered to you in the drive thru. You don't even notice it."[4] The long-term impact on Limbaugh's advertising revenue remains to be seen (see Chapter 4), but it is clear that the Fluke controversy amounted to free publicity for the program and further solidified his standing with his conservative audience.

Liberal organizations and political opinion outlets used Limbaugh's remarks to stoke the anger of their constituents, churning up ratings, traffic, dollars, and votes. MoveOn and Democratic congressional committees used the vitriol as a fundraising tool. Some liberal advocacy groups also used Limbaugh's diatribe to their advantage. UltraViolet, for example, created a political advertisement including footage of Limbaugh to criticize Mitt Romney in an effort to sway the 2012 presidential election. And riding high on moral indignation and the opportunity to dress down one of their audience's favorite villains, the liberal cable news analysis programs lavished airtime on Limbaugh's remarks and the subsequent boycott efforts.[5] Among them was television and radio host Ed Schultz, who interviewed Fluke on his show and expressed dismay at the sexist personal attacks, something he must have been more comfortable with in 2008 when he suggested that vice-presidential candidate Sarah Palin was a "bimbo" and in 2011 when he called conservative radio host Laura Ingraham a "slut."

Given the magnitude of the response to Limbaugh's remarks, an unfamiliar outsider might assume his behavior to be highly out of the ordinary. In fact, what is perplexing is that the attacks on Fluke struck so many as shocking. This is, after all, the same Rush Limbaugh who coined the term "feminazi," called Hillary Clinton a bitch, Chelsea Clinton a dog, and Nancy Pelosi a "ditz"—he who had also suggested that Anita Hill had probably had "plenty of spankings." The is the same Limbaugh who regularly refers to the National Organization for Women as "NAGS," and more recently responded to the multiple allegations of sexual harassment against Herman Cain by suggesting: "You women, why don't you just make it official, put on some burqas, and I'll guaran-damn-tee you, nobody'll touch you. You put on a burqa, and everybody'll leave you alone."[6]

Rush Limbaugh's remarks were outrageous, but such behavior is de rigueur in a political media genre where being offensive (and reliably indignant when offended) is the foundation of most content. Popular conservative radio host Michael Savage has no qualms yelling "take your religion and shove it up your behind" at Muslims on his national broadcast. And liberal radio host Mike Malloy seemed to take great enjoyment in making a mock phone call to Satan to check on conservative blogger and commentator Andrew Breibart, shortly after he passed away.[7] In one of his many ludicrous statements, conservative Glenn Beck told viewers on Fox's morning show that FEMA could very well be building concentration camps for those opposed to the policies of the Obama administration.[8]

Controversial content like this has always existed in small pockets of the media landscape, but in the last twenty-five years this form of commentary has come into its own, as a new genre of political opinion media that we term *outrage*. The genre has several distinctive attributes but is most easily recognizable by the rhetoric that defines it, with its hallmark venom, vilification of opponents, and hyperbolic reinterpretations of current events. With this book, we undertake a much-needed examination of this overlooked development in the political media landscape.

We begin descriptively, identifying the attributes of the genre and documenting its prevalence, showing the ways outrage traverses media platforms and political ideologies. We argue that outrage-based political content cannot be explained by increased political polarization in the United States but rather requires an understanding of the structural changes in the media landscape—primarily regulatory and technological—that have rendered such content newly profitable. This profitability has spurred imitation and unprecedented growth.

The visibility of the genre has been further bolstered by the synergistic relationship between political parties, candidates, social movements, and advocacy groups on the one hand and outrage platforms such as political talk radio, cable news analysis programs, and political blogs on the other. We find that many advocacy groups, social movements, and political operatives draw on the themes and narratives offered by outrage personalities to convince potential supporters to rally behind their cause, party, or candidate. We look, in particular, at how the Outrage Industry shaped the development of the Tea Party, serving as a vital communicative link among disparate independent Tea Party chapters and contributing to the success of their insurgency during the 2010 Republican congressional primaries.

Outrage discourse and programming may be effective at increasing advertising revenues and political support, but our research suggests that the mainstreaming of outrage in American political culture undermines some practices vital to healthy democratic life. Specifically, we show that outrage tactics such as ideological selectivity, vilification of opponents, and fear mongering make talking politics beyond our most intimate circles extraordinarily difficult, complicating our ability to have meaningful discussions about politics in our communities. We also see outrageous voices wielding disproportionate influence in elections, independently vetting candidates, anointing or tarring the contestants, particularly during primaries. This has been most evident on the right, where outrage media are more abundant and mature. Finally, we believe outrage to be increasingly divisive in the world of congressional policymaking, as it works to brand collaboration, open-mindedness, and compromise as weak. This stigmatization of cooperation has particular gravity because public servants are well aware that key votes will be closely monitored by outrage venues and heralded as tests of ideological purity.

OUTRAGE AS A GENRE

We use the term "outrage" to refer to the genre as well as the form of discourse that defines it. While political opinion outlets within the genre are recognizable by a distinct clustering of several attributes, they are recognizable primarily by a hallmark discursive style. Outrage discourse involves efforts to provoke emotional responses (e.g., anger, fear, moral indignation) from the audience through the use of overgeneralizations, sensationalism, misleading or patently inaccurate information, ad hominem attacks, and belittling ridicule of opponents.[9] Outrage sidesteps the messy nuances of complex political issues in favor of melodrama, misrepresentative exaggeration, mockery, and hyperbolic forecasts of impending doom. Outrage talk is not rational-critical discourse in the Habermasian sense, nor is it accurately characterized as deliberation (although users may certainly draw upon or challenge perspectives and information from outrage media during their own political deliberation); instead it takes the form of verbal competition, political theater with a scorecard. What distinguishes this type of discourse is not that it seeks to evoke emotion in the political arena. On the contrary, emotional speech has an important place in political life, and many emotional appeals are not outrageous. What makes outrage distinctive are the tactics used in an effort to provoke the emotion.

Although outrage has some commonality with its conceptual sibling, "incivility," the terms are not interchangeable. Diana Mutz and Byron Reeves use incivility to denote "gratuitous asides that [suggest] a lack of respect and/or frustration with the opposition."[10] In a sense, outrage is incivility writ large. It is by definition uncivil but not all incivility is outrage. Rude behavior such as eye-rolling, sighing, and the like are not outrageous because they do not incorporate the elements of malfeasant inaccuracy and intent to diminish that characterize outrage. In Chapter 2 we delve much more deeply into outrage, identifying thirteen of its most common manifestations.

In addition to its unique discursive style, the genre also has other recognizable attributes. First, it is generally *personality centered*, with a given program, column, or blog defined by a dominant charismatic voice. We can think of liberal columnist Maureen Dowd, conservative television host Bill O'Reilly, conservative blogger Michelle Malkin, or liberal radio and television host Ed Schultz as examples of these distinctive personalities. While many of these programs and blogs include other voices such as those of guests, callers, and commenters, these voices take a backseat to the host, whose charm, emotional sensibilities, and worldview define the content. Unlike a conventional news program, in which the news itself is central and anchors are often replaced, there would be no *Rachel Maddow Show* without Rachel Maddow.

The genre is also recognizably *reactive*. Its point of entry into the political world is through response. The episodes, blog posts, and columns rarely introduce breaking news or political information. Instead they reinterpret, reframe, and unpack news from the headlines, political speeches, or claims made by other outrage hosts. This reactivity is closely linked to another attribute, *ideological selectivity*. Like news programs, producers in the realm of opinion are not expected to address all major political developments but can instead choose to explore what they see as most compelling. However, while conventional commentary might focus on what issues of the day seem most pressing, of particular interest to their audience, or in greatest need of in-depth examination, outrage commentary filters content selections through the lens of ideological coherence and superiority. The preferred focus is stories in which hosts can position themselves or their political compatriots in the role of the hero or can taint enemies, opponents, or policies they dislike as dangerous, inept, or immoral. This often means the emerging content provides additional space for the discussion of issues that concern their audiences. However, because of the approach used in outrage venues, the ensuing attention offers something more akin to the captivating distortions of a funhouse mirror than to the discriminating insights of a microscope. In this arena, issues of import to fans are used for maximum emotional impact, such that tiny niche issues are reshaped into scandals and significant developments that are less ideologically resonant are dismissed as trivial or ignored.

Outrage is also *engaging*. It is easy see why audiences might find their favorite columnists, bloggers, or hosts more entertaining than a conventional commentator. In outrage there is performance. There are jokes. There is drama. There is conflict. There is fervor. There is even comfort, as audiences find their worldviews honored. Adding to this level of engagement is the sense of inclusion offered to those in the viewing, listening, and reading community. As we show in our analysis of talk radio and cable news analysis fans in Chapter 5, hosts help fans feel that they are connected to like-minded others and sometimes even create tangible linkages through blogs, meet-up groups, and social media. In spite of the negative tenor of much of the content, fans feel refreshed by the programs. In many ways, outrage venues serve as political churches. The faithful attend, hear their values rearticulated in compelling ways, and leave feeling validated and virtuous for having participated.

For those seeking to understand the genre, recognizing the various writers and speakers as part of a densely connected web is vital, as outrage is marked by *internal intertextuality*, with personalities from outrage venues constantly referring to one another. This is true for those on the same side of the ideological rift, but it is also difficult to imagine progressive and conservative outrage media being separated, as each plays an instrumental role in creating fodder for the other. Think back to Rush Limbaugh and Sandra Fluke, and consider the ways in which Limbaugh himself became the subject of liberal blogs such as *Daily Kos* and liberal television programs such as the *Ed Schultz Show*. The feedback loop continued to cycle as Limbaugh, in turn, criticized progressive outlets for exaggerating the controversy and using it for political ends.

Finally, we note that although outrage trades in overly simplified stories that paint conservatives and progressives as fundamentally different, the way conservative and progressive commentators *use* outrage unites them. The same rhetorical techniques are deployed by those on both sides of the political divide. Consider practices such as using ideologically extremizing language (e.g., describing someone as "far-right wing" or "far-left wing"), "proving" an opponent is a hypocrite (often with decontextualized quotes offered as evidence), presenting their version of current affairs as the "real story" and other accounts as biased. Taken together, we find remarkable *mirroring* between conservatives and progressives. There are scripts that could easily be rewritten for the other side by simply replacing the nouns. Think, for example, of the reverse characterizations of Tea Party and Occupy activists; in outrage, dissent is brave and admirable (and, analogously, misguided and dangerous) only some of the time.

The attributes of the genre we have just described are best illuminated by example. On September 24, 2011, one week into the Occupy Wall Street protests, amateur videos captured Deputy Inspector Anthony Bologna of the New York Police Department (NYPD) pepper spraying a group of activists after a march against economic inequality. Two of the protesters, 24-year-old Kaylee Dedrick and 25-year-old Chelsea Elliott, were hit at close range. In the video, the use of the spray appears unprovoked: the protesters are shown standing calmly on the sidewalk, behind an orange mesh police fence, at which point Bologna approaches, takes out the canister, and sprays them in their faces. The video next shows both women crumpled on the ground, screaming and crying in apparent anguish, with Dedrick gesturing toward her eyes.

The footage caught the attention of the mainstream news. Joseph Goldstein's September 26 piece in the *New York Times* described it as follows:

> protesters were corralled by police officers who put up orange mesh netting; the police forcibly arrested some participants; and a deputy inspector used pepper spray on four women who were on the sidewalk, behind the orange netting.... The events of Saturday are certain to be examined, especially

since so many protesters were recording the events with cameras; videos of
the pepper spray episode, for example, offered views from several angles.[11]

Goldstein's full story was insightful, framing the police response as related
to both anti-terrorism training and police fears about Seattle-esque lack of
control over crowds of protesters, implicitly suggesting that these factors
may have made police overly reactionary. It offered a fairly detailed account
(roughly 1,000 words), including statements from the chief spokesman of
the NYPD, the chair of the city council public safety committee, a representative from the police union, an officer who had been in touch with Bologna,
and the associate legal director of the American Civil Liberties Union
(ACLU). A response from an affected protester or other activist from
Occupy Wall Street was notably absent. The article indicated there was disagreement over whether the use of force was appropriate, addressed other
protesters' complaints against police, and discussed the role of permitting
in marches.

MSNBC's *The Last Word with Lawrence O'Donnell* offered a different sort
of analysis. O'Donnell devoted nine minutes of airtime to a dramatic monologue on police brutality. He aired four videos of alleged acts of brutality
against Occupy protesters, including the Bologna pepper spray incident.
Differentiating himself from the sedate neutrality of evening news anchors,
O'Donnell grimaced with moral indignation as he offered scathing indictments using the video footage (in slow motion, at one point) as a jumping-off
point for a biting denunciation of law enforcement. His outrage is fully justified if one accepts the premises upon which it is predicated: first, that
these examples of police misconduct are rules rather than exceptions; second, that law enforcement, as an institution, has no interest in serving the
public but rather in perpetrating crimes; and third, that there is methodical
and effective collusion at work ensuring that these crimes go unpunished.

Police brutality is an issue of grave concern, particularly in poor communities of color, but O'Donnell's assertions are hyperbolic and distorting.
Unlike the journalistic account, O'Donnell includes no voices other than
his own. His evidence includes his own insistence that, "As usual, the police
department is defending its troublemakers as having done absolutely
nothing wrong. The department *insists* that the pepper spray was used
appropriately" [emphasis in the original], a statement that mischaracter-
izes the police position. And we find two different forms of outrage
discourse, misrepresentative exaggeration and conspiracy theory, in his
response to the suggestion of an investigation, when he argues that such
efforts are "always a sham designed from the start to the finish to defend
the police conduct."[12]

Further, it was not enough to suggest that the officer or the police department had behaved abusively. O'Donnell framed the issue more grandly. He appears livid as he explains, "I haven't bothered to mention where this took place or what police department was involved because this is an American police work that we're watching.... Every day in America, police are too tough. Every day in America, police cross the line and abuse citizens." Then, to drive his point home, he links Bologna's use of pepper spray to the most notorious case of police brutality of our time, the Rodney King beating. He doesn't simply allude to the case, he replays the original, excruciating video. In it, police officers viciously beat King—assailing him over 50 times with violent baton blows and kicking him—while other officers watch, some offering encouragement. "There's a Rodney King every day in this country," says O'Donnell. Then, with the King beating and subsequent acquittals fresh in our minds he offers, "None of the officers who crossed the line this weekend will be disciplined in any way." The suggestion, of course, is that somehow—defying reason—these two acts of force are equivalent, and that injustice is inevitable.[13]

This is outrage: from the way O'Donnell works to transform the upsetting, yet uninvestigated actions of one police officer into unassailable evidence of widespread police abuse in America that is insidiously covered up as a matter of course (supported by misrepresentative information about the police response), to the sensationalistic way he uses the stomach-turning video of the Rodney King beating to remind the audience of one of the ugliest incidents in law enforcement history, to the controlled rage he exhibits in his delivery. This embodied rage is part of the personality-centered nature of the genre; it is O'Donnell's emotional response that fills the screen as opposed to anger from the affected protesters, other members of the Occupy movement, or bystanders.

In comparing the Lawrence O'Donnell segment to the *New York Times* story, we can see that outrage can be engaging. Viewers are able to see the pepper spray video firsthand and listen to O'Donnell's impassioned commentary, and they have their frustration over the pepper-sprayed protesters validated as it is stoked and blessed with moral authority through the narrative linkages made between this act and larger social problems such as social inequality, corruption, and racial profiling.[14]

The story ricocheted across cable news analysis shows, blogs, talk radio, and social media—at least in the progressive circuit, where it was featured on television shows such as *Countdown with Keith Olbermann* and the *Rachel Maddow Show*, discussed by radio hosts like Thom Hartmann, and featured prominently on blogs such as *Daily Kos* and the *Huffington Post*. Given the genre's tendency toward ideological selectivity, the popularity of the story in these venues is something we would expect since liberal protesters were the ones whose rights were violated. Conservative outlets largely ignored the story.

WHAT'S NEW ABOUT THE NEW INCIVILITY?

Many will rightly note that American political media have always had outrageous elements. Whether we think of yellow journalism in the 1800s, firebrand Father Coughlin on the radio in the 1930s, or belligerent radio and television host Joe Pyne in the 1950s and 1960s, we can see that Glenn Beck and Chris Matthews are not particularly groundbreaking. Yet, while this kind of speech has deep roots in American media, modern incivility is, in many ways, a new ball game. Outrage today is found in a far greater number of venues, circulates quickly, has vast audiences, and often gathers momentum from the attention of conventional news organizations and the synergistic coordination between media organizations, pundits, bloggers, and politicos.

More than anything else, the sheer volume of outrage media today sets it apart from political media of days gone by, giving it density. Even at our most divisive historical junctures, the acrimonious debates and accusations that emerged had few venues beyond the mainstream press. There has always been a small alternative press, but nontraditional venues for dissent were but a modest sliver of all media and had relatively small distribution. By the 1960s, the broadcast networks were at their peak and together with mainstream newspapers and magazines, they dominated the market for political news and commentary. Research suggests that political commentary is increasingly replacing conventional news and much of this commentary is outrage-based.[15] As newspaper readership and nightly national news viewing on networks have declined, outrage news analysis audiences have simultaneously expanded, and the number of outrage venues has grown. The rate of increase in the number of outrage venues is evident in radio where there are 3,795 all-talk or all-news stations in the United States, more than triple the number in existence just 15 years ago.[16] Radio is not an isolated case; the emergence of cable and ultimately satellite television increased the array of television stations exponentially, to be topped perhaps only by the birth and proliferation of blogs in terms of the number of new platforms for outrage content.[17] Of all the news and commentary Americans seek out over the course of a day or week or month, the Project for Excellence in Journalism finds that a significant percentage comes from these alternatives to network news and newspapers, making for a political media environment markedly different from that of just a generation ago.[18]

Another important attribute of the new incivility is its immense popularity. As much as some people might like to think that outrage personalities are fringe figures whose distortions and conspiracy theories are ignored or irrelevant, they have found an audience. Talk radio is the second most popular radio format in the nation, falling only slightly behind the number one format: country music.[19] Data from radio research firm Arbitron indicate that Rush Limbaugh and Sean Hannity draw 15 and 14 million weekly listeners to their respective radio shows.[20] Meanwhile, on television, the *O'Reilly Factor* has over 3 million nightly viewers, not including those tuned in for the repeat showing that airs at 11:00 PM. Although liberal hosts attract a far smaller audience (a difference explained in part by liberals' greater trust in traditional journalism),[21] the *Rachel Maddow Show* still draws nearly 1 million viewers a night, and programs such as *Hardball with Chris Matthews* and *The Last Word with Lawrence O'Donnell* draw close to three quarters of a million viewers according to the Nielsen ratings. As a point of comparison, the offerings on Fox and MSNBC are both routinely rated higher than their more moderate competition on CNN. Glenn Beck's ratings on Fox dropped from their peak of nearly 3 million viewers between the summer of 2009 and the winter of 2010 to 2 million viewers when the termination of his nightly show was announced in 2011, but even with these "low" ratings, he was still trouncing his competitors; at the time he was cancelled Beck was still regularly tripling to quadrupling the viewership of the *Situation Room* with Wolf Blitzer which aired in the same time slot on CNN.[22]

The aggregate audience for outrage media is immense. Our estimate for talk radio, using Arbitron data for the top 12 hosts and extrapolating to the larger talk radio world, roughly 35 million listeners daily. Nielsen data suggest the nightly outrage programs on cable attract close to 10 million viewers. Utilizing figures from Quantcast for the 20 top political blogs and, again, extrapolating to the broader blogosphere, we estimate 2 million people log on to at least one outrage-based political blog on a daily basis. Taken together, this suggests an audience of up to 47 million people daily.[23] The audience is composed largely of those who are most likely to vote, most likely to donate to political causes, and most likely to be politically active in many other ways. For example, 78 percent of listeners to talk radio voted in the 2010 election as compared to 41 percent of the eligible electorate.[24] In short, the outrage audience is quite large, politically active, and valuable to both advertisers and politicos.

Another noteworthy difference between outrage today and incivility of the past is the speed at which it circulates. The voracious appetite of the 24-hour news cycle with blogs and programs in constant need of content, the work of news aggregators such as the *Drudge Report* that curate thematic news stories and blog posts, and the efficiencies of digital technology have given outrage great velocity. In moments past when things got ugly—the partisan press of the early 1800s comes to mind—publication and circulation was much slower. The rate of diffusion has increased over time, but accelerated exponentially in the last 30 years. Consider this comparison. In 2005 President George W. Bush nominated his White House Counsel Harriet Miers for a position on the Supreme Court. On October 3 he made the announcement at 8:00 AM and by 9:00 AM Laura Ingraham was on the air across her 340 radio outlets excoriating Miers. A few minutes after that William Kristol, editor of the *Weekly Standard*, was on Fox Cable att-acking the choice. The conservative onslaught continued throughout the day on cable, talk radio, and the Web. A little more than three weeks later Miers withdrew as conservative opposition was simply too great for her to go forward.[25]

Contrast this with two of President Nixon's nominees to the Supreme Court, Clement Haynsworth and G. Harrold Carswell, who were rejected in the wake of bitter opposition from civil rights groups and other liberal lobbies. Although all three Supreme Court nominations were sidelined by withering ideological opposition, the differences are profound. There was a full debate in the Senate over Haynsworth and Carswell and both went through hearings before their fate was ultimately determined by a floor vote. The blitzkrieg against Miers was so fast and so broad that her weak-nesses metastasized before any hearings could be held. The Bush White House, hardly an inept political operation, was outmatched. Ingraham said it best: "Without alternative media, the [White House] talking points on Miers would have carried the day."[26] And this transpired before the mainstreaming of social media that has occurred since 2005, which has further heightened the rate at which information travels.

Although the columnists, analysts, and writers in conventional news organizations often scoff at the celebrity hosts of the genre, outrage outlets today are closely monitored by mainstream news organizations and often receive significant attention from them. Occasionally, outrage venues bring issues to the fore that had been overlooked or under-covered in the conven-tional press,[27] but more often they enter the news because of the contro-versies they generate. The Limbaugh/Sandra Fluke story and Glenn Beck's public declaration that President Obama was a racist, for example, were covered by mainstream news outlets. And outrage personalities also appear in mainstream news stories as sources, to represent conservative or liberal views on political issues. For example, in its initial story on revelations that GOP presidential aspirant Herman Cain had been accused of sexual harassment, the *Washington Post* addressed the question of conservatives' reaction to the controversy. To reflect conservative thinking about Cain in light of the allegations, the story quoted Rush Limbaugh and fellow talk radio host Laura Ingraham, both of whom said the mainstream press has been racist in their treatment of him. The *New York Times* followed suit in its coverage, using the inflammatory pundit Ann Coulter as its representative of conservative thought. Coulter minced no words in declaring that the story (not yet 24 hours old) smacked of a "high-tech lynching"—Clarence Thomas's evocative phrase from his Supreme Court confirmation hearings.[28] The presence of outrage in mainstream news and opinion venues brings it to audiences who might not seek it out.

When these changes combine they gather force. There is synergy in the complementary incentives shared by outrage commentators, party leaders, candidates, and interest group activists. Producers need guests while candidates, legislators, and interest group leaders want airtime. The Democratic National Committee might host a lunch for leading liberal bloggers and provide them with talking points that Democrats in Congress will be emphasizing that day.[29] The subsequent posts by these prominent bloggers will be picked up by other bloggers across the country, who link to particularly provocative entries. A blogger or Democratic pundit may then show up on MSNBC to discuss the story. MSNBC will incorporate that message on its website as it covers its own story on TV. The repetition of messaging elevates and seemingly adds legitimacy to the content. In sum, there are more Father Coughlins and Joe Pynes today (listing the outrage-oriented hosts of MSNBC alone shows this growth: Al Sharpton, Rachel Maddow, Lawrence O'Donnell, Chris Matthews, Ed Schultz), and these voices have a greater opportunity to find a platform, garner an audience, and have their theories and framings circulate more broadly and more quickly than those in earlier media contexts.

EXPLAINING THE CHANGE

Given the extensive expansion of outrage media and the formidable audience numbers some of these outlets attract, it seems reasonable to assume that a growing number of people share the anger and sharply ideological positions showcased in these venues. If outrage politics are more prevalent today, it seems that this must be a logical outgrowth of our fiercely divided populace.

Yet the relationship between what's offered to consumers, their political ideology, and the nature of their appetite for such content is complex.

The scholarly literature on political polarization in the United States does not align with the growth of outrage commentary. Despite lay assumptions that polarization has increased dramatically, academic research offers a murkier picture of contemporary political culture. Political scientist Morris Fiorina concludes that in terms of its ideological composition "the American public looks much the same as it did a half century ago—centrist more than polarized in its specific positions, pragmatic more than ideological in its general orientation."[30] Alan Abramowitz rejects Fiorina's belief that the polarization that seems so visible in our culture reflects the political beliefs of only a highly active political class. Rather, Abramowitz writes, "Polarization in Washington reflects polarization within the public."[31]

Despite this fundamental disagreement, in some aspects of this problem there is consensus among scholars. Most significantly, we see that the two major political parties have both become more philosophically homogeneous over time. In the wake of the civil rights movement in the 1960s an ideological sorting out of the American electorate took place. White southern conservatives migrated to the Republican Party while newly enfranchised blacks identified with the party of civil rights, the Democrats. The increasingly conservative Republican Party became less welcoming to moderate Republicans and over time many moderates left to become independents or Democrats. This is documented by Matthew Levendusky who finds that public opinion has not shifted markedly toward the ideological poles, but rather that today people have more closely linked their partisanship with their beliefs.[32] This suggests that our beliefs haven't changed significantly; we have simply sorted ourselves more neatly along party lines.

How, then, do we square the vast increase in the number of outrage outlets and the growth of the audience for their content with scarcity of ideologues in the population?[33] Even if Abramowitz is right and the number of Americans who hold polarizing attitudes *has* increased, it is implausible that such polarization can fully explain the current scale of outrage enterprises. Remember the case of radio, where the number of all-talk stations tripled in a period of under 15 years. Changes in public attitudes alone cannot explain such enormous growth; the source of talk radio expansion must derive primarily from other causes.

For a more robust understanding of the growth of the genre, we look to those who produce and distribute outrage-based content. We see outrage as a practical and savvy response to political, technological, and economic shifts that have transformed the media landscape since the 1980s. We detail these wide-ranging changes in Chapters 3 and 4, but for illustrative purposes, we'll consider just one here: the fragmentation of the audience as users have dispersed across the rapidly expanding array of media choices on and offline. Why is a fragmented media environment hospitable to outrage? Think of the case of television: During the era of big-three network dominance, when programming choices were based on garnering the largest possible number of viewers from the mass audience, the goal was to offend the fewest, to program the least objectionable content.[34] Today, the broadcast networks must work to attract a large audience amid an expansive sea of cable channels. In contrast, cable networks can produce content aimed at smaller, more homogeneous audiences. With this niche-orientation, individual cable channels can afford to offend segments of the market that are not their target audience. In fact, many cable television programs, radio shows, and blogs deliver niche audiences to advertisers specifically *through* the use of objectionable programming, which is dramatic, entertaining, and shocking enough to "break through the clutter" in a crowded field of cable choices.

Identifying niche audiences, which exist in cluttered and highly competitive markets, allows advertisers an efficient and cost-effective way to reach these targeted consumers. As a result, agent provocateurs, a nearly unthinkable risk in a least objectionable programming mind-set, now present a far more palatable option. The highly competitive radio and blog universes are similarly focused on niches: If Rush Limbaugh was concerned with attracting a broad audience (presumably including Democrats and Latinos), he would have been unlikely to denounce Sonia Sotomayor as a racist after she was nominated for the Supreme Court or to compare her to Ku Klux Klan firebrand David Duke or to a housekeeper. Of course, there are reasons this particular type of discourse proves culturally resonant, and we return to these shortly, but the point here is that the changing media terrain creates platforms for outrage to become economically viable. Indeed, it is our argument that it has been able to solidify into a genre largely because of this profitability.

The varied structural changes we describe have rendered outrage politically and financially profitable, whether those profits appear in the form of increased advertising revenues (linked directly to ratings and traffic) or fundraising dollars (recall the way Limbaugh's remarks about Fluke were leveraged by the left), or political support, coming in the form of votes, increased support for policy positions, or increased membership in advocacy groups.

OUTRAGE AS AN INDUSTRY

In this book, we highlight the business practices of individual firms in three commercial sectors (cable, radio, and the blogosphere), which, grouped together, create an industry that generates outrage as its product. In addition to explaining the way this industry emerged, we explain how it works, by illuminating the business models used in these three sectors (Chapter 4). In doing so, we hope to outline the relationships between outrage as a genre, the profits that incentivize it, and the business practices that produce it. We believe it is impossible to fully understand the styles of communication and argumentation used on the *O'Reilly Factor* or *Hannity* without linking them to the corporate strategy of News Corp's Fox Cable division. In an enormous multinational corporation with a wide range of properties, some of which do relatively poorly, Fox Cable is highly profitable and earns an outsized proportion of News Corp's overall profits (61 percent for fiscal year 2012).[35]

It isn't simply the media conglomerates reaping the rewards. The personality-centered nature of the genre means that top outrage personalities are able to distribute content across many platforms, creating what feel like their own mini-empires. As noted earlier Sean Hannity reaches 14 million listeners a week with his three-hour syndicated radio show, but he also has a second audience through his Fox News program every evening. Hannity's website is a marketing engine where his fans are encouraged to follow him on Twitter and like him on Facebook, as well as to sign up for his book club and post their comments on any of a steady steam of blog posts. Clicking a link will take visitors directly to Amazon.com where they can purchase a copy of his latest book, *Conservative Victory: Defeating Obama's Radical Agenda*. And golf shirts, mugs, bumper stickers, and Nerf footballs can be purchased directly from the site. If all that fails, you can catch him on tour.[36]

This focus on profits and business strategies might seem odd for a political scientist (Berry) and a sociologist (Sobieraj). We disagree. Recognizing the economic underpinnings of the genre is vital for a more complete understanding of its prevalence, as these insights advance our ability to recognize the phenomena as culturally and politically dependent, but not reducible to culture or politics. Without this lens, the repetition of outrage discourse across media platforms can be read erroneously as an indicator of a landmark shift in political orientation on the part of the audience or of profound cultural intolerance and insularity.

THE OUTRAGE INDUSTRY AND THE PUBLIC SPHERE

What does the entrance of the Outrage Industry mean for the American political public sphere? When we speak of the public sphere, we are invoking the Habermasian version of the concept, referring to the practice of open discussion about matters of common concern, as well as the public spaces that serve as settings for such dialogue (i.e., newspapers, plazas, blogs). It is, then, both a type of dialogue and the fora in which these discussions take place.[37] While such discourse can be direct, as when we discuss neighborhood issues in community centers and at town meetings, the mass media serve as core venues for public discussion in contemporary political culture. As such, our public deliberations are often mediated, rather than face-to-face conversations.

As a genre, outrage-based radio shows, television programs, and blogs serve as new spaces for conversation about public issues of the day, with unique norms in place that shape the discussions that transpire under their auspices. Outrage proffers those participating in these publics a vocabulary, a cadre of tried and true themes, and a preferred style of delivery. In short, the genre structures the discussion, much like the distinctive language, line of questioning, and affect found in broadcast news structures the interactions that transpire when reporters on location interview witnesses at the scene of an accident or those who have survived a natural disaster.

Although mediated and face-to-face publics are analytically distinct, empirically they are deeply entwined. Mediated interactions enter face-to-face political discourse as audiences interpret, react to, and otherwise circulate the content in social settings.[38] Outrage resurfaces in face-to-face encounters when participants reference information gleaned from the programs and blog posts, draw upon the arguments and illustrations they find persuasive, and critique those they find suspect when they talk with friends, family, colleagues, or acquaintances. And it is not only informal, everyday talk that outrage shapes. Instead, we find the residues of outrage in formal publics, coloring the discursive environment in political parties and in the halls of Congress. In these publics, the Outrage Industry is not only relevant because ideas and stories produced there circulate widely but also because outrage outlets monitor political behavior for ideological transgressions, and wield influence in the court of public opinion. In these ways, outrage is enmeshed in water cooler discussions about public issues and hovers over policymakers and party operatives as they do their political work, making outrage relevant even for those unfamiliar with its personalities and platforms.

As a form of discourse, outrage is distinctly emotional, partial, antagonistic, and opinion-based. It stands in stark contrast to the kind of discourse described in normative theories of deliberation, which value political dialogue that is rational, inclusive, impartial, consensus-oriented, and fact-based. Reasoned, dispassionate discourse between open-minded participants is believed to identify the best solutions to issues of shared concern and hence enhance the legitimacy of political decision-making.[39] Critics challenge such visions empirically—even the most well-intended groups struggle with principles such as impartiality, inclusion, and open-mindedness when important decisions must be made—as well as strategically, asking if these counterfactual conditions are an ideal toward which we should even aspire.[40]

While the proliferation of outrage discourse in the media and its concomitant role in direct dialogue about politics is anathema to the values upheld by deliberativists, there are others far more open to diverse forms of political expression. Many have persuasively challenged the privileging of rational-critical discourse as exclusionary and anti-democratic because it elevates a set of voices already at the political center and devalues the contributions of voices that have historically been pressed to the margins, such as those of women, the poor, foreign-born, nonwhites.[41] These critics argue that emotional, opinion-based accounts of lived experience are deemed less legitimate than those drawing dispassionately on facts presented as objective precisely because power has been at play in establishing what we take for granted as common sense. Therefore, as political scientist Jane Mansbridge has argued, under the pretense of inclusion, deliberation may mask domination. Critics focusing on inequalities tend to home in on one or more of the following: calling attention to these subtleties of power in public discourse, broadening the range of political expressions seen as legitimate, and validating the multiple, coexisting publics where those whose needs are not met gather to deliberate independently.[42]

A public sphere open to more diverse types of political expression, then, is arguably better suited to meaningful inclusion, but discourse grounded in emotion and persuasion also may have additional benefits. Specifically, James Bohman suggests that meaningful deliberation requires new ways of framing social reality, suggesting that performative communications including jokes, shared personal stories, and use of irony often help people understand things in new ways, proving pivotal for meaningful political discussion.[43] Even if such devices fail to enhance understanding, it seems likely that they enhance the pleasures of and proclivity toward participation in political life. Sociologists Ron Jacobs and Eleanor Townsley argue that public participation depends on feelings of pleasure, which may be derived from rational argumentation, but also through more "playful forms of argument, such as the clever use of dramatic techniques to place moral conflict into bold (and usually overstated) relief." They suggest that this satisfaction is motivating increasing civic participation: "We want to suggest that if an individual hates George Will or Paul Krugman or Bill O'Reilly, it is more likely that that person will participate in the public sphere."[44] Political communication scholars Kathleen Hall Jamieson and Joseph Cappella's research on Rush Limbaugh listeners suggests this participation thesis is correct. More powerful affective reactions were linked positively to increases in both political participation and feelings of efficacy.[45]

We do not see emotion or opinion in political dialogue as inherently beneficial or inherently problematic. We agree with critics who are unwilling to insist that "good" democratic talk hinges on an ideal that is both counterfactual and apt to devalue certain voices and forms of communication under the guise of neutrality. We see many productive ways to communicate about politics and prefer broad parameters that create space for multiple points of view and for creative forms of expression. Having said that, we are not ready to celebrate outrage on the grounds that it promotes political interest and involvement. While broad parameters are essential and pleasurable political experiences are important to sustain involvement, there are discourses that can be damaging.

Outrage media may offer entertainment, information, a sense of community, and validation. It may inspire more consumption of political information. Our research suggests that outrage is unusually engaging, creating political safe havens for fans in a moment when face-to-face political conversations are extraordinarily daunting. At the same time, these engaging narratives are not neutrally playful or unique ways to tell political stories, but rather they draw on templates that often involve misinformation and render other accounts (and facts in general) suspect. The Pew Research Center found that nearly half of regular Fox News viewers erroneously believed that Obama's proposed health care legislation would include "death panels."[46] The death panel story was one that was perpetuated by several conservative outrage outlets. So, while outrage-based programs do expand discursive space addressing issues often skipped by conventional news outlets, as Jacobs and Townsley argue, we remain less enthusiastic, as this discussion quite often has anti-democratic outcomes.[47] Further, Jamieson and Cappella's research shows that participation in the "insular feedback loop" created by outrage media is not erased by omnivorousness; involvement with conservative opinion media creates resistance to information encountered in other venues.[48]

One of our key concerns is that participation in outrage-based publics (mediated and face-to-face) may very well disrupt participation in other types of publics. By devaluing information available in conventional media, vilifying those with whom we have disagreements, and propagating mis-representative exaggerations in the service of a more robust and persuasive narrative, outrage-based media may limit our willingness to engage in political conversations with people who do not share our worldview, bruise our openness to others' perspectives when we do talk with them, and, per-haps most ironically, leave us valorizing a new ideal that privileges passion-ate argumentation and devalues contributions that are more ideologically neutral.[49]

When evaluating political opinion media with democratic metrics, it is important to acknowledge the uncomfortable reality: most US opinion media are not designed to yield the best possible political deliberation. Instead, most political opinion media are governed by economic impera-tives shaped by our unique historically specific media structures. In this vein, we share Bourdieu's view that social spaces such as the media must be understood in terms of the relations between adjacent spaces. The institu-tions of civil society—be they journalism or voluntary associations or social movements—shape and are shaped by the state and the economy. Importantly, this does not mean that commercial media necessarily pro-duce outcomes that are detrimental to political life or democratic processes, as some, including Habermas himself, have suggested, but rather that they are indifferent to these concerns. Political mudslinging itself offers an excellent example of this neutrality, as commercialization of the press in the 19th century reduced the overt partisanship of newspapers, in the very same way that shifting economic arrangements of the last 25 years have ushered it back in.[50]

In suggesting that we take seriously the role of the market in shaping the mediated public sphere (and, by extension, public spheres that are unmediated), we do not argue that the particular content of the political opinion media is dictated by advertiser influence. On the contrary, such a view would be far too narrow. Instead, we see several factors (e.g., techno-logical developments, ownership, regulatory climate, broader political culture) as key in structuring the media environment. Taken together, they produce a media space with a particular clustering of attributes, such as a largely for-profit production and distribution system yielding a wide variety of consumer choices and a great deal of audience control over what, when, and how viewers/listeners will use available content. The political content existing in this environment is shaped by the economic demands unique to this media space, but the precise forms the content takes are dictated as much by the broader social and political culture as economic pressures.

Holding the economic context constant for a moment, we can see that advertiser interests in reaching target audiences (particularly those with disposable income) could hypothetically be met in a variety of ways. The reorientation toward niche audiences does not mandate outrage-based content. Audiences could be wooed with other fare. We could imagine, for example, a genre of political programming that offers erudite examination of policies related to issues of political concern to specific slices of the public (e.g., immigration; education; lesbian, gay, bisexual, or transgendered (LGBT) rights; labor issues). This would give advertisers a way to reach audiences with specific policy concerns. Or, envision a genre of programs that specialize by region, providing analysis of international political developments in particular parts of the world. In other words, if we considered *only* the fragmentation of the media audience into niches, *LGBT Politics Today* or *South Asian Political Review* could potentially deliver an audience to advertisers and allow producers to sustain their work, but these types of programs are difficult to envision in American media today, even on NPR or PBS. This is because these programs lack the cultural resonance outrage enjoys. We have programs like the *O'Reilly Factor* instead of *South Asian Political Review* because social, political, and cultural forces shape what is financially successful.

Outrage is a genre that works in this cultural moment. The seemingly unscripted format benefits from the prominence of reality television while the faux intimacy fostered by hosts and bloggers with their audiences capitalizes on our infatuation with celebrities. The genre also reflects our pronounced divide along party lines (as opposed to the less-pronounced divide along issue preferences) as well as our two-party system. In this regard, we note that there are no outrage programs featuring socialist, right-to-life, or green party hosts. In other words, the expansion of discursive space has meant more discourse but not necessarily increased diversity of political views, at least on television. Outrage also resonates with audiences because it draws on familiar themes in conventional journalism such as horse-race reportage and opinion pages. And outrage has benefited from the insecurities evoked in dominant groups by the rise of multiculturalism.[51] These factors—and there are others—have facilitated the proliferation of *outrage* in this media landscape as opposed to some other genre of political content. So, in many ways, outrage works. It works because its coarseness and emotional pull offer the "pop" that breaks through the competitive information environment, and it works because it draws on so many of our existing cultural touchstones: celebrity culture, reality television, a two-party system, as well as the conventional news and opinion to which those in the United States have become accustomed. It also, we will show, has resonance in a culture where people feel less and less free to share political ideas in their communities (and harbor anger at this perceived marginalization).

The mediated public sphere, then, cannot be divorced from or reduced to its commercial base. With this understanding in place, questions about the outcomes of the outrage have a different cast as they are undergirded by questions about the relationship between media industries, civil society, and the state (as we are talking about the political public sphere) rather than questions about a public sphere or set of publics that are somehow insulated from the state or the economy. And yet, we push back against visions of a media contaminated by commercialization. We will show that this profitable variant of political opinion media has distinctive consequences at the level of the individual and at the level of politics and policymaking, many of which are concerning, and yet we do so without seeing this as an inevitable byproduct of commercial media. Money can be made in other ways. We will instead show that outrage is an opportunistic genre whose trajectory is unclear, as it is socially embedded and subject to change.

THE PATH FORWARD

We believe this book makes three significant contributions. First, in light of the circulating anxieties about the tone of American political discourse that have been perhaps most evident in the calls for civility that resounded in the aftermath of Congresswoman Gabrielle Giffords's attempted assassination, we believe that a social scientific examination of this muscular negativity is long overdue. We hope our documentation of the volume and nature of extreme political talk today will concretize what has thus far been amorphous. Vague and unnamed, outrage has been lumped under the umbrella of incivility or negativity. It has been *felt*, hence the anxiety around the tenor of American politics, but not fully recognized as a distinctive mode of discourse. We hope our conceptualization and the empirical snapshot presented here will spur more research in this area.

Second, we hope this book will shed light on what it means to have outrage discourse embedded in our political lives. Rather than dismissing this cast of colorful characters as simple entertainment or misrecognizing them as bit players in American political culture, we show how official and informal publics are each shaped by the presence of an Outrage Industry.

We shed light on the ways the genre informs democratic practices as part of the cultural landscape in which fans, advocacy groups, and legislators live and work. At the same time, we work to shift the conversation away from what this type of incivility causes (extant research on this focuses on individuals and is quite divided) and pay more attention to its uses and meanings.

Third, we believe that our insights into the structural underpinnings of this new genre will help us to break free from the notion that we are a hopelessly divided nation unable to communicate about shared priorities by revealing that the prevalence of the genre is a residue of regulatory, technological, and economic conditions rather than a mirror of public political attitudes or antagonisms.

PLAN OF THE BOOK

In the chapter that follows we lay the foundation for the remainder of the book by documenting the prevalence of outrage rhetoric. We also identify the different forms of outrage and explore differences across various media. Chapters 3 and 4 investigate the question of why outrage has surged. Chapter 3 provides historical context and explains how changes in regulation and technology catalyzed the rise in outrage. Chapter 4 links these changes to the business trends that emerged and provided the commercial channels through which outrage is disseminated. In Chapter 5 we introduce you to the fans of outrage-based content on television and radio, and help show why they find this programming uniquely meaningful. What's more, we show how social anxieties surrounding face-to-face political conversations magnify the significance of mediated relationships that form between fans and hosts. We take seriously the Outrage Industry's uneven terrain and turn in Chapters 6 and 7 to look at the role of conservative outrage in broader political life. In Chapter 6 we look at the relationship between the Outrage Industry and the Tea Party, showing the critical role outrage media played in galvanizing the movement and amplifying their concerns, leading to their important impact on the 2010 Republican congressional primary races. In Chapter 7 we focus on the relationship between conservative outrage media, congressional policymaking, and the internal life of the Republican Party (GOP). Here we show the limited but noteworthy ways in which outrage has shaped the development of policies and parties at the national level. Finally, in Chapter 8 we close by pointing at pockets of resistance to outrage and consider its trajectory for the future.

The research draws upon many original data sources, primarily in-depth qualitative interviews, qualitative and quantitative content analyses of outrage content, electoral analysis of the 2010 congressional primary races, detailed monitoring of the 112th Congress (2011–12), and countless hours watching, listening to, and reading outrage. A fuller account of our methodologies can be found in the Appendix.

NOTES

1. See the transcript of Sandra Fluke's statement: http://campaign2012.washington-examiner.com/blogs/beltway-confidential/what-did-sandra-fluke-really-say/408191, as of April 19, 2012.
2. Since the time of the original airing the transcripts from these episodes of the *Rush Limbaugh Show* were edited and some of the remarks in question were removed. For information on this, see the Atlantic Wire: http://www.theatlanticwire.com/politics/2012/03/rush-scrubs-demand-for-fluke-sex-tapes/49643/, as of April 20, 2012. Liberal media watchdog group Media Matters offers their accounting of the original remarks here: http://mediamatters.org/research/201203050022, as of April 20, 2012. Neither record is complete.
3. Brian Stelter, "After Apology, National Advertisers Still Shunning Limbaugh," *New York Times*, March 13, 2012, http://www.nytimes.com/2012/03/14/business/media/ad-boycott-dents-limbaugh-shows-bottom-line.html, as of April 19, 2012.
4. *Rush Limbaugh Show,* March 7, 2012.
5. Stelter, "After Apology, National Advertisers Are Still Shunning Limbaugh."
6. *Rush Limbaugh Show, November* 18, 2011.
7. See http://www.mediaite.com/online/liberal-radio-host-broadcasts-mock-phone-call-to-hell-to-check-up-on-andrew-breitbart/ for a fuller account.
8. Jacques Steinberg, "Boycotted Radio Host Remains Unbowed," *New York Times*, December 17, 2007, http://www.nytimes.com/2007/12/17/arts/17sava.html?-pagewanted=all, as of April 20, 2012; Elana Schor, "Murdoch Intervenes in Olbermann-O'Reilly Row," *The Guardian*, May 19, 2008, http://www.guardian.co.uk/world/2008/may/19/usa.rupertmurdoch, as of April 20, 2012; and "Responding to Krugman, Beck Claimed of FEMA Conspiracy Theories, 'Never Said Anything Like It,'" Media Matters, June 12, 2009, at http://mediamatters.org/research/200906120029, as of April 20, 2012.
9. We first introduced outrage as a concept in Sarah Sobieraj and Jeffrey M. Berry, "From Incivility to Outrage: Political Discourse in Blogs, Talk Radio, and Cable News," *Political Communication* 28 (January 2011): 19–41. The same definitions and framework are used here in Chapter 2.
10. Diana C. Mutz and Byron Reeves, "The New Videomalaise: Effects of Televised Incivility on Political Trust," *American Political Science Review* 99 (February 2005): 5.
11. Joseph Goldstein, "Wall Street Demonstrations Test Police Trained for Bigger Threats," *New York Times*, September 26, 2011, http://www.nytimes.com/2011/09/27/nyregion/wall-street-demonstrations-test-police-trained-for-bigger-threats.html, as of April 18, 2012.
12. A segment of the video can be found at http://www.youtube.com/watch?v=C6J5DuQTHWQ, as of April 19, 2012.

13. Ibid.

14. This is particularly interesting given that the protesters in question were white.

15. There is, of course, ideologically grounded political analysis and commentary that is not outrage-based, such as much of that found in the *National Review* and *The Nation*, which can have very different inputs into democratic processes and are arguably even better at enhancing deliberative practices than mainstream news sources, as shown by Deana Rohlinger, "American Media and Deliberative Democratic Processes," *Sociological Theory* 25 (June 2007): 122–148.

16. The radio station data are from Arbitron and are detailed at greater length in Chapters 3 and 4.

17. See also Ronald Jacobs and Eleanor Townsley, *The Space of Opinion: Media Intellectuals and the Public Sphere* (New York: Oxford University Press, 2011), for a detailed accounting of the expansion of opinion media.

18. "State of the News Media 2012," http://stateofthemedia.org/, as of July 1, 2012.

19. These Arbitron data include all-news stations in this category in its radio classification scheme, but there are actually few all-news stations today because the costs of running such stations are very high. In contrast, it is relatively inexpensive to run an all-talk station as most syndicated shows are distributed at nominal charge or in exchange for advertising, as increased audience size increases ad revenue for distributors.

20. "State of the News Media 2012."

21. William P. Eveland and Dhavan V. Shah, "The Impact of Individual and Interpersonal Factors on Perceived News Media Bias," *Political Psychology* 24 (March 2003): 101–117; Tien-Tsung Lee, "The Liberal Media Myth Revisited: An Examination of Factors Influencing Perceptions of Media Bias," *Journal of Broadcasting & Electronic Media* 49 (June 2005): 43–64; Tien-Tsung Lee, "Why They Don't Trust the Media: An Examination of Factors Predicting Trust," *American Behavioral Scientist* 54 (September 2010): 8–21.

22. Based on Nielsen Media Research ratings widely available on websites such as Media Bistro (http://www.mediabistro.com/tvnewser/) and TV by the Numbers (http://tvbythenumbers.zap2it.com/), as of July 1, 2012.

23. These are aggregates; individuals watching the *Rachel Maddow Show* and reading *Talking Points Memo* are counted twice. For TV we counted viewers for the *O'Reilly Factor, Hannity,* the *Ed Show,* the *Rachel Maddow Show,* and *The Last Word with Lawrence O'Donnell.* We include the audiences for the second showings of the *O'Reilly Factor* and the *Ed Show* at 11:00 PM on Fox and MSNBC, respectively. We acquired these figures from "TV by the Numbers" but they are widely available from many sources. The data for the day we randomly selected are at http://tvbythenumbers.zap2it.com/2011/12/15/cable-news-ratings-for-wednesday-december-14-2011/113914/. For radio, we began with the weekly audience from Arbitron for the top 12 political talk radio figures and divided by 5 for a daily figure. These programs are listed in Table 4.1 in Chapter 4. There are hundreds more talk radio shows, many syndicated. *Talkers Magazine* lists an annual "Heavy 100" of influential and popular talk radio hosts, most of whom do political shows. We believe our broader estimate is a conservative one. Finally, for blogs we used Quantcast.com on December 21, 2011, for the audiences for 10 of the top conservative blogs and 10 of the top liberal blogs. This list is derived from rankings from Technorati, as used in our content analysis (Chapter 2). We had to substitute a handful of new blogs as some used at the time of that research (2009) were no longer appropriate or for which we could not access the comparable data. We

normalized figures to a daily audience rate when the data were not presented that way. There are literally thousands of political blogs, most of them small; our extrapolation from the top blogs is a rough estimate and should be taken as such.

24. Michael Harrison, "Qualitative Aspects of the Talk Radio Audiences," *Talkers Magazine* (October, 2011): 8; and Michael P. McDonald, "Voter Turnout in the 2010 Midterm Election," *The Forum* 6 (January 2011): 1–8.

25. Howard Kurtz, "Conservative Pundits Packed a Real Punch," *Washington Post*, October 28, 2005, http://www.highbeam.com/doc/1P2-86140.html, as of April 20, 2012; and Michael A. Fletcher and Charles Babington, "Conservatives Escalate Opposition to Miers," *Washington Post*, October 25, 2005, http://www.washingtonpost.com/wp-dyn/content/article/2005/10/24/AR2005102401744.html, as of April 21, 2012.

26. Kurtz, "Conservative Pundits Packed a Real Punch."

27. Blogs are particularly important to mainstream news work. Although we do not know how many of the blogs they follow are outrage-based, Richard Davis found that 36 percent of journalists consulted political blogs on a daily basis. *Typing Politics* (New York: Oxford University Press, 2009), 138.

28. Philip Rucker and Nia-Malika Henderson, "Herman Cain Denies Ever Sexually Harassing Anyone, Calls Allegations 'Totally False,'" *Washington Post*, October 31, 2011, http://www.washingtonpost.com/politics/herman-cain-declined-to-address-allegations-that-he-sexually-harassed-two-former-female-employees/2011/10/31/gIQAQ8KNZM_story.html, as of April 20, 2012; and Jim Rutenberg and Michael D. Shear, "Cain Confronts Claim from '90s of Harassment," *New York Times*, November 1, 2011, http://www.nytimes.com/2011/11/01/us/politics/cain-confronts-claim-from-90s-of-harassment.html?pagewanted=all, as of April 20, 2012.

29. One lunch memo we were allowed to see contained three talking points, two of which tarred particular Republicans. We were told that the strategy at that time for these blogger lunches, which were on Fridays, was to build these stories up culminating with the Sunday TV talk shows, where questioning would hopefully follow the lines of attack "initiated" by the blogosphere.

30. Morris P. Fiorina with Samuel J. Abrams, *Disconnect: The Breakdown of Representation in American Politics* (Norman: University of Oklahoma Press, 2009), 20. See also Morris P. Fiorina with Samuel J. Abrams and Jeremy C. Pope, *Culture War?*, 3rd ed. (New York: Longman, 2011).

31. Alan I. Abramowitz, *The Disappearing Center* (New Haven, CT: Yale University Press, 2010), x. For additional evidence of increased polarization, see "Partisan Polarization Surges in Bush, Obama Years," Pew Research Center for the People and the Press, June 4, 2012, http://www.people-press.org/files/legacy-pdf/06-04-12%20Values%20Release.pdf, as of June 26, 2012.

32. Matthew Levendusky, *The Partisan Sort* (Chicago: University of Chicago Press, 2009).

33. See Markus Prior, "Media and Political Polarization," *Annual Review of Political Science* 16 (2013): 101-127.

34. Todd Gitlin, "Television's Screens: Hegemony in Transition," in *American Media and Mass Culture*, ed. Donald Lazere (Berkeley: University of California Press, 1987).

35. Note that this figure is for the Cable Division, which includes other properties like the FX network, in addition to the Fox Cable News. News Corp doesn't break down revenues or earnings beyond the aggregate for "cable" but it is clear from the business press that Fox Cable News is the most lucrative part of this division. *News Corp Annual Report* 2012, p. 12, https://materials.proxyvote.com/Approved/65248E/20120926/AR_141035/images/News_Corp-AR2012.pdf, as of December 18, 2012.

36. See http://www.hannity.com/.

37. Jürgen Habermas, *The Structural Transformation of the Public Sphere: An Inquiry into a Category of Bourgeois Society* (Cambridge, MA: MIT Press, 1991).

38. The discussions transpiring in unmediated publics enter mediated public spheres as well. In outrage outlets, this happens most clearly through the vigilant monitoring of and discussion about the behavior of Congress and the courts, but also when callers and commenters share ideas and analyses from their everyday lives in these mediated exchanges.

39. For some examples, see Joshua Cohen, "Procedure and Substance in Deliberative Democracy," in *Democracy and Difference: Contesting the Boundaries of the Political*, ed. Seyla Benhabib (Princeton, NJ: Princeton University Press, 1996); Joshua Cohen, "Deliberation and Democratic Legitimacy" in *The Good Polity*, ed. Alan Hamlin (Oxford, UK: Blackwell, 1989); Amy Guttman and Dennis Thompson, *Democracy and Disagreement* (Cambridge, MA: Harvard University Press, 1996); Jurgen Habermas, *Between Facts and Norms: Contributions to a Discourse Theory of Law and Democracy* (Cambridge, MA: MIT Press, 1996).

40. For some noteworthy critiques, see John Dryzek, *Deliberative Democracy and Beyond: Liberals, Critics, Contestations* (New York: Oxford University Press, 2000); Nancy Fraser, "Communication, Transformation, and Consciousness-Raising," in *Hannah Arendt and the Meaning of Politics*, ed. Craig Calhoun and John McGowan (Minneapolis: University of Minnesota Press, 1997).

41. Habermas recognizes that power shapes those forms of speech that are deemed legitimate, but believes that status inequalities can be consciously bracketed and left outside of rational-critical discourse.

42. Seyla Benhabib, "Toward a Deliberative Model of Democratic Legitimacy," in *Democracy and Difference: Contesting the Boundaries of the Political*, ed. Seyla Benhabib (Princeton, NJ: Princeton University Press, 1996); Nancy Fraser, "Rethinking the Public Sphere: A Contribution to the Critique of Actually Existing Democracy," in *Habermas and the Public Sphere*, ed. Craig Calhoun (Cambridge, MA: MIT Press, 1992); Jane Mansbridge, "Feminism and Democracy," *The American Prospect* 1 (Spring 1990): 127; Iris Marion Young, "Communication and the Other: Beyond Deliberative Democracy," in *Democracy and Difference: Contesting the Boundaries of the Political*, ed. Seyla Benhabib (Princeton, NJ: Princeton University Press, 2000).

43. James Bohman, *Public Deliberation: Pluralism, Complexity, and Democracy* (Cambridge, MA: MIT Press, 2000).

44. Jacobs and Townsley, *Space of Opinion*, 69.

45. Kathleen Hall Jamieson and Joseph N. Cappella, *Echo Chamber: Rush Limbaugh and the Conservative Media Establishment* (New York: Oxford University Press, 2008), 136.

46. http://pewresearch.org/pubs/1319/death-panels-republicans-fox-viewers, as of September 28, 2011.

47. See Jacobs and Townsley, *Space of Opinion*, for an account of the occupational dis-
    tribution of those with voice in these spaces, primarily academics from elite insti-
    tutions, researchers from think tanks, political analysts, and the like.
48. Jamieson and Cappella, *Echo Chamber*.
49. See, for example, Matthew Levendusky, "Partisan Media Exposure and Attitudes
    toward the Opposition," *Political Communication*, forthcoming.
50. Michael Schudson, *The Good Citizen: A History of American Civic Life* (Cambridge.
    MA: Harvard University Press, 1998); Michael Schudson and Susan E. Tifft,
    "American Journalism in Historical Perspective," in *The Press*, ed. Geneva
    Overholser and Kathleen Hall Jamieson (New York: Oxford University Press,
    2005); and James T. Hamilton, *All the News That's Fit to Sell* (Princeton: Princeton
    University Press, 2004).
51. This is discussed further in Chapter 5.

CHAPTER 2

༺ɔ

Mapping Outrage in Blogs, Talk Radio, and Cable News

You rat bastards are going to cause another Murrah federal building explosion. You are. And then what is Beck—maybe at that point Beck will do the honorable thing and blow his brains out. Maybe at that point, Limbaugh will do the honorable thing and just gobble up enough Viagra that he becomes absolutely rigid and keels over dead. Maybe then O'Reilly will just drink a vat of that poison he spews out on America every night and choke to death! Because that's what's gonna happen. That's what they are pushing these right-wing, nut case, fringe, militia jerk-wads to doing!
    —*liberal radio host* Mike Malloy[1]

O utrage isn't pretty, or difficult to find, yet academic work on this type of political speech is remarkably scant. There is abundant research on "negativity" and "incivility" in American politics, but it has drawn almost exclusively on campaign advertisements and candidate statements in the news in an attempt to measure the impact of this negativity on matters such as voter turnout and faith in government. These inquiries are important but they fail to fully capture the abundant acrimony of our contemporary political culture. To reach a point where we can begin to understand the political consequences of incivility—the question at the forefront of virtually all research on this topic—we first need a more comprehensive understanding of the extent and texture of political incivility itself.

Existing research looks at the statements and advertisements made by candidates and political parties, but virtually no research has examined the ways political incivility penetrates our broader political media landscape—a landscape that is shaped powerfully by entertainment imperatives.[2] Laboratory exposure to advertisements or mock candidates is limited in what it tells us about the real political waters in which we swim, which include news and sometimes campaign advertisements, but also talk radio, political blogs, and cable news analysis programs, all of which have substantial audiences. Questions about negativity in politics must include these spaces in which incivility is elaborated into outrage.

Outrage differs conceptually from its more frequently examined compatriot, incivility, because the discourteous gestures implied by incivility (as defined in most contemporary social science) are considerably less dramatic and demeaning than the remarks and behaviors we define as outrageous. But if outrage is not found in the exasperated sighs and eye-rolls many think of as uncivil, then how do we recognize it? Who uses it? What does it sound like? How do we measure it? In this chapter, we answer these questions, because it is our position that in the absence of meaningful information about *content*, questions of *effects*, which dominate the existing research, are premature. We deconstruct outrage to examine its diverse manifestations and lay out a path for its measurement. We then use these tools to offer a baseline map of the landscape and texture of political outrage speech and behavior, showing that outrage is both plentiful and intense. Finally, we zoom in, moving from mapping the landscape to a closer ethnographic description of one of the most frequently recurring tropes within the genre: vilification.

POLITICAL INCIVILITY

Empirical research in political communication and political psychology attempting to identify the effects of exposure to political incivility—as distinguished from mere negativity, which can exist with or without an uncivil mode of delivery[3]—offers complex and at times contradictory answers, as is the case with media effects research across most content. The reigning presumption is that incivility in politics undermines faith in government and discourages political participation. Findings suggest that exposure to uncivil political discourse in the media erodes political trust, leads to more negative assessments of political institutions and actors, decreases perceived legitimacy of political figures, and triggers increased emotional response.[4]

Yet some research suggests that there may be positive effects of negative political speech, such as Geer and Lau who found that negative (not specifically uncivil) campaign advertisements actually *stimulated* voter turnout in Britain between 1980 and 2000.[5] Similarly, Brader demonstrated that emotional appeals in campaign advertising *engage* audiences, prompting viewers to seek out further information.[6] Some research suggests effects too complex to be viewed as positive or negative. For example, Kahn and Kenney found negative campaign advertisements and negative news coverage increased voter turnout, but that "mudslinging" reduced it and that the impact varies based on the status of the candidate delivering the message as well as the style of the criticism.[7] Similarly, Brooks and Geer find that incivility disturbs the public's sense of the value of political discussion, but that those viewing uncivil messages were also more likely to vote.[8]

The complexity and contradiction embedded in these results make sense; the literature includes researchers who vary in the way they define negativity and/or incivility as well as the way they operationalize these concepts. The researchers also attempt to measure impact in different contexts (laboratory, survey, etc.) after audience members encounter different media and different formats within individual media. It should be of little surprise to find that measurable effects of a mock political talk show viewed in a lab might differ from the survey responses used to gauge the effects of exposure to negative campaign advertisements. Even without these significant methodological differences, it is a daunting task to isolate the impact of one type of political speech given the diverse and complex political and media environment.

Despite these challenges, the effects of uncivil political discourse are worth examining. The problem is that this effects research exists alongside minimal data on the content of actual political discourse. In other words, even if exposure to uncivil political discourse were proven to yield measurable outcomes (e.g., apathy, political engagement, diminished trust), this information is of little use without an empirical account of the degree to which political discourse is actually uncivil. This is an unexpected imbalance, in light of the many corners of media studies in which academic research offers exactly the opposite: numerous analyses of media texts accompanied by conjecture about their likely effects with precious little empirical data on audiences or users.

There is some content analytic work on incivility in political speech, but it is too narrow to provide a meaningful assessment of the state of outrageous political discourse in the media. Beyond the flood of research on negative campaign advertisements[9] and campaign communications via the news,[10] which suggest a downward spiral into negativity cannot necessarily be established, we have little sense of the texture of political discourse more broadly. Jamieson and Cappella offer some valuable qualitative insights into the ways that outrageous personalities present political life to their audiences, but they look exclusively at the conservative opinion media.[11] Herbst's *Rude Democracy* (2010) examines incivility in political life, which she argues is a permanent and not altogether undesirable part of American democracy. Her focus is on the way civility and incivility are deployed strategically by political actors, and she uses Barack Obama and Sarah Palin as case studies. As such, she offers a valuable reflection on incivility and argumentation but is not concerned with the broader media landscape.

Moy and Pfau offer perhaps the most comprehensive content analysis of what we might call the broader political curriculum. The content analysis portion of their study examined depictions of political institutions in 1995 and 1996 across a wide range of media including news, television news magazines, entertainment talk shows, and political talk radio, revealing that negativity varies by format. They demonstrate for example, that political talk radio is most negative on the presidency, while entertainment talk shows depict Congress in the least favorable manner. Their research also reveals patterned differences in media use, with men and women demonstrating different preferences (e.g., men preferring talk radio, women preferring television news magazines), as well as different use patterns among people from different age groups and from different political parties.[12] This reminds us that political discourse is diffuse in society (rather than concentrated in campaign advertisements) and demonstrates that diverse media formats do not create a simple echo chamber in which the same information is articulated and rearticulated by different talking heads. Further, the inter-media variation in content and the patterned differences among audience members suggest that while laboratory experiments allow us to isolate a particular variable, they tell us little about incivility as we experience it. These insights are valuable, but the research pre-dates the transformations in the media landscape that are most relevant to outrage-based rhetoric.

MAPPING OUTRAGE

We map the terrain of outrage in an effort to provide (1) a broader foundation for research on the effects of this type of speech in our political discourse, (2) some sense of what outrage sounds like and how it varies, (3) insights into how political outrage differs on the right and left, and perhaps most critically, (4) a baseline to allow us to monitor changes in outrage discourse over time. At the end of the chapter we discuss the increase in outrage over time, but first we offer a finely grained cross-sectional analysis.

During a 10-week period in the spring of 2009 four researchers coded evening cable TV, national talk radio shows, ideological political blogs, and mainstream newspaper columns.[13] The specifics on each of these four data sources are as follows:

Cable TV. Eight news analysis shows on the three most prominent cable news networks were each watched for one hour per week. The shows were those hosted by Glenn Beck, Sean Hannity, and Bill O'Reilly on the conservative Fox News network; Rachel Maddow, Chris Matthews, and Keith Olbermann on the liberal MSNBC (these data pre-date Olbermann's 2011 transition to Current TV and then off air in 2012); and Lou Dobbs and Campbell Brown who were on CNN at the time. In addition, as points of comparison, an hour of afternoon traditional news programming, the *Situation Room*, with Wolf Blitzer on CNN, and the weekly episode of *Meet the Press* on NBC were included. With the exception of *Meet the Press*, which airs only once each week, we sampled shows on a predetermined schedule that rotated the days of the week for each program.

Talk Radio. With so few liberal talk radio shows we were able to include only those hosted by Alan Colmes of Fox Radio and Thom Hartmann, formerly of Air America. Our choice of conservative radio hosts was dictated in part by the availability of audio archives, but we were able to follow six of the most popular conservatives: Rush Limbaugh, Michael Savage, Hugh Hewitt, Laura Ingraham, Mike Gallagher, and Mark Levin. For comparison we also included NPR's *Morning Edition*, and the *Diane Rehm Show*, a talk show that can be heard on many public radio stations. The first hour of each program was sampled and coded. As with the cable TV programs, days of the week were rotated for each show.

Political Blogs. We followed 10 leading conservative and 10 leading liberal blogs each week. Selecting the blogs was not a simple process. We compiled the entries on three different "Top 10" lists for both conservative and liberal blogs (Technorati's authority rankings, the top conservative and liberal blogs identified on www.blogs.com, and subjective listings provided by Scott Martin and Heather Pidcock), to create master lists including blogs mentioned on any of the lists at least once. After creating a master list for liberal blogs and one for conservative blogs, and removing blogs that were not predominantly political, we utilized Alexa rankings to determine the 10 most heavily trafficked blogs on each list. The conservative blogs in the sample are *Townhall, Michelle Malkin, Hot Air, Right Pundits, Gateway Pundit, Powerline, Hit and Run, Little Green Footballs, Ace of Spades,* and *Moonbattery*. The liberal blogs are *Huffington Post, Daily Kos, Talking Points Memo, Crooks and Liars, Think Progress, Wonkette, Firedoglake, MyDD, Orcinus,* and *Hullabaloo*. Each week we sampled the first post appearing on a rotating day of the week at or after a specified time (as most of these blogs update very frequently).[14]

Newspaper Columns. To compare political speech in cable TV, talk radio, and blogs to that in traditional political commentary, we also coded the country's top syndicated newspaper columnists. We examined the work of the five most widely syndicated conservative columnists at the time (David Brooks, Charles Krauthammer, Kathleen Parker, Cal Thomas, and George Will) and the five most widely syndicated liberal columnists (E.J. Dionne, Maureen Dowd, Ellen Goodman, Leonard Pitts, and Eugene Robinson). We sampled one column per week per columnist, on a rotating schedule.

Outrage and incivility are slippery concepts: hard to define even though we may feel we have an intuitive sense of what crosses the line into outrage. The variables we ultimately used in our analysis were generated through an early wave of inductive research. Each of the authors brought 20 examples we believed to be outrage and several that were borderline and worked through them asking what was going on in each instance. What abstract tactics is the speaker/writer using? What attributes make one example feel clearly outrageous while another feels closer to conventional political discourse? In the end, we were able to identify 13 types of recurring speech and behavior that constituted outrage, and we developed a code-book to define each, provide examples, and address subtleties that might otherwise lead to inconsistent coding. Coders reviewed each case for the following 13 variables: *insulting language, name-calling, emotional display, emotional language, verbal fighting/sparring, character assassination, misrepresentative exaggeration, mockery, conflagration, ideologically extremizing language, slippery slope argumentation, belittling,* and *obscene language.* Summary judgments for *overall tone* (of the case as a whole) and *overall amount* of outrage language (in terms of a percentage of the overall speech used in a given case) were also included.

The operational definitions of the 13 content variables required many rounds of pretesting to construct and are not self-explanatory. Capsule summaries of each are contained in the Appendix, and as we move through the analysis in the pages that follow, detailed descriptions of several variables will be offered. The full operational definitions and illustrative examples are contained in a lengthy codebook available from the authors.

Although the cable television, talk radio, blogs, and columns differ considerably, we created a research instrument that could be used to analyze all four formats. Coders recorded the use of each of these particular types of speech and behavior within each episode, post, and column. Up to six uses of each variable were counted, with the appropriate unit of analysis for most being the "turn" or "chunk." Following Perrin, a "turn" is defined as a contiguous block of speech by a single participant.[15] When there is a back and forth conversation, each speaker's turn is the appropriate unit. If a monologue is prolonged, judgment was made as to appropriate boundaries of a single turn, such as changes in topic, pauses in thought, and disruptions for station information, teasers, or advertisements. For written content, "chunks" are also a contiguous but clearly demarcated block of print, typically a paragraph or section. For four more concrete variables (e.g., obscene language) each discrete use was counted rather than the number of uses per turn or chunk.

Despite the challenges of coding complex variables characterized by a variety of nuanced usages, embedded in rich texts, the level of specificity of the operational definitions in the codebook yielded quite impressive intercoder reliability ratings. Over the course of 10 weeks, 15 cases were randomly selected for intercoder reliability tests in which two of the four coders evaluated the same case independently. The results ranged from a low of 80.43% to a high of 98.6%, with a mean of 91.4% agreement.

HOW MUCH OUTRAGE IS THERE?

The data reveal a great deal of outrageous speech in many diverse forms across political opinion media, suggesting that limiting our explorations of incivility to campaign communications is inadequate. Outrage punctuates speech and writing across all four formats. Whether it was liberal Keith Olbermann skewering conservatives in his "Worst Persons in the World" segment on MSNBC or radio host Michael Savage impugning the character of immigrants, cable television, talk radio, and blogs overflow with outrage rhetoric, and even mainstream newspaper columns are not above the fray.

Excluding the comparison cases such as *Morning Edition*, we find that 89.6% of the cases included in the sample contained at least one outrage incident. If we break this down further and look by medium, 100% of television episodes and 98.8% of talk radio programs contained outrage, while "only" 82.8% of blog posts incorporated outrage writing. Table 2.1 offers some broad measures of the frequency with which outrage is used per case in each of the four media formats. Table 2.2 lists the most outrageous columns, blogs, and hosts overall. Direct comparisons across the four formats are not possible as the one-hour segments of TV and radio are far lengthier than newspaper columns or blog posts (we'll return to cross-format comparisons later), but the unadjusted figures in Table 2.1 are revealing. The number of incidents on TV (23 per episode) and radio (24 per episode) should be viewed within the context of the actual length of programs,

Table 2.1 INCIDENTS OF OUTRAGE RHETORIC AND BEHAVIOR
PER CASE (ROUNDED)

Rates unadjusted for differences in length of shows, columns, and blog posts

	TV	Radio	Columns	Blogs
Mean	23	24	6	6
Median	25	23	5	4
Std. Deviation	10.265	13.739	5.871	6.027

n = 80 n = 100 n = 94 n = 198

Table 2.2 MOST OUTRAGEOUS TV AND RADIO PROGRAMS, BLOGS,
AND NEWSPAPER COLUMNS

Based on average weighted overall outrage score

Format	Name	Perspective
TV	1. The Glenn Beck Show	Conservative
	2. Countdown with Keith Olbermann	Liberal
	3. Hannity	Conservative
Radio	1. Mark Levin	Conservative
	2. Michael Savage	Conservative
	3. Rush Limbaugh	Conservative
Blog	1. Moonbattery	Conservative
	2. Orcinus	Liberal
	3. Wonkette	Liberal
Column	1. Cal Thomas	Conservative
	2. Charles Krauthammer	Conservative
	3. Leonard Pitts	Liberal

which, after subtracting commercial time, leaves approximately 44 minutes of actual content for TV and 36 minutes for radio.

Although the frequency of outrage incidents is striking, our data *understate* the number of incidents for the most egregious cases, as all 13 outrage measures were capped at "6 or more" instances per case, with particularly virulent programs reaching this threshold quite quickly and exceeding that cap by a large margin. Furthermore, there is considerable time devoted to segment setups, teasers, news cut-ins, and nonpolitical talk (e.g., sidebars about taking the dog to the vet), which are devoid of relevant content. Thus, we estimate that outrage rhetoric or behavior is used on average once during every 90 to 100 seconds of political discussion on TV and even more frequently on radio. In particular, two radio hosts, Mark Levin and Michael

Savage, utilize outrage speech or behavior at a rate of more than one instance per minute. The top 10 syndicated columnists were included in the research for the purposes of comparison to more evident provocateurs. Yet even in the newspaper columns we find an average of six instances of outrage rhetoric, even though the tone is often less extreme. This is captured by our summary measure "overall tone."[16] The mean overall tone of columns is 1.05, significantly lower than the mean overall tone for blogs (1.51), radio (1.83), and television (1.92).[17]

These data demonstrate that outrage is common in mediated political discourse, yet they are conservative assessments, and some outrage is missed. During the course of the data collection, the research team found some audacious comments that were not captured by any of the measures. Most glaringly, there is no variable for insults if they do not draw upon some other form of outrage (e.g., insulting language, name-calling, obscenity). Similarly, if we were to replicate this study it would be useful to include a variable to measure conspiracy theories. Conspiracy theories often flirt closely with related variables such as misrepresentative exaggeration, character assassination, and slippery slope argumentation, but some instances did not conform to the strict definitions established for these related variables and were lost. Finally, our variable emotional display was reserved for quite dramatic behaviors (e.g., crying, yelling, slamming down the phone in anger) and does not capture less egregious, but more prevalent behaviors such as eye-rolling, exasperated sighing, and others. If these had been counted, the numbers would have been even higher for radio and television.

WHICH FORMS OF OUTRAGE ARE MOST PERVASIVE?

Table 2.1 aggregates all forms of outrage, but in disaggregating the data we find great variation in the frequency of each of these 13 forms (Table 2.3). In terms of overall use, four types of outrage—mockery, misrepresentative exaggeration, insulting language, and name-calling—each constitute more than 10 percent of all recorded instances of outrage. Ideologically extremizing language falls at 10 percent of all recorded instances of outrage.

Mockery was the most prevalent mode of outrage (N = 1003 instances overall), with hundreds more overall instances than the second most common mode of outrage, misrepresentative exaggeration. Mockery is defined as making fun of the behaviors, planned behaviors, policies, or views of a person, group of people, branch of government, political party or other organization in such a way as to make the subject look bad or to rally others in criticism of the subject. Coders were instructed to weed out

Table 2.3 OUTRAGE INCIDENTS PER CASE: OVERALL, LEFT, RIGHT
(Excluding comparison cases)

Modes of Outrage	Overall (i)	Left (ii)	Right (iii)	Difference (iv)	T (v)
Insulting Language	1.53	1.18	1.81	−0.621***	−2.99
Name Calling	1.54	1.11	1.89	−0.781***	−3.36
Emotional Display	0.99	0.64	1.26	−0.621***	−3.22
Emotional Language	0.58	0.46	0.68	−0.219*	−1.78
Verbal Fighting/ Sparring	0.74	1.1	0.53	0.567**	2.42
Character Assassination	0.56	0.44	0.66	−0.212*	−1.71
Misrepresentative Exaggeration	1.64	0.87	2.26	−1.396***	−6.34
Mockery/Sarcasm	2.56	2.45	2.65	−0.200	−0.81
Conflagration	0.26	0.15	0.36	−0.215***	−2.64
Ideologically Extremizing Language	1.37	0.91	1.74	−0.835***	−3.79
Slippery Slope	0.28	0.17	0.37	0.200***	−2.61
Belittling	0.92	1.06	0.80	0.259*	1.73
Obscene Language	0.64	0.52	0.73	−0.208	−1.45
Total Outrage Incidents	**13.16**	**10.32**	**15.47**	**−5.143***	**−3.76**

Column (i) provides mean statistics for overall sample
Column (ii) and (iii) provide mean statistics for groups of two political orientations
Column (iv) contains the mean differences between the two groups
Column (v) shows t-statistics for equality of means tests
*, **, *** Statistically significant at 10%, 5% and 1% confidence intervals respectively

"affectionate, light-hearted teasing" and to look for humor "designed to make the subject look foolish/inept, hypocritical, deceitful, or dangerous."[18] Radio host Alan Colmes uses mockery to demean the impact of the "Tax Day Tea Parties": "They [onlookers] will go, 'Oh my God, look at all these tea bags ... I just have to act, these people ... must be listened to!'" (4/13/09). Mocking Republicans for ignoring their responsibility for the national financial crisis, columnist Eugene Robinson noted that "They had a decade long toga party, safeguarding our money with the diligence and sobriety of the fraternity brothers in 'Animal House'" (2/24/09).

Misrepresentative exaggeration (N = 615) captures instances of "very dramatic negative exaggeration ... such that it significantly misrepresents or obscures the truth."[19] The conservative blog *Moonbattery* concluded that

"RINO Senator Arlen Specter plans to stab both his party and future gener-
ations of Americans in the back by voting for the outrageous porkzilla
package which appears purposely designed to break capitalism by crushing
our economy" (2/9/09). Exaggeration was coded conservatively, reserved
for cases such as this where the writer states that the stimulus plan is
intended to bring down capitalism. Less dramatic exaggerations are quite
common in political banter and posturing, but are not included in these
numbers.

Insulting language (N = 595) is almost as prevalent as misrepresentative
exaggeration. For this research, the operational definition of insulting language involved use of "insulting words in reference to a person, group of
people, branch of the government, political party, or other organization or
their behaviors, planned behaviors, policies, or views."[20] This variable was
created specifically to capture only insulting words ("idiotic" or "pompous,"
for example), not all insults more generally speaking. For example, describing
someone as "a child" is insulting but does not use insulting words so it would
not be counted as insulting language (it would, however, be captured under
belittling). A blogger at *Firedoglake* used insulting language in posting,
"Jindal, you sucked!" after the Louisiana governor's response to President
Obama's first nationally televised speech to Congress (2/25/09).

Often insulting language was used to name-call, in which case it was
coded only under name-calling, which emerged as the fourth most common
type of outrage (N = 573 instances overall). For example, "asinine" used
in reference to a person or group's behavior was counted as insulting language, but if the person or group is called "asinine," this was recorded as
name-calling. Not stopping with generic names like "moron" or "idiot," or
even with political insults like "partisan hack" or the fresher "hack-in-the-
box" (Dennis Miller to Bill O'Reilly in reference to Nancy Pelosi 2/25/09),
speakers and writers offered quite inventive concoctions. Consider the riffs
on politicians' names: radio host Mark Levin repeatedly referring to then
Illinois governor, Rod Blagojevich, as "Boyabitch" (2/9/09), *Moonbattery*
blogger Dave Blount referring to former senator Arlen Specter as "Sphincter"
(2/9/09), or radio host Michael Savage calling Senator Charles Schumer
"Up-Chuck Schumer." Obama supporters were called names such as
"Obamabots" (*Michelle Malkin*, 3/24/09) and "Obamatards" (*Wonkette*,
2/9/9). Sometimes insulting language and name-calling are strung together
for maximum effect as was the case when TV host Keith Olbermann referred
to the Tea Party protesters as "a bunch of greedy, water-carrying corporate-
slave hypocrites" (4/15/09) or when blogger Digby from *Hullaballoo*
described the defenders of torture practices as "illogical, sadistic scumbags"
(4/17/09).

In coding the cases, there were some surprises. First, direct confrontation, which we term "sparring," is rare. Despite the antagonistic tenor of shows like the *O'Reilly Factor* and the *Rush Limbaugh Show*, sparring scored nearly last among the 13 variables, with just N = 103 instances across all the cases.[21] We anticipated more hostile interruption and conflict between guests or between guests and hosts. This relative lack of jousting is explained by the noteworthy absence of opposing voices within individual programs. Hosts share airtime with ideologically compatible voices, and periodically with moderate or "neutral" visitors, but very rarely with true believers from the other side. We were also surprised how often obscenities were used. We believed naively that foul language would be quite rare—perhaps relegated to a random blog post. Instead, it appears closer to the middle of the rankings.

ARE LIBERALS OR CONSERVATIVES MORE OUTRAGEOUS?

Claiming persecution by those on the other side of the political aisle, and detailing how inaccurate and vindictive they are, is a recurring theme in political talk media. As Table 2.2 demonstrated, the worst individual offenders come from both the left and the right; is one side really worse than the other? In a word, yes. Our data indicate that the right uses decidedly more outrage speech than the left. Taken as a whole, liberal content is quite nasty in character, following the outrage model with accusations, conspiracy theories, and ridicule. Conservatives, however, are even nastier.

Returning to Table 2.3 we see an overview of the number of outrage incidents for the left, right, and as a whole across the 13 modes. The right uses significantly more of 10 of the 13 types of outrage, while the left uses significantly more of only 2 of the 13 types of outrage (verbal sparring/fighting and belittling), and there is no statistically significant difference in the volume of mockery/sarcasm, the 13th type of outrage. Perhaps most important is the marked difference in the overall number of outrage incidents per case, with the right engaging in an average of 15.57 acts per case, while the left engages in 10.32 acts per case, the difference between which is statistically significant at the 1% confidence interval.

Because cases across the four formats (television, radio, blog, and column) are of differing lengths (word count for a column and a radio episode, for example, are quite different), and the cases in our sample are not evenly distributed in terms of political perspective (i.e., we have far more conservative talk radio than progressive talk radio), we cannot simply compare averages. Table 2.4 shows the chances of a personality/author being on the left politically

Table 2.4 WEIGHTED LEAST SQUARES AND PROBIT MODELS
USING AMOUNT OF OUTRAGE TO PREDICT POLITICAL IDEOLOGY

Independent Variables	Dependent Variable = Left							
	WLS				Probit			
	(i)	(ii)	(iii)	(iv)	(v)	(vi)	(vii)	(viii)
Total	-0.007**	-0.009**			-0.008**	-0.009**		
Outrage Incidents	(0.002)	(0.003)			(0.002)	(0.003)		
Total			0.001	0.002*			0.002*	0.002*
Outrage Scores			(0.001)	(0.001)			(0.001)	(0.001)
Other Controls	No	Yes	No	Yes	No	Yes	No	Yes
P	0.0000	0.004	0.1425	0.0400	0.0002	0.0022	0.1376	0.0460

Weighted least squares method in columns (i) through (iv)
Probit maximum likelihood method in columns (v) through (viii)
Coefficients reported are the marginal effects of an infinitesimal increase in independent variables
In even numbered columns we also have controls for the length measure and number of speakers present
Results are for regressions with dependent variable Left. For Right, since Right=1-Left after excluding comparison and neutral cases, the coefficients are the reverse of those for Left
P is the p-value for respective regressions

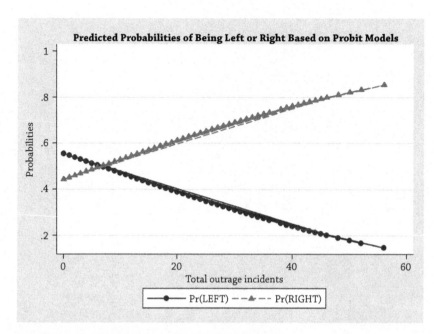

Figure 2.1 Graph of predicted probabilities (fitted values)
(Excluding comparison cases)

This graph is based on the Probit regressions shown in Table 2.4. It shows the predicted probabilities of being left and right given the total outrage incidents. Since we exclude neutral and comparison observations, the probabilities of LEFT and RIGHT must add to 1.

as predicted by both weighted least squares and probit regression analyses. The total number of outrage incidents and the overall outrage scores are used as predictors, controlling for the length in words (to account for differences in length between television episodes, blog posts, and radio programs) and the number of speakers present (as cases with only one speaker will not contain sparring). Both techniques show that as the number of outrage incidents/outrage score increases, the source is less likely to be left of center, and hence more likely to be right of center politically as the comparison cases have been excluded from the analyses. The higher the level of outrage, the greater the likelihood that the personality or author is conservative.

Another way we can assess left–right variation is by examining the predicted probabilities of being left and right in graph form. Figure 2.1 shows the predicted probabilities (fitted values) based on the probit model used in the previous regressions. If the number of outrage incidents in a case is relatively small (5 incidents or fewer), the case is more likely to be liberal. But, as outrage incidents increase in number, the probability that the case is conservative increases dramatically. Those shows with the highest levels of outrage are far more likely to be conservative than liberal. Although the left and right do not use outrage equally, looking at usage across modes, they use techniques that are remarkably similar. This is the mirroring we describe in Chapter 1.

DIFFERENCES ACROSS MEDIA

As stated earlier, there are some differences in the presence of outrage across media formats, with all television episodes and virtually all talk radio programs containing at least one outrage incident (excluding comparison cases), in contrast to the somewhat smaller percentage of blog posts. This is explained in part by the relative civility of political blogs, but the difference is exaggerated by the ways in which blog posts are entered as discrete themed posts. Many radio and television hosts include nonpolitical segments (e.g., a story about lousy service at a restaurant), but these are integrated with political content in each episode. Bloggers, on the other hand, often parcel sidebar commentary/stories into discrete posts. For example, Little Green Footballs had a brief post touting a new iPhone. A few fully nonpolitical posts were selected when their date/timestamps aligned with those outlined in the sampling protocol, diluting the presence of outrage. In other words, we believe blogs do contain outrage less often than cable news analysis and talk radio, but probably not radically less. Taking stock of this information, it is interesting to note that it is television, the most widely used medium in the United States, that is the most likely to contain outrage talk and behavior.

Although we cannot compare outrage frequency within cases across media, we can examine variation in outrage form. The left and right are quite similar in their outrage styles, and the same can be said about variation across format (see Table 2.5). With the exception of mockery and belittling, which have higher rates of usage in blogs and columns than television and radio, most forms of outrage are fairly evenly dispersed across the four formats. Emotional displays show up much less frequently in columns and blogs than in television and radio, but this is to be expected. While print formats have the ability to engage in emotional display through font manipulation, the use of capital letters, dramatic punctuation, emoticons, and so on, they do so infrequently, particularly in newspaper columns.

LISTENING IN

The quantitative data give us a bird's-eye view of the terrain, but qualitative insights are necessary to really explore the nature of the discourse. If you tune in, what do you find? Stepping back and listing the topics covered in

Table 2.5 MODES OF OUTRAGE RHETORIC AND BEHAVIOR (BY FORMAT)

Expressed as proportions for each medium

Outrage Type	Total	TV	Radio	Blog	Column
Mockery	0.20	0.18	0.13	0.32	0.26
Misrepresentative Exaggeration	0.12	0.14	0.14	0.08	0.12
Insulting Language	0.12	0.12	0.12	0.11	0.15
Name Calling	0.11	0.12	0.12	0.09	0.10
Ideologically Extremizing Language	0.10	0.10	0.12	0.08	0.05
Belittling	0.07	0.06	0.04	0.13	0.14
Emotional Display	0.07	0.08	0.11	0.01	0.00
Emotional Language	0.05	0.06	0.04	0.05	0.04
Obscene Language	0.04	0.03	0.06	0.05	0.00
Character Assassination	0.04	0.05	0.04	0.04	0.04
Slippery slope Argumentation	0.03	0.03	0.02	0.02	0.07
Sparring	0.02	0.03	0.03	0.00	0.00
Conflagration	0.02	0.01	0.02	0.04	0.02
Totals	**1.0**	**1.0**	**1.0**	**1.0**	**1.0**

outrage venues, we find that outrage-based political opinion covers many of the same topics that lead the daily news; commentators address bills in Congress, news about the economy, and discussions of political developments and leaders. But whether the subject is health care, unemployment, activity on the part of groups such as the Tea Party or the Occupy movement, or new proposals about immigration, the purveyors of outrage transform and intensify the conversation by drawing on a range of tools that dramatize the buffoonery, intrigue, and perilousness of the news at hand. A new bill on the floor of Congress enters the picture as a jumping-off point for escalating rhetoric rather than as the subject of careful policy analysis. Outrage hosts, then, do offer insight into the political world, but with a kaleidoscope-like vantage that provides a captivating and colorful lens through which to view current affairs, albeit one that is also riddled with distortions that often obscure rather than illuminate the issues at hand.

Writers, hosts, and producers filter the news through the lens of ideological selectivity. Events that can be used to suggest that policies, beliefs, or people from the other side are ignorant, dangerous, or inept—an embarrassing mistake, for example, such as Rick Perry's awkward inability to remember the third federal agency he would cut if elected during the 2012 primary season debate or Herman Cain's cringe-worthy straining to remember how President Obama had intervened in Libya—are amplified and raked relentlessly over the coals. But if such points of vulnerability fail to occur naturally, outrage outlets divine them. We find that routine political behaviors are regularly presented in ways to create the impression that views or people are ignorant, dangerous, or inept. While there are many techniques hosts can use to "spin" something benign into an indictment, there are a few favorite, tried-and-true tools hosts use regularly to get the job done. We turn now to look in detail at one of the most commonly recurring themes in outrage discourse: vilification.

Nazis, Fascists, and Racists: Unveiling the Enemies

Outrage trades in hyperbole, doling out comic book narratives in which users almost always cast themselves in the role of intrepid hero ready to fight for "the American People," although this character position is occasionally swapped for that of innocent victim. Like Clark Kent or Peter Parker, the celebrities of political opinion media are good guys who would prefer to restrain their fury, but who are noble enough to stand up and shine a spotlight on danger if necessary (and it's almost always necessary). This danger most often takes the form of bad guys determined to put an end to the American way of life. So that the audience is perfectly clear who the villains are, hosts and bloggers use semiotic shortcuts, attempting to symbolically pollute their enemies by linking them to the groups most reviled by American audiences. In this section, we examine these attempts at vilification via symbolic pollution, to illustrate the intensity of the rhetoric and the ways in which the conventions of the genre reappear across venues.

No One Looks Good in a Hitler Moustache

Of the available evil stock characters, Hitler is the overwhelming favorite among outrage pundits. One headline in the *Telegraph* during the summer of 2011 read: "Glenn Beck likens Obama administration to the Third Reich." It begins with the lead: "Glenn Beck, the American broadcaster who compared Norwegian massacre victims to the Hitler youth, has defended his use of Nazi analogies and likened the Obama administration to the Third Reich."[22] On one hand, we can understand why statements this offensive would capture the attention of the international news media. Such analogies might plausibly even give fans pause, as it seems possible that likening *anyone* to a leader responsible for the genocide of over 10 million people might raise a red flag—strain fans' faith in the credibility of the speaker, perhaps, or come across as so ludicrous as to be interpreted as unintentionally funny, or be seen as unconscionably irresponsible—but if this is the case, no one has mentioned it to the gurus of outrage opinion media. Indeed, the use of such analogies has become so frequent that news stories such as the one in the *Telegraph* almost feel naive, detached from the realities of a media environment in which evoking Hitler approaches the mundane.

Glenn Beck, at the center of that article, uses such analogies often. Beck has compared Barack Obama to Hitler on more than one occasion. For example, in comparing the Obama administration's approach to the present US debt crisis with that of the early days of the Nazi government in the late 1930s, Beck said: "I'm telling you—it's the same situation.... Hitler and all of the people in the Third Reich—they were all doing the same thing," by blaming their failings on having inherited a "bad situation" from the Weimar Republic just as Obama suggested that the economic turmoil facing the United States is a legacy from George W. Bush.[23] Beck also suggested that Al Gore's environmental speeches in schools were designed to indoctrinate American children in the tradition of the Brown Shirts:

> When I finish this story you may believe we're on the road to the Hitler Youth.... You're all working hard right now to raise your kids right and it seems like everything is stacked against you.... Now you've got the former vice president of the United States—and a Nobel Prize winner—looking *your kids* in the eye and telling them, you know what, *you* know things that your dad and mom don't.... The government and its friends are indoctrinating our children for the control of their minds, your freedom of choice, and our future. It must stop, because history—when properly taught—has already shown us where it leads. This is what the Nazi Joseph Goebbels said about the Hitler Youth: "If such an art of active mass influence through propaganda is joined with the long-term systematic education of a nation and if both are conducted in a unified and precise way, the relationship between the leadership and the nation will always remain close." Well what's next?[24]

There are times Beck makes Nazi analogies while simultaneously suggesting that he is not making such a tactless comparison. For example, on one episode of his radio show, Beck insisted: "I'm not comparing" Obama to

Hitler, but "please read *Mein Kampf*." This is valuable, suggested Beck, because those who do will see that the Germans ignored the fact that Hitler—like Obama—gave clear foreshadowing of his horrific plans, but was not taken seriously. Americans should learn from the German mistake.[25] But whether or not Beck sees these references as comparisons, he regularly links those he finds ideologically objectionable to Hitler, usually in an effort to help the audience recognize the potential danger before it is too late, with statements such as: "most people... when they say they are progressive, they don't think they're headed here [points to the words "Nazis" and "Communists" on his blackboard]. But progress—baby steps— you are moving toward something! You are moving toward one of these. This is why they called George Bush a fascist. Because progressives know what's at the end of the progressive road: Nazis or Communists!"[26]

Beck may most frequently press the Nazi panic button, but he is not alone. For example, Rush Limbaugh suggested there were "gazillions of similarities between National Socialism in Germany and Obama's healthcare plan," but made clear, "Nobody is saying that Obama is Hitler.... What we're saying is that this healthcare plan mirrors Nazi Germany's. And the Nazi Germany healthcare plan was the foundation from which they built the rest of their socialist paradise." And Bill O'Reilly once described liberals who support gun control as "today's totalitarians," saying: "In the past, right-wing extremists like Hitler and Mussolini were in the forefront of state control.... [T]oday's totalitarians are primarily on the left. Certainly that's the case in the U.S.A."[27] And conservative radio host Michael Savage has been even more explicit in his use of such analogies to fear-monger:

> The fact of the matter is that Obama may be getting ready to organize his own personal army—not of brown shirts, but of green shirts—that's why he's given this street thug, Van Jones... this all-important job. If Obama should appoint thousands or more than thousands of people to the environmental green czar to work for him and then he deputizes them and gives them guns and then gives them federal powers over the local police, you will know that we are repeating in the United States of America. There was another man, in another country who rose to power on an army of street thugs... the Obama appointees actually have almost the same exact policies as the Nazi Party did.... The brown shirts, as I said, under Hitler were used to intimidate Germans who opposed Hitler. My fear is that Obama will be using green shirts—these street agitators—in order to control the police and the people.[28]

And while conservative hosts use Nazi analogies more often than liberals, progressives also use such comparisons periodically. Consider the remarks made by liberal radio host Mike Malloy[29] when talking about former vice president Dick Cheney: "You know, I listen to this monster, and all I see is underneath his suit, I see the SS uniform. And if he were to open up his collar, there would be the death's head."[30] And in the 2012 election season, the liberal outrage outlets enjoyed raking Mitt Romney over the coals for commenting publicly and favorably on Hitler's liquefied coal technology.[31]

Elected leaders are not the only Nazis in our midst. Outrage commentators often depict their competitors as Nazis or Nazi sympathizers. Listen to Ed Schultz of MSNBC as he comments on a clip of Rush Limbaugh speaking to the conservative political action conference:

> Now if you watch Limbaugh with the sound down, the drugster, he looks like Adolf Hitler! His animation is amazing! It's—the parallel is so striking. And then, of course, Rush is now the angry American. The *angry* American.... They are so out of touch, just like Hitler was out of touch.... I think there are parallels drawn by some of the things Hitler was saying and some of the things that were at the CPAC convention. They are not Americans. They don't care about the greater good of society.[32]

Similarly, conservative Bill O'Reilly once said of Arianna Huffington, from the liberal *Huffington Post*, "I don't see any difference between Huffington and the Nazis.... There's no difference between what the two do."

These repeated references to Nazis showcase the substantial difference between conventional political "incivility"—in which a speaker is not treated respectfully—and outrage. These examples illustrate both the vitriolic nature of the genre and also the way in which users play on the worst fears of the audience. Not only is Obama, or Cheney, or Limbaugh described as a terrible leader or broadcaster, they are described as capable of genocide. The direction of influence is notoriously challenging to pin down in media effects research, but in 2010 a Harris Interactive poll found that a remarkable 38 percent of Republicans (and 20 percent of all people polled, regardless of party affiliation) reported believing that President Obama "Is doing many of the things that Hitler did."[33] Suggesting that this astounding finding is in no way related to the repeated connections between Hitler and the Democrats that have been made by conservative political opinion leaders feels difficult to accept.

McCarthy's Resurrection

The Nazis may be the most dramatic of the villains evoked in political opinion media, but they are not evoked as often as groups such as communists, socialists, fascists, and anarchists. These groups are referenced in a variety of ways. Sometimes they appear in analogies (e.g., often in reference to the path a leader wishes to take), other times they are used more directly as a form of name-calling (e.g., in referring to the Occupy movement), and they are also used as adjectives in an attempt to radicalize the appearance of policies deemed objectionable (e.g., Obama's "communist" health care legislation). With the exception of the less commonly used "anarchist," these terms (socialist, communist, fascist) are deployed daily— and usually inaccurately—with nary a raised eyebrow. Sean Hannity calls the Democrats "The Socialist Party of America" and President Obama "The Socialist in the White House."[34] Rush Limbaugh says the National Lawyers Guild is a "communist front group."[35] Such characterizations are so common as to be unremarkable.

While Barack Obama has been the subject of many accusations of socialism and communism by conservative outrage commentators, liberals commonly referred to George W. Bush as a fascist (he was also often labeled "terrorist"). For example, Keith Olbermann addressed then President Bush through the camera:

> If you believe in the seamless mutuality of government and big business, come out and say it! There is a dictionary definition, one word that describes that toxic blend. You're a fascist! Get them to print you a T-shirt with fascist on it!…You, sir, have no place in a government of the people, by the people, for the people. The lot of you are the symbolic descendants of the despotic middle managers of some banana republic to whom "freedom" is an ironic brand name, a word you reach for when you want to get away with its opposite.[36]

But under the Obama administration, there are still plenty of fascists to go around. Here conservative radio host Michael Savage offers a similar assessment of Barack Obama:

> He's a fascist. I know that you don't want to hear this, but the man is a neo-Marxist fascist dictator in the making. He is not using his fascism yet, because he doesn't have enough power to wield the fascist instruments of power, but he is aggrandizing enough power to become a very dangerous president.[37]

This mirroring is one of the most noteworthy attributes of outrage, with techniques remaining consistent regardless of the ideological orientation of the venue. The specific language is even often the same such that the villain on MSNBC is presented as a "right-wing extremist" while the villain on

Fox News is described as a "left-wing extremist." This is why two such different presidents can find themselves equally open to these vilifying labels. This is because the labeling, the analogies, the rhetorical tools are a product of the genre, not attributes of the targeted subjects, who are easily replaced. We see this vividly in the way the right and left differently narrate the actions of the Tea Party and Occupy movements. One group of protesters is made of fringe lunatics fawned over by the media and the other is composed of patriotic freedom fighters treated unfairly by the media, but the Tea Party and Occupiers float freely between being depicted as good or evil, depending on the political inclinations of the speaker.

Racists Are Everywhere (Else)

Racism appears in outrage venues, which are overwhelmingly dominated by white male voices. Sometimes it is very explicit, as when Michael Savage rants about the white male being pushed around by "multicultural people" who are "destroying the culture in this country."[38] The racism changes focus and tenor with changes in the political context (e.g., a surge of anti-Islamic rhetoric after the 9/11/01 terrorist attacks in the United States). In recent years racism has been particularly pronounced in discourse regarding (1) President Obama's racial and national identity as illustrated in racialized comments such as Rush Limbaugh's suggestion that the new Oreo with chocolate and vanilla filling be called the O-Bam-eo,[39] or Chris Matthews's seeming delight when he realized that he "forgot he [Obama] was black tonight for an hour!"[40] as well as in more extended conversations such as the questioning of Obama's citizenship spurred by the "birthers"; it has also appeared (2) in virulent discussions about undocumented immigrants, many of which have involved the use of pejorative terms and have blamed immigrants for draining welfare, spreading disease, stealing American jobs, and committing crimes. This anti-immigrant rhetoric was particularly interesting in a November 2011 episode of *Lou Dobbs Tonight* when a guest worked to taint Mexican immigrants by linking them to a more stigmatized ethnic group, suggesting that they may actually be Middle Eastern terrorists who have "gone through training to look like Hispanics."[41]

Matthews came under fire for his remarks about President Obama, as have others. This makes sense in an outrage context, because while racism itself appears regularly in outrage discourse, *allegations* of racism are even more commonplace. It seems many of these same hosts are deeply committed to uncovering racists wherever they might lurk. For example, in analyzing a fairly benign statement made by Limbaugh that the Republicans should be able to roll back Democrats' accomplishments, Chris Matthews said: "Here's Rushbo with his agenda....He wants to get rid of the integration we did under Harry Truman in the United States Armed Forces. That was what Truman did in '46. That was 65 years ago. He wants to get rid of the *Brown case*, of course, integrating our schools, at least the public schools."[42] Jack Coleman, a blogger with the conservative blog *NewsBusters* singled out Rachel Maddow after she referred to Obama as the "boy king." Coleman introduced the clip of her making the remark by saying, "Listen for yourself from the embedded video while Maddow takes off her KKK hood just long enough to commit this utter outrage."[43] While examples abound, Glenn Beck's July 2009 comments received particular attention as they offered double shock value by calling a sitting president and a person of color a racist: "This president [Obama], I think, has exposed himself over and over again as a guy who has a deep-seated hatred for white people or the white culture....I'm not saying he doesn't like white people, I'm saying he has a problem. This guy is, I believe, a racist."[44]

Having been accused repeatedly of not supporting Obama because of his race, conservative commentators lashed out eagerly at liberals for their criticisms of Republican primary contender Herman Cain in 2012. On *Hannity*, conservative pundit Ann Coulter sounded the racist alert:

HANNITY: Both Herman Cain and Clarence Thomas used the term "high-tech lynching." Is that high-tech—is that accurate?

COULTER: Yep. It absolutely is. It absolutely is, and it's coming from the exact same people who used to do it the lynching with ropes. Now they do it with a word processor.

HANNITY: You mean the Democratic Party.

COULTER: Yes. Yes. We had to have national federal civil rights laws to protect blacks from Democrats.[45]

Rush Limbaugh made similar allegations:

After all of these years, none of us should be surprised, but I still am. Look at how quickly what is known as the mainstream media goes for the ugliest racial stereotypes they can to attack a black conservative...[begins a Bill Clinton impersonation] *"They're going after him with some of the ugliest racial stereotypes I have ever seen. That's how our side does it; we get away with it. I just love it. I love watching it."* What's next, folks? A cartoon on MSNBC showing Herman Cain with huge lips eating a watermelon?[46]

This line of criticism is not new to Limbaugh who has called many people and groups of people racist, President Obama and Supreme Court Justice Sonia Sotomayor among them.

Outrage commentators share mainstream news analysts' penchant for horserace coverage focusing on strategic choices made by political figures. As a result, outrage personalities are quick to challenge behavior interpreted as racist, as well as the deployment of race-baiting as a political tactic. For example, one blogger from the *Daily Kos* suggests not only that Tea Partiers have a penchant for "racist conspiracy theories" but also that these theories are used to gin up support: "apparently prejudice is the only thing that can reliably rally conservatives to meetings."[47] Such racism-as-a-tactic commentary is particularly common because virtually *all* suggestions of racism made by opponents can be read as strategic rather than as authentic expressions motivated by concern. The same is true, though, of the outrage hosts whose outcry over racism appears to have little to do with concern about racial equality or discrimination.

Conservatives, who are more often charged with racism (this will be discussed more in Chapter 5), are particularly defensive about such allegations and express greater frustration with accusations they perceive to be strategic. This is illustrated well by Mark Levin's rage-filled commentary on the use of cries of racism as a political ploy intended to discredit those who oppose health care legislation:

Whenever the white, left wing democrats are in trouble, they try to stoke racism or race battles in this country....Always seems to work for them. It upsets minorities, keeps them in the fold so to speak. Keeps conservatives on the defense....They get cornered. Like rats, and so this is what comes up....And so now we have Jimmy Carter, right on schedule. The anti-Jew. The anti-semite. That's what he is....Let's hear what the anti-semite had to say, Jimmy Carter. Let's go.

(Clip plays) "*I think an overwhelming portion of the intensely demonstrated animosity toward President Barack Obama is based on the fact that he is a black man, that he is African American. I live in the South and I've seen the South come a long way and I've seen the rest of the country that shared the South's attitude toward minority groups at that time, particularly African Americans that racism in connection still exists and I think it's bubbled up to the surface.*" (Clip ends)

[Levin screaming] That's enough! Shut up you idiot. You damn fool!...How dare you pass judgment on anyone who questions Barack Obama....This is sickening. Absolutely sickening. What is it that these folks are trying to do? What's their end game? They want some kind of a race war?...And the willingness to use that tactic repeatedly is so contemptible and irresponsible.

His commentary is delivered with a palpable fury that is lost in transcription, but which is a hallmark of Levin's broadcasts.

We see then that attempts are made to discredit opponents by painting them as racist and as race-baiting. However, this concern about racism appears much as other important social and political subjects appear in outrage—not as serious issues in need of examination but as golden opportunities to gain footing in the ongoing contest to re-inscribe the sense of political superiority and aggrieved solidarity that proves effective in validating audience preferences and winning the ratings game. These attempts to vilify are sometimes built upon empirical evidence of political maliciousness, but more often they build upon stock characters—evoking images of murderous dictators, cold war communists, and bumbling southern ne'er-do-wells slinging the "n" word (Islamic terrorists are another regular, though we have not offered examples here). These hyperbolic analogies would seem ludicrous to dispassionate observers, but most loyal followers are not dispassionate.

Don't Trust a Word They Say

It can be difficult to maintain these accusations and assertions in the face of news outlets that circulate less outrageous interpretations of public affairs. Conventional journalists' narratives are easily dismissed, however; since there is incontrovertible evidence that conventional news outlets— the liberal media or the corporate media, depending on your politics—are *not* to be trusted. Debunking the lies of the mainstream news media and revealing their bias is an essential accessory to the dramatic stories crafted in outrage venues. As a result, growling at conventional news media (usually just called "the media," as if these speakers and writers are somehow outside that umbrella) is another recurring theme in outrage discourse.

Both liberal and conservative outrage personalities sound the bias alarm, claiming that they are victims of the hidden ideological ambitions of traditional journalism. While conservatives may find Al Sharpton or Rachel Maddow objectionable, and liberals may find Bill O'Reilly or Sean Hannity objectionable, these hosts work in opinion media and are not expected to be free from ideological perspectives. The legitimacy of journalists and conventional news outlets, however, hinges on the appearance of objectivity, even though "objectivity" has been long dismissed as an unattainable fiction, and in more provocative critiques it is considered an undesirable journalistic ideal leading to news that privileges neutrality over information quality. In spite of this, notions of objectivity continue to shape journalistic practices today in powerful ways, as news organizations must demonstrate their neutrality. While fairness and accuracy remain important to most news organizations, objectivity lingers as a performative ritual in which journalists and editors showcase these attributes, by doing such things as acknowledging that a particular source was asked to comment and declined or failed to return messages rather than allowing the absence of their inclusion to suggest a failing in the reportage.

Polls show that trust in journalism is at a record low. In September 2011, Gallup reported, "The majority of Americans still do not have confidence in the mass media to report the news fully, accurately, and fairly. The 44% of Americans who have a great deal or fair amount of trust and the 55% who have little or no trust remain among the most negative views Gallup has measured." What's more, 60 percent of those polled reported sensing media bias.[48] We cannot discern whether these attitudes toward conventional news are related to real changes in the quality of reporting, shifts in perception unrelated to news quality, or an artifact of something unrelated such as an increase in diffuse cynicism or overall distrust in social institutions. If the decreased trust in news media has been produced by a non-content-related shift in public perception, such a shift could be happening concurrently to outrage purveyors and lay people, or the purveyors could themselves be driving this distrust with their seething indictments. Jonathan Ladd finds that listening to talk radio is negatively correlated with trust in the media, as is use of the Internet for acquiring political information, with the effect stronger for Republican users, although he is not examining outrage venues specifically, making it difficult to know the impact with certainty.[49]

Whether or not the outrage hosts drive distrust, they certainly capitalize on it, ranting about the conventional news media in a way that stokes the fear and anger of the audience and lends credence to their own accounts when they fail to align with the reports made in conventional news and opinion venues.[50] In reference to the sluggish response of the press to the earliest Occupy protests, Keith Olbermann threw his hands up in frustration: "Why wouldn't that get extensive news coverage?" adding that the question is "self-answering"; anyone with a good head on his shoulders could see that the invisibility was attributable to the corporate ownership of the news organizations, as such entities would not be supportive of the movement goals. Olbermann said:

> After five straight days of sit-ins, marches, and shouting and some arrests, actual North American newspaper coverage of this...has been limited to one blurb in a free newspaper in Manhattan and a column in the *Toronto Star*....Why isn't any major news outlet covering this? Do we have the crowd shots by any chance? Where you can see the dimensions? That one!

(photo showing a large group of protesters) That's the one. If that's a Tea Party protest in front of Wall Street about Ben Bernanke putting stimulus funds into it, it's the lead story on every network newscast.[51]

For Olbermann, mainstream news is biased—it would cover the Tea Party, but avoids Occupy—and the bias is politically motivated. Olbermann, however, has a bias that serves as a corrective, restoring equilibrium to the conservative view of the world presented by conventional news. At least that's how he presents it.

Conservative voices in the Outrage Industry are even more apt to condemn conventional news media. Conservatives' relationship to mainstream news is one fraught with hostility that became visible during the Nixon administration (as we describe in the next chapter), and which has been aggravated in subsequent decades by high-profile wounds from events such as General William Westmoreland's libel suit against Mike Wallace and CBS in the early 1980s and the scandal surrounding the damaging but unauthenticated documents about President George W. Bush's military service that Dan Rather presented on *60 Minutes Wednesday* in 2004. The distrust in and distaste for the conventional news media is a staple of conservative outrage programming. Indeed, whereas progressives generally imagine MSNBC as the avowedly liberal network, and Fox News as the avowedly conservative network, and the bulk of conventional media as ideologically neutral, the conservatives we spoke with in our research imagine a different map in which it is a full-blown liberal onslaught—ABC, NBC, CBS, PBS, CNN, *New York Times*, *Washington Post*, NPR, and so on, with only Fox to provide a neutral lens. Hannity, for example, has a weekly segment called "Media Mash," which he generally introduces as a "weekly opportunity to expose the most outrageous examples of the mainstream media's liberal bias." This segment includes a discussion between Sean Hannity and the president of the conservative Media Research Center, Brent Bozell. And recurring references to the "drive-by media" are part of the Limbaugh argot. Hannity, interviewing Limbaugh, once asked him to explain the concept for those not familiar with it. Limbaugh offered:

> It's like a drive-by shooter except the microphones are the guns—and they drive into groups of people, they report a bunch of totally wrong libelous stuff about people. They create a giant mess. Sometimes people get really harmed. They go out and try to destroy people's careers. Then they get in the convertible, head on down the road and do it all over again, while people like you and me are left to clean up the mess with the truth.[52]

Criticism of the mainstream media was a frequent topic of conservative outrage during the 2012 election. Obama's persistent lead in the polls seemingly contradicted the messaging that these media had offered over the past four years. Despite the near unanimity of major polling firms showing Obama ahead in the swing states, leading media figures on the right simply denied what the surveys were saying. In the run-up to the election, Dick Morris, a frequent commentator on Fox, declared on the network that the polls were mistaken and Romney was actually ahead. As to why this was so, Morris simply said that the data were wrong. Rush Limbaugh smelled conspiracy. He told his listeners that the polls "are designed to do exactly what I have warned you to be vigilant about and that is to depress you and suppress your vote."[53]

At moments, the anger at conventional media feels closer to unbridled rage. Glenn Beck illustrated such ferocity when he gutted a fish he named "Larry" on his Internet TV show (which also became available a la carte on the Dish Network in late 2012) as a symbolic disemboweling of the press. "Just like Larry the fish, they're full of crap," Beck said of the conventional news media as he disemboweled the fish. Beck hacked the fish with a meat cleaver as he vented about the mainstream media's treatment of Herman Cain and of the Occupy protests. He gutted the fish with a playful violence as he celebrated the fact that the conventional news "is going to go extinct because—they suck....We [at Glenn Beck TV] know you see the end of what's going on...it doesn't work anymore...and we know you know that." The gruesome stunt went on, with Beck taking out the fish's eyes and putting his finger through the eye socket after reminding the audience that the fish was the press. In this bizarre scene, we are reminded of how much Beck dislikes the conventional news media, but also of how vital their debasement is to his success online; in the midst of the tirade, Beck says, "We think GBTV [later renamed TheBlaze] is the future."

Because Beck is available only by subscription or a la carte via satellite television, it is particularly vital to his success that the audience makes a break from conventional news, but all outrage hosts—left or right—need their audience to accept their view of current affairs as valuable. Discrediting other accounts helps privilege their own. Thus, hosts' genuine frustration with conventional reporting merges with a need for loyal fans to make critique of mainstream news a mainstay of the genre.

CHANGE OR MORE OF THE SAME?

Taken together, these data demonstrate that outrage is plentiful, but also that it is outlandish, strategic, and predictable—marked by recurring discursive devices. But since the data offered here are cross-sectional, do we really know that outrage is more prevalent than in years past or that the nature of mediated analysis of political life has truly shifted? We cannot go back in time to take comparative measurements of cable, talk radio, or blogs, and there are no historical archives of talk radio shows that we're aware of, and cable TV opinion shows and political blogs are relatively recent in origin. Again, we know of no repository of such shows or posts that go back many years in time.[54]

What can be analyzed over time are newspaper columns. The most widely syndicated conservative and liberal columnists were included in our analysis as a point of comparison to the three other media sources. The research objective was to see to what degree the presumed sources of outrage commentary in TV, radio, and blogs compared with this more conventional form of journalism. It was hardly surprising that the newspaper columnists used less outrage than those in other formats. But we were surprised to find that outrage language is now also common among the nation's leading newspaper columnists. Charles Krauthammer may be a steely intellectual, but he can also be nasty. And Maureen Dowd has become known for brandishing derisive mockery with little sympathy.

To determine whether outrage is new in prominent newspaper columns, we studied 10 widely syndicated columnists during 10-week periods for both 1955 and 1975.[55] We chose these dates assuming that if there was a precedent for outrage it would appear during the tumultuous period of the 1960s and early 1970s, with the civil rights movement, the Vietnam War protests, and the Watergate scandal, all of which raised the country's political temperature to a fever. As illustrated in Figure 2.2, the answer is no. Outrage is virtually absent from both the 1955 *and* the 1975 columns. This contrasts to the columns from our 2009 research, which contain, on average, nearly six instances of outrage per column. In short, the titans of American journalism in 1955 and 1975 remained restrained in their language despite the impassioned controversies of the times.

In addition to this longitudinal data, other relevant research supports our presumption that outrage is on the rise. The tone of talk radio also seems to have changed over a relatively short period of time. The Times Mirror Center for People and the Press conducted a substantial study of talk radio during the early 1990s. To be sure, talk radio then leaned right but Andrew Kohut and his research team described talk radio as a mix of conservative and moderate views and through interviews determined that despite the presence of Rush Limbaugh as a high-profile counterexample, hosts were on average more moderate than their audiences. Politically, the radio hosts themselves were a mix of ideological and partisan backgrounds

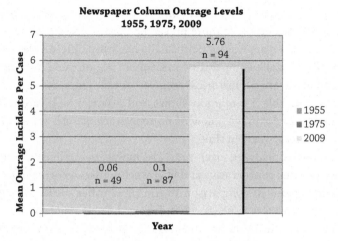

Figure 2.2 Newspaper Columnists' Use of Outrage Over Time
Mean outrage incidents per case

and more were actually Democrats than Republicans.[56] What they describe is like nothing we find today. There is a handful of liberal and moderate talk shows at the local level but all the leading nationally syndicated shows today are sharply conservative. While talk radio is becoming more conservative and the audiences increasing, a significant market has yet to emerge for liberal talk radio.[57]

The most powerful hint that outrage is on the rise is the emergence of new platforms. Cable news analysis shows and political blogs were not even in existence a decade ago, and political talk radio did not begin its dramatic growth until the 1990s. Father Coughlin may have spawned controversy decades ago, but programming of that ilk was rare. Now outrage venues abound and their audience continues to grow. The blog world is splintered into a staggering number of sites, though the top sites (which include the ones we studied) attract a lion's share of the traffic.[58] Today the number of outrage media outlets and the size of outrage audiences are both impressive and unprecedented. In the next chapter, we describe the historical transition that has helped outrage proliferate.

THE INADEQUACIES OF INCIVILITY

Cheney has had five heart attacks, and history of heart trouble—well, I guess they're one and the same. The cause of his latest health problem is not clear. I think I know. (long pause) He's done too much cannibalism, drunk too many cups of blood! Cheney's in the hospital. Ah, the first good news all day....I'm not going to feel anything but intense gratitude that this miserable bastard has finally stepped off this earthly coil!

Really!...Cheney is a murderer. He's a killer. He's a torturer. He is evil personified! He is a walking mass of horror and when he's gone, this planet will be cleaner!
— *liberal radio host* Mike Malloy[59]

It is our hope that this chapter accomplishes two key tasks. First, that it demonstrates that incivility is a useful concept, but that it is conceptually incapable of bearing the weight of this new genre of political media. Not all participants are as virulent as Mike Malloy or Mark Levin, but none of them are adequately described as uncivil, by virtue of their strategic and persistent emphasis on diminishing their opponents and valorizing their compatriots. Second, we hope these data illustrate that outrage speech and behavior are not just different from incivility, but that they are also abundant. Prior work on incivility has focused on candidate (or mock candidate) statements, debates, and advertisements, but these data make clear that this is not the only place political acrimony resides. Those who concern themselves with the effects of uncivil, negative, or outrageous political discourse should cast a broad net. Indeed, our own could be even broader, and should look at the relationship between political media and political conversation that is not mass mediated.

We also hope that the modes of outrage we identify and the baseline numbers offered here will encourage other social scientists to take this new genre seriously. Although we have emphasized measurements of outrage commentary, what is ultimately important are the larger implications of these behaviors and trends. But before we can consider the impact of incivility or outrage on the audience, on political culture more broadly, or on policy making, we must have measures that assess how much of this discourse we encounter and quality audience research that helps tease out the ways we interact with this content and the meanings we make as we do so. We will address all of these questions, but first we unravel another mystery—why outrage speech and behavior has increased so precipitously.

NOTES

1. *Mike Malloy Show,* March 26, 2010.
2. For a noteworthy exception, see Kathleen Hall Jamieson and Joseph Cappella, *Echo Chamber: Rush Limbaugh and the Conservative Media Establishment* (New York: Oxford University Press, 2008).
3. There is a long history of research on the impact of negativity in politics, particularly negative campaign advertising, in which negative information is relatively undifferentiated, with messages coded as broadly positive or negative. The benchmark research on this is Stephen Ansolabehere and Shanto Iyengar, *Going Negative: How Political Advertisements Shrink and Polarize the Electorate* (New York: Free

Press, 1995), but critics have suggested that without more information about *types* of negativity, the findings from negativity effects research are difficult to interpret. Much recent research, therefore, examines negativity with more nuance, differentiating between such characteristics as negative information about issues versus negative information about people and civil versus uncivil modes of delivery. See the citations on incivility appearing earlier in this chapter as well as Deborah Jordan Brooks, "The Resilient Voter: Moving toward Closure in the Debate over Negative Campaigning," *Journal of Politics* 68 (August 2006): 684–696 as well as Lee Sigelman and David Park, "Incivility in Presidential Campaigns 1952–2000," Working Paper (2007), for critiques of negativity research.

4. See, for example, Richard Forgette and Jonathan Morris, "High-Conflict Television News and Public Opinion," *Political Research Quarterly* 59 (September 2006): 447–456; Kim L. Fridkin, and Patrick J. Kenney, "The Dimensions of Negative Messages," *American Politics Research* 36 (September 2008): 694–723; Diana C. Mutz, "Effects of In-Your-Face Television Discourse on Perceptions of a Legitimate Opposition," *American Political Science Review* 101 (November 2007): 621–635; and Diana C. Mutz and Byron Reeves, "The New Videomalaise: Effects of Televised Incivility on Trust," *American Political Science Review* 99 (February 2005): 1–15.

5. John Geer and Richard R. Lau, "Filling in the Blanks: A New Method for Estimating Campaign Effects," *British Journal of Political Science* 36 (April 2006): 269–290.

6. Ted Brader, "Striking a Responsive Chord: How Political Ads Motivate and Persuade Voters by Appealing to Emotions," *American Journal of Political Science* 49 (April 2005): 388–405, and Ted Brader, *Campaigning for Hearts and Minds* (Chicago: University of Chicago Press, 2006).

7. Kim Fridkin Kahn and Patrick J. Kenney, "Do Negative Campaigns Mobilize or Suppress Turnout?," *American Political Science Review* 93 (December 1999): 877–889, and Kim Fridkin Kahn and Patrick J. Kenney, *No Holds Barred: Negativity in U.S. Senate Campaigns* (Upper Saddle River, NJ: Pearson, 2004).

8. Deborah Jordan Brooks and John G. Geer, "Beyond Negativity: The Effects of Incivility on the Electorate," *American Journal of Political Science* 51 (January 2007): 1–16.

9. See, for example, Emmett H. Buell Jr. and Lee Sigelman, *Attack Politics: Negativity in Presidential Campaigns*, 2nd ed. (Lawrence: University Press of Kansas, 2009); John Geer, *In Defense of Negativity: Attack Ads in Presidential Campaigns* (Chicago: University of Chicago Press, 2006); Timothy B. Krebs and David B. Holian, "Competitive Positioning: Deracialization, and Attack Speech," *American Politics Research* 35 (January 2007): 123–149; and Darrell M. West, *Air Wars: Television Advertising in Election Campaigns*, 1952–2004 (Washington, DC: CQ Press, 2005).

10. Richard R. Lau and Gerald M. Pomper, *Negative Campaigning: An Analysis of U.S. Senate Elections* (Rutgers, NJ: Rutgers University Press, 2004).

11. Jamieson and Cappella, *Echo Chamber*.

12. Particia Moy and Michael Pfau, *With Malice toward All* (Santa Barbara, CA: Praeger, 2000).

13. Some of these results were first reported in Sarah Sobieraj and Jeffrey M. Berry, "From Incivility to Outrage: Political Discourse in Blogs, Talk Radio, and Cable News," *Political Communication* 28 (January–March 2011): 19–41.

14. Sampling posts from some blogs, such as the *Huffington Post*, which have more complex structures and many nested blogs required additional instructions, which are available from the authors but too detailed to enumerate here.

15. Andrew J. Perrin, "Political Microcultures: Linking Civic Life and Democratic Discourse," *Social Forces* 84 (December 2005): 1049–1082.

16. Coders assessed Overall Tone subjectively, in conjunction with extended definitions of both outrage speech and conventional political speech (available in the codebook, upon request). The coding instructions read: This variable asks your assessment of the overall tone of the program, column, blog, etc. This particular variable is about the <u>intensity</u> of the outrage. The variable OAMOUNT should be used to assess the <u>amount</u> of outrage. The coders were asked to consider the following: Taken as a whole, describe the case you have just analyzed: 00 Overall tone is more aptly described as conventional political speech (Content and form OVERALL are more aptly described as "conventional" political speech, even if there are moments that technically count as outrage), 01 Light intensity outrage (Close to the border of "conventional" political speech), 02 Moderate intensity outrage (Outrage is present, but not overly emotional in form and/or content), 03 Intense outrage (There are windows of reason, but the content and/or form is generally quite emotional), 04 Very intense outrage (Content and/or form may match, but infrequently exceeds this level of emotionality).

17. Using an unpaired, unequal variance t-test, we can reject at the .001 significance level that the overall tone mean of columns is the same as the other formats, and accept that radio, TV, and blogs have a higher mean overall tone than columns.

18. As per the codebook.

19. As per the codebook.

20. As per the codebook.

21. Conflagration, which appeared in N = 100 instances overall, was the least commonly found mode of outrage.

22. Jon Swaine, "Glenn Beck Likens Obama Administration to the Third Reich," the *Telegraph*, July 27, 2011, World News, online edition.

23. *Glenn Beck Show*, July 26, 2011.

24. *Glenn Beck Show*, February 4, 2009.

25. *Glenn Beck Program*, August 12, 2009.

26. *Glenn Beck Show*, March 1, 2010.

27. *O'Reilly Factor*, March 2, 2010.

28. *Savage Nation*, March 12, 2009.

29. Please note that although Mike Malloy is the most outrageous liberal radio host, he is not in the quantitative sample because of his considerably smaller syndication (13 markets).

30. *Mike Malloy Show*, January 7, 2009.

31. http://www.dailykos.com/story/2012/09/26/1136903/-Mitt-Romney-Praises-Adolf-Hitler-s-Energy-Ideas

32. *Ed Schultz Show*, March 2, 2009.

33. Humphrey Taylor, 2010, "Wingnuts and President Obama," Harris Interactive, http://www.harrisinteractive.com/NewsRoom/HarrisPolls/tabid/447/ctl/ReadCustom%20Default/mid/1508/ArticleId/223/Default.aspx, as of November 15, 2011.

34. *Sean Hannity Show*, February 9, 2011, and March 31, 2010, respectively.
35. *Rush Limbaugh Show*, November 15, 2011.
36. *Countdown with Keith Olbermann*, February 14, 2008.
37. *Savage Nation*, February 5, 2009.
38. *Savage Nation*, September 20, 2009. For the context in which these particular remarks were made, see the opening quote in Chapter 5.
39. *Rush Limbaugh Show*, August 17, 2011.
40. MSNBC State of the Union telecast January 27, 2010.
41. *Lou Dobbs Tonight*, November 4, 2011.
42. *Hardball with Chris Matthews*, August 10, 2011.
43. Jack Coleman, "Apparent Closet Racist Rachel Maddow Describes Obama as 'Boy King,'" *Jack Coleman's Blog*, September 9, 2011, http://newsbusters.org/blogs/jack-coleman/2011/09/09/apparent-closet-racist-rachel-maddow-describes-obama-boy-king.
44. *Fox & Friends*, July 28, 2009.
45. *Hannity*, October 31, 2011.
46. *Rush Limbaugh Show*, October 31, 2011.
47. Michael Lazarro (aka "Hunter"), "Florida Tea Party Locked in Pointless Battle with CAIR Claims Boycotts Are Sharia Law," *Daily Kos*, November 5, 2011, http://www.dailykos.com/story/2011/11/05/1032998/-Florida-Tea-Party-locked-in-pointless-battle-with-CAIR;-claims-boycotts-are-Sharia%20Law?detail=hide&via=blog_1.
48. Limari Morales, "Majority in U.S. Continues to Distrust the Media, Perceive Bias," *Gallup Politics Blog*, http://www.gallup.com/poll/149624/Majority-Continue-Distrust-Media-Perceive-Bias.aspx.
49. Jonathan M. Ladd. *Why Americans Hate the Media and How It Matters* (Princeton, NJ: Princeton University Press, 2012).
50. Matthew Levendusky, "Why Do Partisan Media Polarize Viewers?," *American Journal of Political Science*, forthcoming.
51. *Countdown with Keith Olbermann*, November 21, 2011.
52. *Hannity*, January 19, 2009.
53. Jonathan Martin and Alexander Burns, "The Parallel Universe Where Mitt Romney Leads All Polls," *Politico*, October 1, 2012, http://www.politico.com/news/stories/0912/81845.html, as of December 19, 2012.
54. For an interesting look at references to political vitriol over time, see Daniel M. Shea and Alex Spoveri, "The Rise and Fall of Nasty Politics in America," *PS: Political Science & Politics* 45 (July 2012): 416–421.
55. The five leading syndicated liberal columnists for 1975 were Joseph Kraft, Mary McGrory, William Raspberry, Anthony Lewis, and Tom Wicker. The conservatives were Vermont Royster, William F. Buckley, George Will, William Safire, and Rowland Evans/Robert Novak. For 1955 we found the leading columnists to be mostly moderate in tone. Based on their home papers and reputations, we chose these columnists: Stewart Alsop, Joseph Alsop, Walter Lippman, Arthur Krock, C. L. Sulzberger, William Henry Chamberlin, Roscoe Drummond, Philip Geylin, and John Chamberlin.
56. Andrew Kohut, Cliff Zukin, and Carol Bowman, *The Vocal Minority in American Politics* (Washington, DC: Time Mirror Center for the People and the Press, 1993).

57. William G. Mayer, "Why Talk Radio Is Conservative," *Public Interest* 156 (summer 2004): 86–103.
58. Matthew Hindman, *The Myth of Digital Democracy* (Princeton, NJ: Princeton University Press, 2009).
59. *Mike Malloy Show,* June 25, 2010.

CHAPTER 3

The Perfect Storm

Michele Bachmann kicked off her 2012 presidential campaign in Waterloo, Iowa, where she was born and spent most of her childhood. During the speech announcing her candidacy, Bachmann emphasized her connections to the community, a theme she continued in subsequent interviews. In one interview with Fox News, Bachmann suggested that she shared the spirit embodied by John Wayne, Waterloo's other native son. Unfortunately, the candidate's facts were incorrect; John Wayne hailed from Winterset, Iowa, not Waterloo. This would have been a small detail, except that another nationally known John Wayne, John Wayne Gacy—who raped and murdered 33 boys in the 1970s—did, for a time, live in Waterloo. This left some in the media assuming that she had confused the two men. In an information environment rife with outrage outlets, it was more than a gaffe. It was political pornography.

If you are an outrage-based liberal blog, headlines such as *Wonkette*'s "Michele Bachmann Launches 2012 Presidential Campaign by Praising 'Killer Clown' John Wayne Gacy,"[1] are great for traffic, even if they are patently inaccurate. The video clip of Bachmann's blunder hit YouTube and was posted on several liberal blogs including the *Huffington Post* and the *Daily Kos*, and reappeared on the left-leaning cable news analysis shows. After Keith Olbermann aired it on *Countdown*, he quipped (in response to Bachmann's reference to her "spirit"), "The kind of spirit that mixes fact, fantasy, and often sheer stupidity in a potent blend that is really all her own." He then went on to ridicule other errors made by Bachmann while in the public spotlight. Olbermann quickly returned to the John Wayne mistake, working the subject over with a guest on the show, belaboring this trivial and politically irrelevant mistake for nearly 10 minutes.

A case could have made that Michele Bachmann was unqualified to serve as president, but that isn't what *Countdown* or *Wonkette* or any of the other outlets where terms like "moron" and "idiot" flow cheaply and quickly set out to do. On the day she announced that she would be running for president, it seems possible that liberal venues would take up something of greater substance, her policy positions perhaps, but that's not their modus operandi. Instead, they perseverated on an error about an actor's hometown. And although that error could have been explored in less adolescent directions—interrogating the depth of her Iowan roots, for example, or speculation about how Iowan voters might react to the error—liberal outrage personalities opted for playground-level mockery.

Like Sarah Palin's "refudiate" or Anthony Weiner's repeated sexting faux pas, Bachmann's serial killer faux pas was tantalizing click-bait—a snarky jab at a favorite target—too good to pass up. Indeed, according to the Project for Excellence in Journalism's New Media Index, a full third of the newslinks on blogs from the week of the John Wayne Gacy error were about Michelle Bachmann, with her candidacy and the John Wayne Gacy gaffe noted as sharing the spotlight.[2]

This political mudslinging is not new, but over the last 25 years outrage as a genre has grown exponentially. In this chapter we dispel the myth that the outrage we see today has always been present—an unfortunate but unavoidable side effect of American democracy—showing that while outrage as a rhetorical style was not recently invented, its emergence as a genre is new. Its popularity and prevalence have grown in the political arena much like reality television grew in the entertainment arena during the mid 2000s. We will also work to dispel a second myth—that the emergence of the genre is a simple byproduct of an increasingly polarized populace pounding their fists for more red meat. While a plausible and tidy hypothesis, it is nonetheless flawed. As we note in Chapter 1, the research on polarization is conflicting. Even if polarization has deepened, the level of increase is not enough to explain the dramatic growth of outrage. What's more, the history of commercial mass media in the United States does not suggest it is particularly responsive to audience desires. Social change is rarely simple, and the development of the Outrage Industry is no exception. We offer a more complicated accounting of its rise, showing that outrage has been propelled by a synergistic confluence of economic, technological, regulatory, and cultural changes that converged to create a media environment that proved unusually nurturing for outrage-based content, "Bachmann praises serial killer" isn't as simple as it seems.

BEFORE THE STORM

Fire and brimstone political inflammation was first brought to mainstream American media by a Catholic priest, Charles Coughlin, who captured the rapt attention of an estimated third of the country during his radio show's peak in the 1930s. Remarks such as "When we get through with the Jews in America, they'll think the treatment they received in Germany was nothing" remind us that the vitriolic personalities we know today are not the first of their kind.[3] And yet, Coughlin's work came long before outrage could be understood as a genre.

For his time, Coughlin was more aberration than exemplar. American mass media have not always delivered an abundance of such voices. The new popularity of today's outrageous political personalities comes in the wake of a golden age of journalism when the most visible voices in political television were known for their sobriety rather than their sensationalism. In the 1960s and 1970s political information was dominated by the three broadcast networks and the leading newspapers, especially the *New York Times* and the *Washington Post*, which reached new heights in the quality and depth of reporting. Although news gathering by such organizations today is undertaken with leaner staffs and budgets than in the 1980s, the spirit of the work done in large conventional news organizations creates a product that remains profoundly different from the political information circulated by the colorful giants of political opinion media.

It may seem unfair to draw this contrast—there is, after all, an important, if blurry, distinction between news and opinion and people certainly still get news from traditional news organizations. Access to conventional political reporting has become ever easier in the Internet era and more people today read content produced in a newspaper newsroom than at any time in American history.[4] But political news and commentary must be discussed side-by-side as both make up vital pieces of our broader political curriculum via the media, and the information, arguments, and stories presented in both venues work their way into public political discourse, becoming part of the cultural landscape even for those who do not tune in directly.

Political news and commentary were born and remain in dialogue with one another. While it is not necessary to revisit the entire history of American journalism, we see the history of network news as a particularly important point of reference for placing contemporary political commentary in context. Unlike early American newspapers, which were born teeming with opinion and persuasive content (having pre-dated our socially constructed notions of journalistic objectivity and, indeed, pre-dated even our notion of journalism), broadcast news was mindfully presented as unbiased from the outset.[5] This attempted objectivity had little to do with the new medium but rather reflected a complex history of postwar anxieties about the use of newspapers as political tools. Journalists and editors began to frame their profession in general, and news products in particular, as objective in order to build their credibility. This commitment to neutrality was then canonized through the growing ranks of journalism schools, professional associations, and awards, most notably, the Pulitzer Prize.[6] In the process, value-neutrality became not only the hallmark of high-quality news but also a requirement for ethical reporting. This objectivity imperative transferred to both radio and television news.[7]

The beginning of televised news in the late 1940s was less than auspicious. In 1948 NBC and CBS each initiated 15-minute news programs, but with few television sets in American homes, broadcasters invested only modest resources in these early news shows. Radio dominated the networks' news divisions and radio newshands protected their budgetary turf with great vigor. John Cameron Swayze (NBC) and Douglas Edwards (CBS) became the first anchors of nightly network news shows on TV, each of which used a format aimed at emulating the movie newsreels.[8] The NBC show evolved into the *Camel News Caravan*. The cigarette manufacturer generally avoided involvement in news content but did forbid any mention of cancer. If someone died of the disease, they would be described on NBC as passing away from "a long illness."[9] While imperfect, the *Camel News Caravan* was considerably more dignified than NBC's other notable initiative, the *Today Show*, which paired a chimpanzee (J. Fred Muggs) with host Dave Garroway.

As television sets became commonplace in American households in the early to mid 1950s, network news began to serve as a source of social cohesion as well as a source of information, by linking inhabitants of the United States in a way that was unprecedented. Wire services and radio networks had provided limited national news reporting, but families increasingly tuned in, watching the same content at the same time, as part of an evening ritual that formed a connective common stock of knowledge. The novelty could have worn off, but the nightly news ritual instead gained traction as CBS and NBC began to expand their TV news operations, gradually building in nightly news programs that offered more reliable reporting and eye-catching images in a straightforward manner; the viewer need not be particularly sophisticated to understand the information presented.

TV news gained gravitas through the investigative journalism of CBS's Edward R. Murrow who took on Senator Joseph McCarthy at the height of the senator's power on Murrow's program *See It Now*. The most critical episode, in which Murrow interviewed McCarthy himself, opened the senator up to national scrutiny and ultimately contributed to his censure. Given the tenor of the times, Murrow's work, and CBS's support of that work, was extraordinarily brave. Murrow demonstrated the potential of the medium and set a new standard of excellence that the networks failed to meet with their pedestrian evening newscasts.

The pairing of Chet Huntley and David Brinkley on NBC marked the transition to contemporary newscasts. Teamed together for the national nominating conventions in 1956, they took over the nightly news in October of that year. They were an unusual duo. Huntley was pensive and serious if not downright somber; Brinkley always seemed slightly amused by the absurdity of the human comedy. As television historian Barbara Matusow notes, "Brinkley's irreverent, offbeat sense of humor [played] well against Huntley's air of settled authority."[10] The odd chemistry worked and together with a small number of regular correspondents, their 15-minute program led CBS in the ratings. Their trademark was their signoff; broadcasting from Washington, Brinkley would say "Good night, Chet," and in New York Huntley would then respond, "Good night, David" (or vice versa). NBC executive Reuven Frank, who crafted the simple lines, recalled that the two newsmen hated the closing, believing that it was effeminate.[11] To Huntley and Brinkley's dismay, their signoff became a national punch line and they could not abandon it.

As Huntley and Brinkley's stature grew over time, CBS executives became increasingly concerned about the bland Douglas Edwards and his lackluster ratings. In 1962 they replaced him with veteran journalist Walter Cronkite. A year later both networks expanded their evening news broadcasts to 30 minutes. To staff this expansion, both NBC and CBS opened bureaus in key US cities and devoted more resources to existing foreign bureaus. Ratings improved; in 1970 three quarters of those who had a TV on in their house at the appropriate time (6:30 EST) had it tuned to a network news show.[12] The point is not that the ratings were high—given the limited alternatives on television, finding a lower percentage would be surprising—but it is significant that so many people shared the nightly news ritual. There was reason to tune in. The 1960s were replete with extraordinary and often traumatic events, all of which middle America watched in their living rooms. This decade of reporting included the Kennedy-Nixon debates, the moon landing, the Cuban Missile Crisis, the civil rights protests, the Kennedy assassination, the Vietnam War and the domestic protests against it, the assassinations of Robert Kennedy and Martin Luther King Jr., the tumultuous protests at the Democratic convention in 1968, and race riots in urban America.

Firing Line emerged in the context of these dramatic and often divisive events. The program was a one-hour debate-style public affairs show hosted by conservative William F. Buckley, during which Buckley posed challenging questions of the day to high-profile guests ranging from Hugh Hefner to Noam Chomsky. The interviews were interesting, with a more adversarial tone than found in network news and yet markedly more civilized than today's cable news analysis shows. Questions were thoughtful, answers tended to be substantive, and those involved treated one another respectfully. Disagreement was ever present, but disparagement was rare. *Firing Line* is noteworthy not only because it created space for extended exchange of political opinion on television, but also because it aired for over 30 years. *Agronsky and Company*, which debuted a few years later, but had less durability, also began to offer opinion-laden public affairs programming on television with a recurring slate of combatants who would reliably disagree with more personality than was typical of other news-based content of the time, though still in a far more respectful manner than is characteristic in similar formats in the outrage era.[13]

The tumultuous events of the 1960s combined with technological improvements and increased financial support culminated in broadcasts that paired compelling storylines with arresting visuals from the location of the unfolding events. Americans turned to the news to witness these historic events in real time. Media events such as these are atypical and have a distinctive disruptive dimension—commanding the viewers' attention in a way that routine news does not, yet this string of pivotal moments characterized by a norm of viewing altered our relationship to televised news in its more mundane forms.[14] By bringing these historic events into American living rooms, TV news networks became both the filter and amplifier through which Americans observed the political world. Watching these pivotal events live as they transpired heightened the sense of trust in news anchors and correspondents. Over time, many in the viewing public developed a sense that they had experienced the events first-hand rather than through the lens of editorial judgment. When Walter Cronkite ended his show with his signature tagline, "And that's the way it is," that was the way it was for many viewers.[15]

Cronkite became a towering figure in American journalism, widely respected as a paragon of common sense and integrity. For 20 years he anchored the CBS evening news and narrated the live events that drew Americans to the program, helping them to make sense of turbulent times. There are few moments in the history of TV journalism more poignant than when Cronkite told viewers that President John F. Kennedy was dead. As he made the announcement, he took off his thick glasses and struggled to retain his composure, communicating both his professionalism and his humanity. A poll in 1973 ranked him as the most trusted figure in America.[16] When Cronkite came to believe that the war in Vietnam was a mistake, President Lyndon Johnson told an aide, "If I've lost Cronkite, I've lost Middle America."[17]

In spite of the high level of trust in broadcast news, or perhaps because of it, the 1960s were also the early days of conservative antagonism toward the networks and, more broadly, toward the "eastern establishment" press. The Nixon administration seethed at CBS, the *Times*, and the *Post* (even before Watergate). In the words of Theodore H. White, "the hostility of the Liberal Press obsessed Nixon."[18] Nixon transformed his resentment of an elite that he believed used every opportunity to undo his career into an institutionalized response. His White House created an office led by firebrand Pat Buchanan that monitored press enemies and responded emphatically to what was regarded as biased coverage. CBS reporter Daniel Schorr made the infamous White House "enemies list" and CBS White House beat reporter Dan Rather was also a particular irritant to Nixon.

What was important about the Nixon response to adverse press coverage was that it appeared to tap into a broader resentment by conservatives, especially those who lived away from the East Coast and regarded the perceived values of the eastern establishment (whatever that was to them) to be contrary to traditional American values, values they believed they embodied as middle-class Americans. The attack on the news media did not end with Nixon but would become a staple of conservative rhetoric. Indeed, there has been no more enduring theme in the conservative sector of the Outrage Industry than criticizing the perceived liberal bias of the mainstream news media. As addressed in Chapter 2 and as we explore further in Chapter 5, the antagonism has culminated today in a constant drumbeat of criticism of the mainstream media on Fox News and on conservative talk radio.[19] Distrust of the conventional news reverberates through liberal political commentary as well, though the criticism is less frequent and usually framed as concern about corporate influences rather than political ideology, even if those influences are thought to map fairly well onto conservative policies and priorities.

Perhaps somewhat ironically, these charges of bias helped to expand the role of opinion in mainstream news. This is most visible in the growing opinion and editorial pages of the major national newspapers during the 1970s. Creating more robust opinion sections helped editors highlight the distinction between fact, which was idealized, and opinion, which was suspect. This strategy also saved money because contributors were happy to have visibility and did not demand a regular paycheck. Thicker op-ed pages also created space for a greater diversity of voices, which provided editors tangible evidence of political openness in the face of the alleged liberal or corporate bias.[20]

Despite conservatives' dissatisfaction with the network news, these programs dominated the political media landscape until the proliferation of cable. With cable came exponential growth in the number of channels from which audiences could choose, and with these choices came a steady stream of viewers switching from the network news to the entertainment available on new rival networks. The introduction of cable television exposed the fact that a large segment of the news audience had been attracted by the time rather than the programming, tuning in because that's what happened to be on when they wanted to watch TV.[21] Even though cable offered news channels of its own, such programming appealed primarily to those with great interest in politics who wanted more news to watch and not to the previously casual or even accidental audiences lost by the networks.

The fortunes of network news have only continued to decline, as shown by a 2012 poll conducted by Pew Research Center for People and the Press, which found more Americans using the cable channels for news about the elections than the network news; the results further confirmed the continued decline in the number of adults who report getting campaign news from newspapers, and local and network TV news.[22] What do they value in cable news? In 2010, a poll on campaign information sources conducted by *Politico* and George Washington University found that among cable hosts, Glenn Beck scored the highest among respondents for having a "positive impact" on political debate in this country.[23] Even optimists among TV industry insiders do not envision the legacy networks recovering their lost audience as each heads toward being just another channel among the hundreds that now flow into the home.

But if audiences want alternatives to network news for their political information, why has outrage-based political material, in particular, emerged as such a successful political genre across media platforms? Why has a hyperbolic, politically superficial, and often inaccurate species of political commentary taken hold in place of something more trustworthy and penetrating? If there is interest in political commentary, rather than "value-neutral" political news, why not a growth in more reliable and informative opinion formats, which examine political issues in detailed, compelling ways? Or, at the very least, why not greater diversity among the political alternatives?

THE PERFECT STORM

The standard industry response to critical questions about media content is that programming is a response to audience demand, but in practice most decisions are governed by a slightly different question. Rather than asking what the audience wants, producers and distributors focus on how to attract an audience. The difference between these two questions is substantive rather than semantic. Audience interests are often not met, even the interests of quite large segments of the population, when those segments lack the disposable income desired by advertisers. The viewing preferences of African Americans, for example, or viewers over 65 are regularly overlooked in favor of shows positioned toward white, middle-class viewers under 50. Programming is determined by many factors, including recent media success stories, cultural norms, historical context, and media practices and regulations. To the extent that radio and television concern themselves with meeting needs, the needs met are those of advertisers. The content offered by public radio and public television, which are supported by government funds, private donations, and underwriting, rather than advertising, serve as a useful point of contrast.[24]

If audience preferences drove content, we would look to the political opinion media and learn that the American public is highly polarized, with the vast majority of us at the far end of the conservative pole. Yet this stands at odds with the empirical research on political identification in the United States. Although the use of red and blue state maps during election return analysis creates an impression of a country that is of two strident minds, more careful analysis suggests that while we identify strongly with parties, we are a far more moderate—more purple—nation than such bottom-line red and blue analyses imply.[25] This is no coincidence; the very perception of a polarized populace is undoubtedly supported by the high visibility of the most extreme voices in the political opinion media. Whether or not we are more polarized, there is certainly no evidence to suggest that Americans are overwhelmingly conservative as the balance of outrage offerings might suggest. Media content cannot be understood as a simple barometer of the tastes and preferences of the citizenry.

But if outrage has not come to flourish by virtue of heightened polarization of the American public or a change in party politics, what has led to its emergence and expansion? The disparate changes we outline here coalesce to produce economic and organizational incentives to showcase—and attempt to nurture—outrage. These deeply entwined changes defy easy categorization and resist linear description, but we work to show how the clustering of a diverse array of economic, regulatory, technological, and cultural changes have created a media environment that is uniquely supportive of outrage-based political opinion.

The Changing Media Landscape

The media environment over the last 30 years has been marked by two divergent trends. First, we see a set of media industries that have moved away from a relative diversity of ownership toward industries that are overwhelmingly controlled by a handful of major media conglomerates.[26] When Bagdikian wrote the first edition of his landmark book, *Media Monopoly* in 1983, he expressed concern about the consolidation of media into the hands of 50 owners. By 2004 he argued that the overwhelming majority of media properties are controlled by only five corporations: Viacom, Bertelsmann AG, News Corp, Time Warner, and Disney.[27] The sheer size of these conglomerates was highlighted in 2011 by News Corp's phone-hacking scandal when Rupert Murdoch told reporters, "I didn't know, I'm sorry....*News of the World* was 1 percent of our company."[28] At the same moment, the public was keenly aware that News Corp was poised to grow even further, via a bid to purchase British Sky Broadcasting, which they were quickly pressured to drop. These events brought the magnitude of the corporation center stage, when they are usually obscured by the numerous brands and holdings that feel distinct to the consumer.

At one end of the production and distribution spectrum there is a concentration of control while at the level of the individual user, we see a media space that is increasingly democratic, though by no means egalitarian. Barriers to entry at the lowest levels have been reduced by the increase in computer ownership coupled with a series of sweeping technological developments. While concentration and democratization are miles apart—at the largest and smallest ends of the media landscape—they each support outrage politics. We turn first to issues of deregulation and the concentration of ownership.

Deregulation and Concentration

The Communications Act of 1934 established the Federal Communications Commission to work on behalf of "the public interest, convenience, or necessity,"[29] but what is thought to best serve the public interest is a matter of socio-historical context and political worldview. As a result, the role of the FCC has shifted over time in step with prevailing political forces. The early work of the commission is best understood as protectionist. Since the electromagnetic spectrum used for broadcasting was conceptualizd as a natural resource belonging to the public and channels were a finite commodity, the commission worked to see that the licenses were distributed in a way that would best serve the public. From the beginning, public airwaves were viewed as essential for protecting the public citizenry in the event of emergency and as a resource that could enhance public life. It is in this spirit of enrichment that the commission considered not only public preferences, but also social needs in their licensing and regulatory decisions. These concerns were at the root of such regulations as the non-entertainment guidelines, which required that a minimum percentage of broadcasting time be devoted to news and public affairs programming.[30]

Early documents and court decisions make clear that the public interest was viewed as something that could be threatened by corporate interests. These excerpts from a 1928 statement on the public interest from the FCC's predecessor, the Federal Radio Commission, are illustrative:

> While it is true that broadcasting stations in this country are for the most part supported or partially supported by advertisers, broadcasting stations are not given these great privileges by the United States Government for the primary benefit of advertisers. Such benefit as is derived by advertisers must be incidental and entirely secondary to the interest of the public.... Advertising should be only incidental to some real service rendered to the public, and not the main object of the program.... The emphasis must be first and foremost on the interest, the convenience, and the necessity of the listening public, and not on the interest, convenience, or necessity of the individual broadcaster or the advertiser.[31]

Most of the regulations put in place on radio and (eventually) television, such as the numerous ownership restrictions, were intended to ensure that corporate needs did not usurp broadcast diversity, as the "marketplace of ideas" was seen as a cornerstone of democracy. This interest in diversity emerged from a First Amendment tradition that emphasized the "Widest possible dissemination of information from diverse and antagonistic sources."[32] The marketplace of ideas, then, was seen as fostering informed decision making, cultural pluralism, and the legitimacy of democratic processes.

As the broader political tide transitioned away from corporate oversight toward deregulation, this protective approach, in which the role of the commission was seen as helping to protect and provide for the public interest, shifted toward a corporatist approach. In a marked reversal in step with the wave of deregulation that began in other arenas such as transportation, energy, and telecommunications, the FCC's new operating assumption seemed to be that the public interest would be *advanced* rather than *undermined* by the relatively free operation of market forces.[33] With this new, benevolent view of corporate outcomes, the guiding orientation of the FCC changed. Rather than intervene and protect, the government would need to step back and get out of the way.

While the first winds of deregulation were felt under Nixon, Ford, and Carter, Ronald Reagan made it his trademark, and he had a kindred spirit in his appointed commission chair, Mark Fowler. Since the mid 1980s, mass media have been increasingly deregulated, particularly around issues of broadcast diversity.[34] The financial interest and syndication ("fin-syn") rules that attempted to foster broadcast diversity and limit television network control (by minimizing vertical integration of production, distribution, and exhibition of media content) were gradually relaxed beginning in 1983 and completely erased by 1995. Policies capping ownership of radio and television stations were gradually reduced, reaching a pinnacle in the Telecommunications Act of 1996, which significantly liberalized ownership limits in national and local television as well as national and local radio. In 2003, even the prohibition on simultaneous newspaper and broadcast ownership ("cross-ownership") was relaxed (although this decision was overturned in appeals court in 2011, on the grounds that the FCC had not allowed adequate time for official notice and public comment).[35] And in 2007, FCC Chairman Kevin Martin further eased cross-ownership limits in the top 20 markets.

This deregulatory wind has not gone unchallenged, often resisted by interest groups that rarely collaborate. Sometimes these efforts are effective, as was the case in 2003 when the left and right worked together and collectively generated 3 million letters to Congress and the FCC after the commission decided to further ease television ownership caps. The controversial decision permitted broadcast companies to accumulate stations reaching 45 percent of the national audience, rather than the 35 percent cap put in place by the Telecommunications Act of 1996 (prior to 1996, the limit had been only 25 percent). The public outcry led the House to vote 400 to 21 in favor of repealing the FCC's decision. Even so, five months after this landslide victory, Congress increased the cap to 39 percent through a rider on an omnibus spending bill. This allowed Viacom/CBS and News Corp to keep the stations they already owned.[36]

This relaxed regulatory environment fueled concentration of media ownership in virtually every sphere. Looking at print, music, film, and television, Eli Noam showed that the market share of the top five media firms *doubled* between 1996 and 2001. And in spite of our perception of the Internet as more diversified, Noam finds similar patterns of concentration of ownership in Internet service providers (ISPs), web portals, search engines, browser software, and the like, arguing that rapid change in the sector is speeding consolidation rather than slowing it down. In his words, "This pours cold water over the hope that the Internet will solve the media concentration problem."[37]

Even industries historically marked by lower levels of concentration, such as the newspaper industry, have been reshaped as massive chains now own an increasing number of newspapers. Gannett, for example, now owns 82 daily newspapers in the United States alone, including *USA Today*. In addition, the company owns a large number of newsweeklies, more than 20 television stations, and an expanding digital business.[38] The overarching trend, as noted by the Project for Excellence in Journalism, has been from local ownership to chain ownership, to publicly traded company.[39]

Political content has been reshaped by the transitions in news prompted by consolidation of ownership. Scholars have argued that changing ownership arrangements have transformed news into a consumer-driven commodity, whose corporate overseers work from a market model in which success is assessed by profit margin rather than a public interest model in which success is linked to information quality.[40] During the Reagan administration, television was reimagined as a generic commodity. This was infamously evinced by former FCC Chairman Mark Fowler's assertion that in terms of regulation, the television is "just another appliance—just a toaster with pictures." To understand the paradigm shift represented by this statement, consider Supreme Court Justice Frank Murphy's perspective in 1943:

> Although radio broadcasting, like the press, is generally conducted on a commercial basis, it is not an ordinary business activity, like the selling of securities or the marketing of electrical power. In the dissemination of information and opinion, radio has assumed a position of commanding importance, rivaling the press and the pulpit…because of its vast potentialities as a medium of communication, discussion and propaganda, the character and extent of control that should be exercised over it by the government is a matter of deep and vital concern. (*National Broadcasting Co. v. United States*)[41]

This is quite different from Fowler's insistence that "The perception of broadcasters as community trustees should be replaced by a view of broadcasters as marketplace participants."[42] In the new ethos, mass media are not seen as linked to democratic practices but rather as entities to be mined for profit—and hopefully improved in the competitive market—like a consumer good.

The increased emphasis on profitability has transformed news gathering. This has been particularly visible in the centralization of news production, in which "nonessential" bureaus (e.g., international, rural) are closed, staff members are winnowed, and local communities are left relying on national news outlets.[43] Centralized news production, of course, also means fewer news sources.[44] As a result, the major networks offer relatively interchangeable "product" in terms of substantive news content and increasingly seek to stand apart by incorporating principles of entertainment into their programs.

Deregulation has affected more than ownership. In terms of political opinion media, it is particularly significant that this transition also wrought the elimination of the Fairness Doctrine in 1987. The Fairness Doctrine required broadcast licensees to present controversial public issues in an equitable and balanced manner. "Fairness" might suggest newscasts in which opposing parties are given opportunity to comment, but the doctrine defined balance more broadly: opposing viewpoints did not need to be presented within a particular broadcast, but contrary views had to be included across a television network or radio station's programs and program segments. Thus, the key was balancing programming overall. This was intended to create flexibility, but the doctrine inadvertently created a disincentive for broadcasters to offer political programming since a show that was commercially viable might require airing a balancing program that was not. The Fairness Doctrine also required that a certain percentage of airtime be devoted to public affairs programming.

Today, an overall inventory of media content does not demonstrate balance, particularly in radio, where conservative talk radio programs dominate, with more than 10 times as many on-air minutes as progressive talk radio.[45] Given the dominance of only two political parties, the media space would be well served to incorporate a broader range of ideological perspectives, and yet, political opinion media—which is overwhelmingly dominated by conservative voices—is even more narrow than electoral politics. Left to the market, this "marketplace of ideas" lacks the broadcast diversity deemed so vital during the first 50 years of the FCC.

Incivility can and does exist in spaces where opposing views are presented side-by-side, but the removal of this requirement for balance promoted outrage in two ways. First, because the Fairness Doctrine required licensees to devote a significant amount of time to controversial issues of public importance, the Doctrine's demise has been accompanied by a significant decrease in public affairs and news programming in traditional radio and television formats. Today coverage of substantive issues is remarkably thin. One study examining 112 commercial television stations demonstrated that on average, the stations offered 3.59 hours of public affairs programming over the course of a two-week period.[46] At the same time, talk radio and political blogs have exponentially increased the amount of available substantive discussion about public policy. To their credit, these parts of the media industry offer citizens an enormous array of venues containing analysis of pressing issues, many of which are productive and participatory.

The elimination of the Fairness Doctrine has also promoted outrage because the removal of the "personal attack" and "political editorial" corollaries in 2000 created a space where outlandish attacks flourish with little threat of rebuke (and great potential for financial reward). As we will show in the next chapter, there is a reason that Keith Olbermann would spend 10 minutes ridiculing Michele Bachmann's every error, relentlessly documenting each with video evidence of her "stupidity" rather than discussing the policy positions that those on the left might find objectionable.

Proliferation: Infotainment, Niche Markets, and Formulas

The trend toward hybrid news-entertainment programming is driven by the desire to attract audiences that are increasingly elusive. The exponential growth of television and radio stations introduced by the development of cable television and satellite radio fundamentally altered the way executives and advertisers conceptualize the audience. Until the emergence of cable, the three broadcast networks were an unassailable oligopoly. As described briefly in Chapter 1, with few networks vying for viewers, programming choices were predicated primarily on an interest in garnering the largest possible audiences and, as a result, the most successful television shows were those offering the least objectionable programming, those shows that interested the broadest range of people while offending or distancing the fewest.[47] The expansion of cable channels has fragmented the audience, dispersing them across the array of newly available networks, and greatly reduced the expectations that networks have for the audience share. The same proliferation of stations has transpired in radio since the advent of satellite radio and the Internet offers countess options to users, creating a similar phenomenon. In essence, users have choice overflow—options so numerous that they exceed any individual's capacity to independently explore and evaluate their choices before making a decision.

The acceptance of necessarily smaller audiences on the one hand and improved market research techniques on the other have refocused programming choices on niche audiences. Cable networks offer advertisers slivers of the public, but well-planned programming can link advertisers to audiences with their desired demographics for considerably lower advertising rates than are required to reach large audiences that may contain only small numbers of the target market. MSNBC's *Rachel Maddow Show*, for example, does not attract the large audiences that the *NBC Nightly News with Brian Williams* attracts, but her viewers are more homogeneous and have higher levels of education and considerably more disposable income.[48] This target marketing environment is one in which networks can afford to offend because they are no longer speaking to a broad audience. The viewers of AMC's *Mad Men*, ESPN's *SportsCenter*, and Nickelodeon's *Victorious* have distinctive attributes that draw specific advertisers. Although we tend to think of audiences in terms of demographic characteristics such as age, gender, and level of education and income, political preferences also shape viewing choices. It is intuitive that political preferences would shape political programming choices, but party affiliation also influences nonpolitical program choices. Recent market research that explores top television shows for Democrats and Republicans finds quite different entertainment preferences, as Figure 3.1 illustrates. The fragmentation and reclustering of the once-national audience into smaller, more homogeneous subgroups means that programming no longer needs to please everyone.

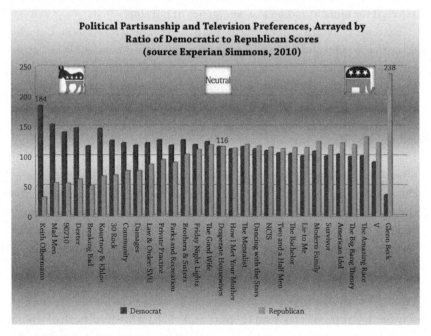

Figure 3.1
Source: Chris Uggen

In fact, many networks generate revenue by using "objectionable" programming strategically. This is readily apparent in nonpolitical entertainment media. Consider MTV, which has successfully deployed controversial material (particularly highly sexualized content and edgy appropriation of urban violence) to attract tweens and teens. The term used in the industry is "pop"; producers strive to create pop to break through the clutter and draw the eyes and ears of the audience. Pop comes in many forms, the two most familiar being violence and sex, but carefully negotiated shock is not far behind.[49] In entertainment, pop might take the form of sexually explicit content in music videos or the over-the-top battles in professional wrestling. In advertising, it takes the form of shock advertising (or "shockvertising") in an effort to entice jaded viewers and listeners to pay attention to their missives.[50] In political media, pop takes the form of agent provocateurs and their outrageous appeals.

Outrage options are not succeeding *despite* offending some segments of the audience but *because* they do so. Bill O'Reilly and Ed Schultz with their brash personalities and ideological fervor would have been unthinkable hosts in the era of the three big networks, but a shift to niche markets means that ideologues, ill-suited for the least objectionable programming model, now have a home on television. We contend that these shifts in regulation and technology and the accompanying transitions in media terrain are vital for understanding the emergence of outrage.

Extreme incivility is desirable in this hypercompetitive context, but why do so many radio and television programs use similar formats? Why has an entire genre emerged? The proliferation of this kind of talk is best explained by the mainstream media's heavy reliance on successful formulas. We may think of television and radio as creative, innovative spaces, but in practice, producers tend to imitate content that has proven successful in an effort to reduce risk. This is why *CSI* spawned *CSI: Miami*, and *CSI: New York*. Even when the mimicry is not as explicit as sequels and spinoffs (although it often is—consider the *Law and Order* franchise, *The Real Housewives* franchise, and so on), we still find "new" content paying heavy homage to the themes, settings, and concepts that have proved profitable, as anecdotally evinced by the flood of vampire television spawned by the success of the *Twilight* series and why *American Idol*'s ratings gave birth to shows such as *The X Factor* and *The Voice*.

Because political programming, like televised dramas or sitcoms, is also expected to draw profits, Rush Limbaugh's commercial success paved the way for imitators such as Sean Hannity and Michael Medved, both of whom increased their exposure as guests on Limbaugh's show. And beyond any one program, it is this preference for tried-and-true commercial successes that fueled the development of conservative outrage on the right. On the left, Rachel Maddow cut her teeth as a contributor and fill-in host on MSNBC before she was awarded her own show. As little as possible was left to chance—the type of program (politically liberal news analysis replete with outrageous rhetoric), the time slot, and even the host have been pre-vetted. Indeed, most hosts are tested at length before being hired, as was the case in 2011 as MSNBC sought to fill the time slot vacated after Olbermann left the network and Ed Schultz was shuffled from 6 to 10 PM. Both Cenk Uygur and Al Sharpton guest-hosted at the 6:00 PM slot before Sharpton was selected.[51]

The sheer number of cable and radio channels creates an impression of increased choice in terms of political content and information (as well as in entertainment), but in reality we have an array of options with limited substantive diversity. Ideologically, we see only two political perspectives represented, and those voices come from the ends of the spectrum, not closer to the center. The diversity is narrow in non-opinion formats too; local television news perhaps provides the best example of formulae at work, as network programs are virtually interchangeable with strikingly similar content, pacing and placing of segments, and appearance and demeanor of the on-air personalities.

Democratization: Erasing Barriers to Entry

The expansion of high-speed Internet access, diffusion of mobile devices, and emergence of more accessible user-generated content vehicles have democratized the production and distribution process and given outrage another platform. Self-publishing, formerly an expensive endeavor pre-senting significant distribution challenges, is now possible even for those without coding skills or special equipment. And Internet users who wish to share their self-published content need not even fund their own web host-ing space, as they can use a wide array of platforms that function as free distribution networks. These diverse venues include sites such as *Indymedia* (in the case of citizen journalism), *YouTube* or *Vimeo* (for video), and *Flickr* or *Instagram* (for photos), in addition to *Facebook*, *Twitter*, and *Tumblr* among other microblogging and social networking sites. Bloggers can post their content at no charge through venues such as *Wordpress* or *Blogger*. Attention is often paid to political entrepreneurs on the Web, such as Matt Drudge of *The Drudge Report* and Markos Moulitsas of *Daily Kos*, who began as amateurs with a website and blog, respectively, only to garner vast audi-ences (*Daily Kos* receives an estimated 1.4 million visitors per month, and *The Drudge Report* attracts 5 million).[52] But beyond these giants are countless lower-profile bloggers and web developers who also create and distribute political content.

Blogging, in particular, has exploded from a minor outpost of the Internet to more than 181 million blogs (as of March 2012), up from 50 million in July 2006.[53] BlogPulse indicates that although the rate of growth has slowed somewhat since the late 2000s, over 100,000 new blogs are still created in each 24-hour period. Early research and mainstream media attention to blogging often described blogs as online diaries or journals, and this metaphor shaped public perceptions of the practice by constructing them as emotional outlets for exhibitionists, dismissing bloggers who sought public influence.[54] But political and social commentary are rampant, and the goals of these bloggers vary. In their 2010 study of widely read political bloggers, Ekdale and colleagues found that while the group in the beginning was most interested in intrinsic motivators such as "to keep track of your thoughts" and "to let off steam," over the course of their blogging, extrinsic motivations such as to provide "an alternative perspective to the mainstream media" and "to influence public opinion" overtook these initial interests as bloggers' primary motivations.[55] These extrinsic rewards require respectable traffic levels, demanding engaging content.

Declining circulation of magazines and newspapers and the introduction of digital video recorders have combined such that the impact of many traditional advertising venues has weakened. This has led advertisers toward more creative marketing strategies, including product placement, a variety of viral marketing techniques, and narrowcasting. Research shows that political blog readers are sorting themselves into ideological niches even more aggressively than viewers of left and right political television.[56] Indeed, Kerbel and Bloom argue, "[people in the blogosphere] divide into ideological camps in a manner that resembles the narrowcasting of cable television on steroids."[57] And they often share social as well as political attributes. In an interview the marketing manager for a prominent conservative blog described his readership to us in the following way:

> 34% make 100K or more. 35% make between 60K and 100K. 47% college, 33% grad school. So, this is a very attractive demographic. And they're attractive not just because of where they are in society but by dint of the fact they read [our blog], which, even though it has 3 million monthly readers, is kind of an inside baseball thing. It means these people are influencers in their neighborhoods. Their neighbor seeks out political advice or news advice or business advice from our people. They are those sorts of people.

This readership, which he indicated also skews heavily white and male, is a valuable one for "general brand enhancement" because their readers are respected in their communities. When a luxury car brand is associated with this demographic, it benefits the brand, so advertisers want to reach this audience. Reader homogeneity and desirability make advertising on heavily trafficked blogs attractive.

Advertising networks like Google's Adsense and BlogHer have emerged to link advertisers and smaller bloggers, while advertising firms like BlogAds and Intermarket connect advertisers looking to place products and services on higher-profile blogs. These relationships have worked to create an elite subset of independent probloggers and a larger contingent of quasi-probloggers, who bring in modest sums of money through pay-per-post arrangements (e.g., product reviews) or pay-per-click ("click through") advertisements, with a host of websites (*ReviewMe*, *PayPerPost*, *SocialSpark*, *Blogvertise*, etc.) available to facilitate these relationships between advertisers and bloggers. Like ratings in the television industry or circulation in the magazine trade, traffic determines blog income, creating incentives similar to those present in the crowded television or radio environment. But as we discuss in the next chapter, blogging is not lucrative; most bloggers find that attempts to monetize their content fail, and even some of the higher-profile political blogs are barely able to cover operating expenses as a result of the unending options available online for advertisers and those surfing the Web.

This is a media environment exploding with options for users. Media companies and Internet entrepreneurs compete for an audience that enjoys (1) a multiplicity of media options (on television, online, in print, and on the radio) and (2) extensive control over their choices (thanks to digital video recorders, Really Simple Syndication (RSS) readers, MP3 players, smart phones, e-readers, and services such as Hulu and Pandora). This combines with infotainment, formulaic content, and a desire to court niche audiences such that outrage-prone commentators are attractive not in spite of their propensity for inflammatory speech but because of it. Even in niche markets, there is competition for eyes and ears, so content must stand out from the barrage of stimuli that compete for attention.

Radio: A Case Study in Convergence

The impact of the sweeping technological and regulatory changes in the mass media is perhaps best illustrated by the remarkable growth of talk radio. As noted in Chapter 1, there are now around 3,800 all-talk or all-news stations in the United States, roughly triple the number in existence before the dramatic wave of regulatory and technological shifts (see Figure 3.2).[58] Prior to the Telecommunications Act of 1996, radio station ownership was limited by media cross-ownership rules and by restrictions on the number of stations any one company could own. The liberalized cross-ownership rules now have little relevance to radio stations, and the national limits on the number of radio stations under one owner have been eliminated entirely. Today the limits placed on station ownership in a single market are set along a sliding scale. At the smaller end of markets—those metro areas with 14 or fewer radio stations—no one entity can own more than 5 stations. For markets with 45 or more stations, the limit is 8 stations.[59] But these restrictions are not a problem for large radio companies as there is sufficient opportunity within this regulatory framework to own enough stations in a market to collectively target most major audience niches.

Before 1996, the radio industry was largely composed of "mom and pop" stations. A small company or family would own a station or two in a single market and would often have a strong presence in the community in philanthropy and civic affairs. But after deregulation a tidal wave of corporatization hit. Consider the case of Clear Channel Communications, which owned 43 radio stations in 1995. By 2010, it owned over 800 stations. Aufderheide documented this transformation, noting that in the year and a half following the passage of the Telecommunications Act of 1996, more than 25 percent of US radio stations had been sold, and many more than once.[60] Cumulus Media, the second largest in the industry, owned approximately 350 stations until late 2011 when it acquired Citadel Broadcasting

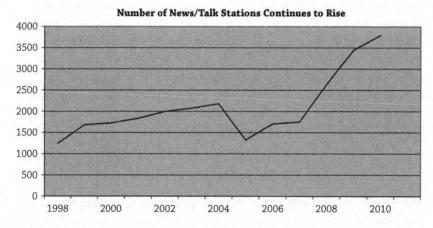

Number of News/Talk Stations Continues to Rise

Figure 3.2
Source: Arbitron via Pew Research Center's Project for Excellence in Journalism
State of the News Media 2012

and its stable of stations, increasing its holdings to 570 radio stations in 120 markets.

Clear Channel is also the dominant purveyor of talk radio programs. Its subsidiary, Premiere Radio Networks, syndicates Rush Limbaugh, Sean Hannity, and Glenn Beck, three top radio personalities, along with many others. Thus the company is vertically integrated, owning stations across the country while also providing programming to them. The company's revenues are in the neighborhood of $5 billion a year, half of which are from radio. None of this would have been possible before the FCC changes ushered in since the 1980s. But while deregulation allowed radio giants to form, these giants might have done any number of things with their content. Why *talk* radio? The answer lies in our new audio technologies.

With the emergence of new media technologies, terrestrial radio seems more and more like an antique ready for the museum. Indeed, with the exception of political talk, terrestrial radio is teetering. Emerging technologies have delivered new ways of listening and options abound. MP3 players, smart phones, Pandora, Spotify, Rdio, Sirius, and Internet radio stations have made listening to terrestrial radio seem increasingly inefficient and impersonal. Why tolerate least common denominator song choices punctuated with commercials when there are so many better ways to enjoy music? On Pandora, users enter a favorite song, symphony, or performing artist and the site creates a personal radio station that plays content Pandora's algorithms predict listener preferences. The website's "music genome project" maps 400 musical attributes for each song, creating detailed profiles that allow the service to offer a stream of music tailored to the tastes of each individual listener. A listener can continually update her preferences by giving a thumbs up or thumbs down to individual songs, as well as by adding new songs or artists to the station, allowing Pandora to further pinpoint her particular tastes. This specificity and interactivity is also portable via Pandora applications for mobile devices that allow users to stream custom stations whenever they like.

Given the ability to customize and the range of commercial-free stations available online and through satellite radio, audiences for musical formats on terrestrial radio have dwindled precipitously, leaving a disproportionate number of listeners without the resources and/or technological comfort required to make these news modes of consumption part of their routines. Not coincidentally, these audiences come disproportionately from less desirable demographics from the point of view of advertisers. From an advertising perspective, the virtue of terrestrial radio is that an individual station can deliver a demographically defined slice of residents in a particular geographic area. In short, Dave's Used Cars only wants to pay for ad placements that reach listeners in the area where Dave's Used Cars is located. Local stations can, of course, run commercials for national advertisers but that has not been their bread and butter. Radio business consultants we interviewed estimated that local sources provide 80 percent of all terrestrial advertising. Since the size and "quality" of the audience listening to music on terrestrial stations is in decline and advertising rates are based largely on the characteristics of listeners, music stations' ad revenues are in free fall. In an interview, radio analyst Holland Cooke noted:

> Why do you need an FM station to get music? You can get everything you need in your pocket. For a station, no matter how few commercials you play, the iPod still has fewer and on the iPod you get to pick your songs. And stations can't get the number of commercials down because their owners paid too much for them. They're selling more commercials than listeners will tolerate.

If terrestrial radio wasn't having enough problems, the recession of the past few years delivered another grievous blow. Total radio revenues (billings) in 2000 were around $20 billion but the recession cut revenues to only $14 billion in 2009, and forecasts by BIA/Kelsey (2010), a leading media research firm, estimates that revenues won't return to the $17 billion range until 2014. During this period Clear Channel's finances declined precipitously, Cumulus staggered, and Citadel fell into bankruptcy (before being acquired by Cumulus in 2011).

Large radio companies have tried to generate more national advertising and attempted to create synergies with new technologies. To date this approach has generally failed. Two other strategies aimed at reviving the industry have been more successful. The first is cost cutting. With terrestrial music stations drawing smaller audiences, the stations themselves have had to reduce expenses. Smaller stations may play nothing but preset playlists without live personalities. Other stations utilize a fake local presence via "voice tracking," in which a personality might over the course of an hour insert a few sentences to indicate that he or she is in Boston. But after the show is done the same disc jockey will re-record the few comments that are location-specific. "Hey Boston, we're all rooting for the Celtics tonight" will be edited, replaced with something such as "What a great day for a stroll along the River Walk here in San Antonio." The reduction in the number of on-air personalities and program managers has trimmed personnel expenses but in some cases has expedited the downward spiral as the lack of strong, on-air personalities and distinctive musical selections whittles away the few remaining attributes that make radio special.

A second popular strategy has been switching stations to a political talk radio format. The foundational strength of talk radio is that it has an audience that is attractive to advertisers. The audience for political talk radio—even the outrageous iterations—is relatively well educated and possesses enough discretionary income to attract sponsorship to these shows. These listeners are also thought to be uniquely attentive, as they are fully engaged in the program, less likely to channel surf than those listening to music formats.

For local stations, syndicated national programs are especially desirable because they are generally distributed at little to no cost to the individual station. It is largely a bartering relationship: local stations receive the programs and are allotted some open air time they can sell to local advertisers, while the syndicator increases the size of the audience it can offer its national advertisers. This is a business model that has proven to be profitable. It may be that the industry is approaching the saturation point in the conversion of music stations to talk radio (a subject we explore in the following chapter). However, the allure of music-to-talk conversion was well illustrated in an interview we conducted with a radio business consultant. He offered this example:

> In Albuquerque, which is the 68th largest market, we took a music station and converted it into the 4th talk radio station in the market. We got programs for no cash at all. So even as the 4th talk radio station in the 68th market we got enough programming that wasn't being played here and are able to make a profit.

Newer technologies have had only a modest impact on the way people listen to talk radio. For the most part the audience still listens on their local AM or FM station, either in their car, at home, or at work. Although one can get an app for Rush Limbaugh for a mobile device or listen to the national programs online, such alternatives have not yet changed the basic dynamics of the market. Some believe that the future may be Stitcher, winner of a "best app ever" award for allowing the listener to patch together all his or her favorite talk radio programs.[61] Pandora itself has said it is working on a spoken word alternative to accompany its music choices. For the time being, the same forces that have eviscerated music-based formats have bolstered the rise of political talk radio.

ROUGH WATERS

In sum, the widespread outrage identified in Chapter 2 cannot be accounted for with simple theories of increased political polarization. Such a hypothesis

is suspect, because empirical evidence of significant increases in polarization has yet to emerge and because the audience rarely exercises such
influence over programming. Reducing the genre's emergence and success
to a logical outgrowth of heightened polarization or acrimony between
parties misses the underlying structural foundations that support this
amped-up incivility. Polarization, much like the contested culture war of
the 1990s, may offer a partial explanation of this emergent genre, but it is
by no means the only contributing factor. We see instead a perfect storm of
political transitions, regulatory shifts, and technological advances that
have fundamentally altered the relationship between producers, advertisers, media content, and the public. In this new climate, outrage speech
and behavior prove to be a sound strategy for profits in a way that would
not have been true 30 years ago.

We describe the business model that supports outrage in detail in our
next chapter yet do not wish to say that the genre exists strictly because of
economic factors. It is the coalescence of the forces we describe here that
built the platform on which the colorful characters of political opinion
media stand. Without the exponential growth of outlets across media
(hundreds of cable networks, countless music delivery options, the
explosion of blogs), there would be no place to distribute this content.
Without the erosion of the Fairness Doctrine, Fox News and MSNBC could
not justify ideological one-sidedness. Media organizations, pundits,
political leaders, and advocacy groups are indeed clamoring for profits,
broadly defined, but the way in which they pursue their goals, the attributes of the technological environment in which they work, the media
through which they communicate, and the political culture in which they
work shape the nature of the genre.

In light of the structural foundations of the genre, it makes little sense
to blame an angry populace or to think of this discourse as the disappoint-
ing fruit of a debased public sphere. The existing arrangements are such
that even if we were to see a marked increase in bipartisanship or less con-
tentious political conversation at Thanksgiving tables across America, outrage media are quite unlikely to fade, as such changes do not disturb the
social arrangements beneath their surface.

NOTES

1. Wonkette Jr., "Michele Bachmann Launches Campaign with Praise for 'Killer Clown'
   John Wayne Gacy," *Wonkette*, June 27, 2011, http://wonkette.com/448389/michele-
   bachmann-launches-campaign-with-praise-for-serial-killer-john-wayne-gacy, as of
   July 5, 2011.

2. The New Media Index is a weekly report that tabulates the leading topics addressed on news-focused blogs and social media sites. This information is drawn from "Social Media Users Debate a Tea Party Favorite," http://www.journalism.org/index_report/social_media_users_debate_tea_party_favorite, as of July 8, 2011.

3. http://www.fathercoughlin.org/father-coughlin-anti-semitism.html, as of June 13, 2013.

4. Natalie Jomini Stroud, *Niche News: The Politics of News Choice* (New York: Oxford University Press, 2011), 46.

5. Early colonial newspapers were assembled by printers, rather than journalists, who printed the material submitted to them rather than seeking out information and sharing that information in the form of news stories as we know them today. For additional information about the fascinating start of colonial newspapers, see Michael Schudson, *The Good Citizen: A History of American Civic Life* (New York: Free Press, 1998) and Paul Starr, *The Creation of the Media: Political Origins of Modern Communication* (New York: Basic Books, 2004).

6. On the economic incentives that led newspapers to pursue objectivity, see James T. Hamilton, *All the News That's Fit to Sell* (Princeton, NJ: Princeton University Press, 2004), 37–70. See also Matthew Gentzkow and Jesse M. Shapiro, "Competition and Truth in the Market for News," *Journal of Economic Perspectives* 22 (Spring 2008): 133–154.

7. Schudson, *The Good Citizen*, 194–196.

8. Harry Castleman and Walter J. Podrazik, *Watching TV*, 2nd ed. (Syracuse, NY: Syracuse University Press, 2003). ABC was slower to develop as a network and lagged far behind NBC and CBS in building a national news capacity.

9. Jeff Kisseloff, *The Box: An Oral History of Television, 1929–1961* (New York: Viking, 1995), 366.

10. Barbara Matusow, *The Evening Stars* (Boston: Houghton Mifflin, 1983), 71.

11. Kisseloff, *The Box*, 389.

12. Markus Prior, *Post-Broadcast Democracy: How Media Choice Increases Inequality in Political Involvement and Polarizes Elections* (New York: Cambridge University Press, 2007), 1.

13. See Ronald Jacobs and Eleanor Townsley, *The Space of Opinion: Media Intellectuals and the Public Sphere* (New York: Oxford University Press, 2011) for more detailed description and analysis.

14. See Daniel Dayan and Elihu Katz, *Media Events: The Live Broadcasting of History* (Cambridge, MA: Harvard University Press, 1992) for more information.

15. When he said this he added the day's date at the end of the sentence.

16. Bart Barnes and Joe Holley, "America's Iconic TV News Anchor Shaped the Medium and the Nation," *Washington Post*, July 18, 2009, http://articles.washingtonpost.com/2009-07-18/news/36865941_1_walter-cronkite-oliver-quayle-president-obama, as of June 11, 2013.

17. Barnes and Holley, "America's Iconic TV News Anchor."

18. Theodore H. White, *The Making of the President 1972* (New York: Athenaeum, 1973), 261.

19. See also findings in Kathleen Hall Jamieson and Joseph N. Cappella, *Echo Chamber: Rush Limbaugh and the Conservative Media Establishment* (New York: Oxford University Press, 2008).

20. Jacobs and Townsley, *The Space of Opinion*, 83.

21. Prior emphasizes that these inadvertent viewers learned from the TV news and such learning led more of them to vote. *Post-Broadcast Democracy*, 87.

22. http://www.people-press.org/2012/02/07/cable-leads-the-pack-as-campaign-news-source/.

23. Keach Hagey, "Poll: O'Reilly Popular; Maddow Unknown," *Politico*, September 26, 2010, http://www.politico.com/news/stories/0910/42738.html, as of January 9, 2013.

24. Underwriting is governed by a set of rules established by the FCC that do not apply to advertising. For example, underwriting announcements are intended to inform the public about what sponsors do in the interests of full disclosure and are not supposed to include qualitative assessments of their goods or services, information about pricing, comparisons to other merchants, manufacturers, or service providers, and so on.

25. See, for example, maps that allow for greater variation such as those here: http://www-personal.umich.edu/~mejn/election/2008/ and here: http://www.princeton.edu/~rvdb/JAVA/election2008/.

26. See Ben H. Bagdikian, *The New Media Monopoly* (Boston: Beacon Press, 2004), Robert McChesney, *The Problem of the Media: US Communication Politics in the Twenty-First Century* (New York: Monthly Review Press, 2004), and Robert McChesney, *The Political Economy of Media: Enduring Issues, Emerging Dilemmas* (New York: Monthly Review Press, 2008).

27. Bagdikian, *The New Media Monopoly*.

28. Anothony Fiaola, "Rupert Murdoch, Son Apologize to Lawmakers, but Deflect Phone-Hacking Blame," *Washington Post*, July 19, 2011, http://www.washington-post.com/world/rupert-murdoch-james-murdoch-to-appear-before-parliament/2011/07/19/gIQAUMQUNI_story.html, as of August 1, 2011.

29. This was the same language used when the FCC's forerunner, the Federal Radio Commission, was established.

30. Marc Sophos, "The Public Interest, Convenience, or Necessity: A Dead Standard in the Era of Broadcast Deregulation?" *Pace Law Review* 10 (Summer 1990): 661.

31. Statement Made by the Federal Radio Commission on Aug. 23, 1928, Relative to Public Interest, Convenience, or Necessity, 2 Federal Radio Commission Annual Report 166 (1928), as cited by Sophos (1990).

32. *Associated Press v. United States 1945*, p. 1424, as quoted in Philip M. Napoli, "Deconstructing the Diversity Principle," *Journal of Communication* 49 (December 1990): 7–34.

33. Charles Fairchild, "Deterritorializing Radio: Deregulation and the Continuing Triumph of the Corporatist Perspective in the USA," *Media, Culture, and Society* 21 (July 1999): 549–561; and Martha Derthick and Paul J. Quirk, *The Politics of Deregulation* (Washington, DC: Brookings Institution Press, 1985).

34. See David Croteau and William Hoynes, *The Business of Media: Corporate Media and the Public Interest* (Thousand Oaks, CA: Pine Forge Press, 2006) for a complete description of the changes in industry regulation and their subsequent fallout.

35. Bill Carter, "Court Overturns F.C.C. Cross-Ownership Rule," *New York Times* July, 7, 2011, http://www.nytimes.com/2011/07/08/business/fcc-cross-ownership-rule-is-overturned.html, as of January 9, 2013.

36. For more information, see William Kunz, *Culture Conglomerates: Consolidation in the Motion Picture and Television Industries* (Lanham, MD: Rowman & Littlefield, 2006).

37. Eli Noam, *Media Ownership and Concentration in America* (Oxford, UK: Oxford University Press, 2009), 5.

38. For an exploration of media holdings, see the Columbia Journalism Review's *Who Owns What* web tool, http://www.cjr.org/resources/. This consolidation of

newspapers has also meant that smaller operations have been forced out of business. Bagdikian, *The New Media Monopoly*, lists thousands of cities that no longer have a daily newspaper and shows that of those with dailies, the overwhelming majority are one-paper cities.

39. Project for Excellence in Journalism, "State of the News Media 2010," http://stateofthemedia.org/.
40. See, for example, Lance W. Bennett, *News: The Politics of Illusion* (New York: Pearson Longman, 2007) and Croteau and Hoynes, *The Business of Media*.
41. Extracted from his dissenting opinion and cited by Sophos, "Public Interest, Convenience, or Necessity." Also available in full text here: http://en.wikisource.org/wiki/National_Broadcasting_Company_v._United_States_(319_U.S._190)/Dissent_Murphy.
42. Lori A. Brainard, *Television: The Limits of Deregulation* (Boulder, CO: Lynne Reinner, 2004).
43. For information on centralization, see Project for Excellence in Journalism, "State of the News Media 2010" and Eric Klinenberg, *Fighting for Air: The Battle to Control America's Media* (New York: Metropolitan Books, 2007).
44. In one striking example, CBS considered outsourcing reporting to CNN. See Tim Arango, "CBS Said to Consider Use of CNN in Reporting," *New York Times*, April 8, 2008.
45. John Halpin, James Heidbreder, Mark Lloyd, Paul Woodhull, Ben Scott, Josh Silver, and S. Derek Turner, "The Structural Imbalance of Political Talk Radio," http://www.americanprogress.org/issues/2007/06/talk_radio.html, as of August 10, 2009.
46. Philip M. Napoli, "Market Conditions and Public Affairs Programming: Implications for Digital Television Policy," *Harvard International Journal of Press/Politics*, 6 (March 2001), 15–29.
47. Todd Gitlin, "Television's Screens: Hegemony in Transition," in *American Media and Mass Culture*, ed. Donald Lazere (Berkeley: University of California Press, 1987).
48. Pew Research Center for People & the Press, "Trends in News Consumption 1991–2012. "http://www.people-press.org/2012/09/27/section-4-demographics-and-political-views-of-news-audiences/.
49. Playing this edge isn't without its challenges. Interpersonal conflict, when real, makes many uncomfortable and must be domesticated in order to retain viewers. See Kevin Arceneaux and Martin Johnson, "The Tone of Televised Political Discussion: Norming Studies for Communication Research" (paper presented at the annual meeting of the American Political Science Association, Boston, MA, August 28–31, 2008). This may explain the near extinction of what Jacobs and Townsley (2011) call the "dueling host" format (e.g., *Crossfire*).
50. Reviewing advertising agency websites will yield as many promises to "break through the clutter" as weight loss websites yield promises of remarkable results in "just two weeks!"
51. In a rather dramatic exit, Uygur said that he left the network because he did not want to acquiesce to political pressure to "tone it down." MSNBC did not deny asking him to tone down some of his performances but asserted that the reason they did so was because his loose cannon tendencies were making it difficult to book guests. See Brian Stelter, "Sharpton Appears to Win Anchor Spot on MSNBC," *New York Times*, July 20, 2011. Either way, Uygur's high ratings at the time Sharpton was deemed better suited serve as another reminder that audience interests are not the only factor taken into account in determining content.

52. There are many ways to measure traffic (e.g., page views, unique visitors, hits) and a great deal of squabbling about such measures. Drudge, for example, claims over 20 million visitors per day, but critics have argued that this is an artifact of the automated page refresh that is embedded in site, which refreshes the page every three minutes. For examples of this discussion see http://valleywag.com/tech/traffic-tricks/matt-drudges-spin-243614.php and http://www.personaldemocracy.com/node/1320. Alexa rankings are becoming the standard but mean less to outsiders as they are comparative rather than absolute numbers. We have used http://www.trafficestimate.com here for standardization and clarity.

53. "Buzz in the Blogosphere," *Nielsen Wire*, http://blog.nielsen.com/nielsenwire/online_mobile/buzz-in-the-blogosphere-millions-more-bloggers-and-blog-readers/, as of July 4, 2012. The 2006 data are taken from Dave Sifry's State of the Blogosphere report on *Technorati*. http://technorati.com/weblog/2006/11/161.html. This number does not include the 70 million Chinese blogs estimated to have existed at that time.

54. danah boyd, "A Blogger's Blog: Exploring the Definition of a Medium," *Reconstruction* 6 (2006).

55. Brian Ekdale, Kang Namkoong, Timothy K. F. Fung, and David D. Perlmutter, "Why Blog? (Then and Now): Exploring the Motivations for Blogging by Popular American Political Bloggers," *New Media & Society* 12 (January 2010): 217–234.

56. Eric Lawrence, John Sides, and Henry Farrell, "Self-Segregation or Deliberations? Blog Readership, Participation, and Polarization in American Politics," *Perspectives on Politics* 8 (2010) 1: 141–157.

57. As cited in Ekdale, et al., "Why Blog?," 219.

58. Jeffrey M. Berry and Sarah Sobieraj, "Understanding the Rise of Talk Radio," *PS: Political Science and Politics* 44 (October 2011): 762–767.

59. http://www.fcc.gov/guides/review-broadcast-ownership-rules, as of May 10, 2011.

60. Patricia A. Aufderheide, *Communications Policy and the Public Interest: The Telecommunications Act of 1996* (New York: Guilford Press, 1999).

61. At the time of this writing, however, NPR programs are the most popular downloads at Sticher, and conservative talk radio does relatively poorly. This reinforces our sense that the success of political talk radio remains tied to actual radios, http://stitcher.com/stitcher-list/, as of December 20, 2012.

CHAPTER 4

✦

It's a Business

When we think about outrage media we think about the competition between left and right. We see those with whom we agree working to promote worthy ideas that compete with those advanced by the other side. The real competition in the Outrage Industry, though, is for advertising dollars. Each day producers, hosts, and bloggers try to fashion content to draw more viewers, listeners, and readers so that they can at least survive financially, if not prosper. This discussion of business practices within the cable, talk radio, and political blog sectors provides some context for determining why outrage has surged in recent years. The perfect storm may have provided greater opportunity for outrage but entrepreneurs had to find formats and content that would attract advertising revenue, which can only be done by delivering audiences.

We begin with a fundamental problem that all types of individual businesses face: How do you differentiate your product from those that are already in the marketplace? In a competitive world with more supply than demand, which businesses win out? And how are business decisions made about the type and level of outrage that is produced? From product differentiation, we turn to profitability. Developing a product and making money from it are two different things. The financial underpinnings of each of the three sectors are examined in turn.

We also look at brand identity to try to better understand how outrage is marketed. In this context we ask how portable is outrage—can companies build beyond the personalities that define their programs or blogs? Finally, we place the new incivility within the framework of competitive advantage. How and why does outrage, delivered day-in, day-out by host or writer, provide advantages in the marketplace? Given the harshness of outrage talk, are there any limits to what hosts and writers can say? Are there constraints imposed by the market on the language that is used?

PRODUCT DIFFERENTIATION

Facing competition, businesses within each sector must find ways of building a loyal clientele and, they hope, expand upon their base. That's no small challenge. In cable television, product differentiation is abundantly clear: There is MSNBC on the left, Fox News on the right, and CNN in the center. CNN itself has only episodically offered outrage programming but did well with Glenn Beck before he left for Fox and with Lou Dobbs who railed incessantly against illegal immigration on his financial news program before he abruptly quit the network in 2009. In the evenings when cable news viewing is at its highest, CNN has struggled against Fox and MSNBC.

Fox has dominated in the evening, and the network's the *O'Reilly Factor* at 8:00 and repeated at 11:00 is the highest rated political show on cable, with its daily showings averaging more than 3 million nightly viewers. Rachel Maddow, who has become the face of MSNBC, draws under a million viewers at the 9:00 slot, many fewer than Fox's Sean Hannity (more than 2 million viewers a night) at the same time.[1] From the start, Fox was intended to be a conservative voice, fitting comfortably within parent News Corp's worldview and that of its head, Rupert Murdoch. MSNBC, however, has gradually transformed itself into a liberal alternative to Fox. General Electric, NBC's corporate parent at the time, received a cable channel as part of compensation from cable distributors who needed to pay to carry NBC and other GE cable properties. In 1994 GE first used the new cable network slot for *America's Talking*, conceived of as a cable alternative to talk radio. When that failed, the corporation looked for alternatives. Said one cable consultant in an interview, "For ten years they have been experimenting with it, throwing things up against the wall and seeing what sticks. MSNBC really had no place else to go but to appeal to liberals." MSNBC put an exclamation point on its long-term strategy when in the fall of 2010 it unveiled a new corporate slogan, "lean forward."

In the past few years Fox has turned even further right and MSNBC has tacked more to the left. Glenn Beck, who joined Fox in 2009, was unlike anyone else on cable.[2] Although he is widely criticized for his conspiracy theories and crying on the air in despair about America, he gave Fox's previously sleepy 5:00 time slot impressive ratings until Fox chose not to renew his contract in the summer of 2011. Liberal Alan Colmes was let go from *Hannity and Colmes* as the show traded its left-right format for a strictly conservative outlook. Meanwhile MSNBC has added more liberal programming, with evening hosts Al Sharpton, Ed Schultz, and Lawrence O'Donnell picking up the departed Keith Olbermann's belligerence. In discussing Mitt Romney's campaign during the GOP primaries in 2012, O'Donnell described the Mormon Church as an institution created by a man who "got caught having sex with the maid and explained to his wife that God told him to do it."[3] It is rhetoric like this that led Bill Clinton to call the network "our version of Fox."[4]

A study by Pew of media coverage in the 2012 presidential election found that MSNBC was sharply more negative toward Mitt Romney in its coverage than was Fox Cable in its coverage of Barack Obama.[5] There were some concerns that when corporate behemoth Comcast purchased NBCUniversal in 2009, it would clip MSNBC's liberal wings. Whatever the political views of Comcast's hierarchy, it seems to have done little to inhibit MSNBC. As we discuss below, MSNBC is highly profitable and has grown its audience as it has turned even more to the left.[6]

Similar, Not Different

Although it is easy enough to tell the difference between conservative and liberal talk radio programs or blogs, the product differentiation within each ideological grouping is modest. Talk radio is particularly notable in that the competition is largely conservative versus even more conservative. Almost all the top syndicated shows feature a conservative host (see Table 4.1). More broadly, tune in any talk radio station in the nation and the likelihood is that you'll hear a conservative commentator. Since cities of any significant size typically have more than one (non-sports) talk radio station, a conservative program on one station is likely to be competing against one or more conservative commentators running at the same time.

Business School 101 would lead us to expect that any store or vendor would work hard to distinguish its products and services from competitors. Talk radio hosts would probably dispute our characterization of their programs as formulaic, but the basic approach, format, and political point of view of the programs is remarkably similar. Two questions emerge. First, why the dearth of liberal hosts to offer a contrast to conservative talk radio? Second, why is conservative talk radio generating such homogeneous product?

The paucity of liberal talk radio became ever more apparent after the collapse of Air America, an ambitious effort to create a progressive talk radio

Table 4.1 TOP TALK RADIO HOSTS, MILLIONS OF LISTENERS (WEEKLY)

Host	Political Leaning	2003	2007	2012
Rush Limbaugh	Conservative	14.5	13.5	14.75
Sean Hannity	Conservative	11.75	12.5	14.0
Michael Savage	Conservative	7.0	8	8.75
Glenn Beck	Conservative	*	5	8.25
Mark Levin	Conservative	*	4	8.25
Dave Ramsey	Financial Advice	*	4	8.25
Neal Boortz	Conservative	2.5	4	5.75
Laura Ingraham	Conservative	1.25	5	5.75
Jim Bohannon	Ind./Moderate	4.0	3.25	3.75
Jerry Doyle	Conservative	*	3.0	3.75
Mike Gallagher	Conservative	2.5	3.75	3.75
Michael Medved	Conservative	*	3.75	3.75
Doug Stephan	Ind./Moderate	2.0	3.25	3.75
Bill Bennett	Conservative	*	*	3.5
Clark Howard	Consumer Advice	*	*	3.5
George Noory	Supernatural, Paranormal	*	*	3.5

Source: Arbitron ratings as published in *The State of the News Media, 2010*, Pew Project for Excellence in Journalism, at http://www.stateofthemedia.org/2010/audio_talk_radio.php#audio_toptalkhosts; and "The Top Talk Radio Audiences," *Talkers*, August 17, 2012, http://www.talkers.com/top-talk-radio-audiences/
* Information unavailable or talk host not nationally broadcast

network. It was a highly visible initiative with well-known personalities such as Al Franken and Janeane Garofalo taking to the airwaves. Air America never attracted an audience, and without an audience there was no reason for advertisers to buy commercial time. When it finally stopped broadcasting in January of 2010, *Daily Kos*'s Markos Moulitsas mocked its demise, tweeting: "Air America was still really on the air?"[7]

Yet there is some liberal talk radio. Although the nationally syndicated shows are almost all conservative in outlook, liberal talk radio can be found on local stations. Some hosts with liberal views are syndicated (Stephanie Miller, Randi Rhodes, and Ed Schultz, for example), though no one on the liberal side approaches the audience size drawn by the conservative stars.[8] There is also some presence of moderate or non-ideological hosts at the local level.

One basic reason for the modest size of the market for liberal talk is that much of the potential audience listens to other types of radio. Together African Americans and Hispanics constitute somewhere near 30 percent of the nation's population, but they constitute a much larger proportion of the nation's liberal population, and these listeners can choose programming that is specifically targeted toward them.[9] Talk programming is particularly popular among African Americans and there have long been stations catering to that market in urban areas. There are also Spanish-language alternatives that appeal to many Hispanic listeners. The potential audience for liberal talk radio is further reduced by the popularity of National Public Radio (NPR), which is more popular with liberal listeners than with conservatives.[10] NPR rejects the charge that it reports news from a liberal point of view, but conservatives consistently deride NPR as biased. Ratings put the weekly audience for NPR at around 34 million and it is a major force in radio nationwide.[11]

Political scientist William Mayer points to a fundamental difference between conservatives and liberals in their attraction to talk radio. Surveys consistently show that conservatives are much more distrustful of the mainstream media than are liberals.[12] Indeed, conservative hosts on talk radio emphasize this bias as the raison d'être for their programs. This bias is frequently illustrated by hosts who will use coverage of a story in the *New York Times* or other mainstream outlet as a jumping-off point for conversation.[13] Talk will then focus on why the story must be understood in a different context. In short, conservatives like talk radio because they believe it tells them the truth, while liberals appear to be much more satisfied with the mainstream media and are more likely to conclude that it is accurate in its reporting.

In very general terms there appears to be a broad personality difference in those who are attracted to conservative talk radio and those who shun it. As Marc Hetherington and Jonathan Weiler write, "The vast audiences of Rush Limbaugh, Sean Hannity, and Michael Savage, espousing deeply emotion- and symbol-laden views of American politics speak to the place in American life of the political style that we believe is best explained by an authoritarian divide."[14] "Authoritarian" refers to a personality and attitudinal style that believes there is a clear right and wrong. Individuals who embrace this belief are more attracted to aggressive rhetoric in political commentary, which narrates the world in black and white. This Worldview fits contemporary conservative politics more than it does contemporary liberal politics.[15]

Conservative dominance of political opinion radio, then, has both demand-side and supply-side explanations. On the demand side, conservatives' greater distrust of mainstream media and greater interest in black and white narratives, and the niche talk alternatives for African American and Hispanic audiences help us to understand why conservative audiences might be larger than liberal audiences. Meanwhile, on the supply side, the early success of Rush Limbaugh, spurred executives—prone to build on financially successful models—to develop more programs in this vein. The format is inexpensive. For an individual show, only a modest level of preparation is needed—often nothing more than constructing a brief list of discussion topics—and, thus, staffing needs are minimal. A host may have a sheaf of news clippings and will use them as take-off points. Rush Limbaugh, who could spend lavishly on a staff if he so desired, works in his small, nondescript studio in Palm Beach with a sound engineer, an assistant who transcribes the show, and a staffer he refers to on the air as Bo Snerdley. During the ample commercial breaks Limbaugh searches websites like the *Drudge Report* for material to use.[16]

Not only is there evidence that edgy conservative talk radio can be profitable but Air America's demise has suggested that liberal talk radio is a bad investment. Ironically, that may not be the case. Air America may have just been too much too soon—an entire network of liberal programming from scratch—and failed for this reason. On television, MSNBC began with one liberal show, adding new shows tentatively with carefully vetted hosts. Air America was far less cautious from a commercial perspective; the network was founded during George W. Bush's presidency, driven quite explicitly by a political (rather than economic) goal: to influence the presidential election.[17] Whether or not Air America would have had success if a more judicious approach had been used, its failure has had a chilling effect. Given the rampant preference to replicate commercially successful programming that we described in the previous chapter, it follows that the Air America legacy is likely to prolong the ideological imbalance in the political talk radio arena, a cautionary tale for potential investors.

While new modes of distribution have emerged—one can listen to talk radio streaming, online via mobile devices, on Sirius XM, or by podcast—the industry still offers the same shows produced in the same fashion. The talk radio format revolves round a host (sometimes two) talking at length, periodically ranting, taking some calls from listeners, and occasionally, talking to a guest over the phone. Almost nothing has changed since the format was first instituted. Although a listener can now go to the website and send in a comment, the new technologies have not led to substantive changes in the content of the programs themselves. The programs are virtually identical in format and similar ideologically. The conservative viewpoints expressed on radio are not particularly diverse. The host and/or writers mine the day's news, finding an item that will work well as a jumping-off point. The hosts gravitate toward similar perspectives and express them with the hallmarks of the genre. Indeed, financial success is what created the genre. Cable news exhibits considerably more product differentiation. Instead, in a sea of similarly structured conservative content, what differentiates one talk radio show from another is the personality of the host. Some may prefer Glenn Beck's professorial explanations of history, while others favor Mark Levin's venom.

The Entrepreneurial Spirit

The political blogosphere is vast, and generalizations about its nature are problematic. Our research examined two important sectors of this universe. First, we monitored the content of the most popular independent political opinion blogs (Chapter 2). By "independent" we mean that they were not part of a larger media organization exerting editorial control over content. As such we did not look at blogs embedded in press entities like the *New York Times* or the *Atlantic*. Second, as part of the research for Chapter 6 we followed the coverage of the 2010 congressional primaries by state and local political blogs. (We did not include candidate or party blogs.) The analysis here focuses on these two subsets of the blog world.

In terms of creativity the small staff of most political blogs could be a good thing.[18] Lacking a corporate hierarchy and a heavy hand of management, blogs might be expected to demonstrate a variety of formats and an inclination to experiment, and indeed we see this if we look at the blogosphere writ large; but among the most heavily trafficked political blogs, there is less diversity than we might expect. Political blogs have their own personalities, owing largely to the style of writing by the administrators and bloggers. Despite this distinctiveness, there is similarity in the strident tone of the commentary across the blogs we examined in Chapter 2. Both large and small, conservative blogs rely heavily on outrage. Although our data demonstrate that the liberal outrage outlets utilize outrage less often than conservative ones, the liberal blogs are still biting in their mocking of conservatives. Reexamining the blogs from our 2009 content analysis 18 months later (a long time in Internet years) we found that little had changed in terms of their operation. Most still appear to be modest business enterprises. We did notice a bit of change among a few. The liberal blog *Orcinus* stopped posting in April of 2010.[19] *PowerLine*, a conservative blog, had stopped taking comments. This simplified the site and certainly reduced ongoing maintenance.[20] The most dramatic change has been in the *Huffington Post*, which was independent when we first monitored it. In February of 2011, however, it was purchased by AOL. In terms of substantive content, though, the blogs continued to offer the same basic product. The continuing popularity of the blogs we studied in 2009 does not necessarily reflect a superior product as they are advantaged by getting into the business relatively early and establishing a presence. This does not keep competitors out but new entrants have a challenge in breaking through an enormous clutter of websites devoted to politics. Anyone can start writing, using simple software to establish a blog, and join the "pajamadeen."[21] As Scott Johnson of *PowerLine* told us, they started with "that free blogger software, so our investment was zero. Our monetary outlay was zero."

Even though little capital is required to launch a blog, many blog owners would surely like to have access to capital to enhance their asset. For example, most of the blogs we examined could use both "face lifts" to improve their web design and improvement and expansion of their interactive features. But money to pay for improvements must come from within as blogs are unattractive investments for third parties. Potential investors look at the market and see a profusion of competitors, no real barrier to entry to new competitors, and weak advertising revenues. The attrition rate for blogs is exceptionally high, and one study found that close to 60 percent of new blogs are inactive just four months later.[22]

Consequently, blogs are supported by the investment of human capital of their owners.[23] With the exception of those developed as supplements to major publications or for standing organizations, blogs tend to be personal vehicles driven forward by their founders. The writers of the most successful political blogs become personalities in their own right. Everyone who reads conservative Michelle Malkin's eponymous blog knows that it is a vehicle for her conservative views. Charles Johnson of the oddly named *Little Green Footballs* is known for both his conservative outlook and his fondness for feuding with other conservatives. *Talking Points Memo* is liberal Josh Marshall's outlet. The reward for their labor is certainly not a high salary but, rather, attention and influence. The blogs are vehicles that make successful bloggers political celebrities who receive requests to appear on television, make speeches, and write for other forums.

PROFITABILITY

The income of the top outrage hosts and personalities demonstrates just how lucrative talking about politics can be. At the very top of the business is Rush Limbaugh whose yearly income approaches $60 million. Fifty million dollars of this comes from his syndicated radio show.[24] Glenn Beck has built a remarkable empire in a relatively short period of time and derives his fabulous income from many more platforms than does Limbaugh. *Forbes* estimated Beck's annual paycheck prior to his departure from Fox at $32 million. His largest source of income was publishing and his cumulative book sales through Simon and Schuster stood at 3.5 million in 2010. He receives another $10 million annually from Premiere Radio Networks for his daily show and was being paid just $2 million a year from Fox. The Beck website garners $4 million from merchandise sales, his insider newsletter, and advertising. His public appearances net $3 million annually.[25] As noted in Chapter 2, since leaving Fox he's established TheBlaze TV, a web-based television channel and quickly built an audience of 300,000 subscribers paying $9.95 a month or $99.95 a year. In 2012 Beck contracted with the DISH Network, a satellite broadcaster, which brings him back to television.[26] The deal with DISH marks another innovative step for Beck and some financial analysts predict that Beck will soon be grossing over $100 million annually.[27] Beck is exceptional, but there are others who do well. From research conducted by *Newsweek* for a ranking of the highest earning political figures, we've culled those who are employed by the companies that fall into our outrage classification and make at least $2 million a year (see Table 4.2).[28]

These, of course, are the top earners, and all is not riches in the world of outrage. There are striking contrasts among the three industries. The cable networks are extraordinarily profitable, easily besting the rate of return that can be typically found in talk radio or in the blogosphere. As noted in Chapter 1, Fox Cable earns more than half the profits at News Corp, a huge enterprise. Although MSNBC is much smaller, it is highly profitable as well.[29] Cable television benefits from two income streams, advertising and the subscription fees that cable providers must pay to the networks for the privilege of carrying their programming.

Mad Men

Ad buys for cable, talk radio, and blogs are determined not only by audience size but also by audience quality. In the eyes of advertisers, not all viewers, listeners, and readers are created equal. Consequently, ad rates differ for each individual radio show, TV program, and blog. As we've noted, the perfect storm of technological change and deregulation that provided fuel to the growth of the Outrage Industry also created new channels for advertisers. The oldest joke in advertising—"I waste half of my money advertising, I just don't know which half"—is now a historical curio, just like the ad agencies on *Mad Men*.

Table 4.2 RICHLY OUTRAGEOUS

(Estimated annual income, in millions of dollars)

Figure	Income
Rush Limbaugh Talk radio	$59
Glenn Beck Fox cable, talk radio	33
Sean Hannity Fox cable, talk radio	22
Bill O'Reilly Fox cable	20
Keith Olbermann MSNBC	8
Laura Ingraham Talk radio	7
Mark Levin Talk radio	5
Joe Scarborough MSNBC	4
Rachel Maddow MSNBC	2

Source: "The Power 50: The List," *Newsweek*, November 1, 2010.

In the past, half an advertiser's commercial would be wasted because an expensive 30-second commercial on, say, the *NBC Nightly News* would be shown to a very large and diverse audience, some of whom had little interest in products that were being marketed. What the perfect storm hath wrought is efficiency. For the advertiser who is interested in a particular demographic (which is most advertising), a smaller niche medium will be more economical.

Marketers would find network news a bad investment for most political books because they would be paying to reach a broad audience for an item of interest to a small audience. But a liberal political blog such as *Daily Kos* offers an inviting opportunity for a book antagonistic toward Fox News.

The sheer number of options available has driven down the price of advertisements and made competition for ad dollars cutthroat. A common metric known as the CPM (cost per thousand of impressions) provides a basis of comparison of alternative placements across different shows and different media. On cable, MSNBC has a CPM of a little more than $3.00, Fox is around $4.00, and CNN is higher at close to $6.00. By way of comparison, the Weather Channel's charge is $4.61 and Comedy Central's is $7.46. The CPM for ESPN, however, is around $15.00.[30] The disparity reflects the challenge in reaching young males. This demographic watches little television but does tune in to watch sports, and for advertisers selling beer, cars, and action movies, ESPN is worth the premium CPM.

Fox's relatively modest CPM stands in contrast to its powerhouse image and its ratings superiority over the other cable news networks. "From an ad point of view it's a crappy demographic," says cable consultant Rob Davis. "What is an advertiser going to show 50 to 70 year olds? GEICO?" Fox has the oldest audience among the major cable networks, news or otherwise, with an average viewer age of 65. CNN's daily average is 63 years and MSNBC's is a relatively spry 59.[31] Advertisers interested in reaching adults are generally aiming at the 25- to 54-year-old demographic, an age group where incomes are rising, needs are expanding as families grow, and retirement and health concerns are not yet paramount. In this regard, the cable news networks are less efficient than ad buys for shows popular with younger audiences. At the 8:00 PM block, 40 percent of the O'Reilly Factor's audience is over 65. MSNBC's Rachel Maddow has a hip, younger image but even 25 percent of her viewers fall into this category.[32] The ability of the three cable news networks to actually improve their demographics appears limited.[33] Said one advertising executive, "If you're talking about cable channels that are on 24/7, you're going to get an older audience." Retirees and others with lots of time on their hands are clearly the core audience of the cable news networks.[34]

Without a particularly attractive audience, why are the cable news networks the most profitable segment of the Outrage Industry? First, there are some advertisers who do want to reach older consumers (more on this later). Second, the revenue from the networks' subscription fees charged to TimeWarner, Comcast, and other cable distributors, is an enormous boost. Fox Cable News has the seventh highest charge of all cable networks, receiving .82 cents per month for every cable subscriber.[35] This is a testament to how strongly its viewers prize access to the channel. Third, the production costs for the evening talk shows are modest. Most guests are not paid and staffing needs are not extensive.

Cable's profitability is but a distant dream for political bloggers. Consider the CPMs. For the premium display ad spot, usually the top right or top left of the opening web page, the rates for even the most highly trafficked blogs are quite low. The controversial and highly visible conservative, Michelle Malkin, lists a premium (optimally placed) ad on her blog at just $1.28 per CPM. Outside the Beltway, a conservative blog with a highly educated audience charges $1.74. Moonbattery, another blog popular with conservatives lists its premium space at $1.14.[36] Moreover, these stated rates are soft. In an interview, ad analyst Brandon Coleman noted that as the last opportunity to purchase advertising for each day approaches, websites have to consider whether they should lower their price so they can sell at least some of their considerable empty inventory of ad space. "Every day, once that day goes by, you've lost that inventory that you didn't sell. You can't get it back. It's like empty airline seats."

Even a cursory glimpse at most political blogs shows plenty of empty seats. The number of ads that run down the left or right side tends to be small, and consumer goods are conspicuous by their absence. Even the most widely visited political blog sites have sparse advertising. A peek at *Crooks and Liars* (liberal) showed an ad for La Quinta hotels but little else. At the conservative *Ace of Spades*, a display ad for HP computers sat in the middle of the lead post.[37] *Wonkette* has 5 million page views a month but struggles to attract advertisers; the lack of ads would lead one to believe it was a rather obscure website rather than one of the most popular political blogs. "We're all fighting for the same shrinking pool of advertisers," one editor told us.

CPM rates aside, in terms of demographics the audience quality for the top blogs is far superior to that of cable news viewers. The low CPM for *Michelle Malkin* cited above belies an audience that advertisers should find attractive. Fully 75 percent of her readers have a college degree and 66 percent have an annual income of more than $75,000.[38] The primary reason that advertising is so cheap on political blogs is that there are just so many of them. Since the vast majority of blogs are personal vehicles for their writer-owners, they can survive with a little bit of advertising revenue to supplement the discounted or even free labor that generates the content. The writer-owner who cares little about making a profit drives down the CPMs for all in the industry. With so few barriers to entry, new supply easily supplants those who tire of the game and quit. Perversely, political blogs also suffer financially because they attract people who have serious interests in politics. One advertising executive noted, "[You] go to a blog wanting to know what it's saying about Obama. You likely block out any advertisements that are there.... You're not going there to buy things. It's harder for me as an advertiser to penetrate your mind space." This view is supported by research, which shows that on news sites the "click rate" on display ads is very small.[39] As we'll discuss, the nature of the content can also scare away advertisers worried about irritating consumers who regard blogs on the other side of the political fence to be offensive.

To make matters worse for blogs, the growing popularity of social networking sites is placing additional pressure on CPMs. Facebook and other social networking sites soak up a considerable amount of all online display advertising. The result is downward pressure on prices. Says *Advertising Age*, "it's supply simply outstripping demand."[40] This low demand ultimately works to support outrage. An editor and publisher of one of the top liberal blogs described the situation as follows:

> We're competing for the same ads that are on popular political blogs that are in political and policy publications, things that are in liberal and alternative media like *Mother Jones* or *Alternet*.... They are ads for things like CSPAN, or PBS documentaries, or political books. The ad market has never been very robust for political media in this country. It's a strange thing because the audience is pretty big for political media and tends to be better educated, employed at higher levels, and has more consumer dollars to throw around, but there is a kind of long tradition of political media in America being constantly under funded. Look at the *Nation*. The *Nation* has been around for I think a century or so and they are literally begging people for money right now. So, to survive in that climate, we try to be a little more entertainment-based. We're not putting out 10,000 word dry foreign policy articles on partitioning Iraq or whatever (although we'll make fun of those!), but we're still reaching that audience and that audience has not been appreciated nearly enough by advertisers or marketing companies. Maybe it's because they're smarter—maybe they're not as likely to be fooled by sports drinks or something.

And so even blogs that are heavily trafficked find themselves searching for "click bait." One conservative blog editor called anything on Sarah Palin the equivalent of political pornography and described trying to stay away from compromising what they want to say politically by populating the site with low-hanging fruit. "Why do you think *Huffington Post* has so many photos of celebrities in bikinis?" he asked.

Trust Me

As described in Chapter 3, terrestrial radio is struggling. One advertising executive put it bluntly, "Radio is on its deathbed. Limbaugh, he's it." Another ad analyst said derisively, as if he were talking about dead people, "You're talking about a 55 plus audience." For a dying industry, though, radio has a lot of customers. The combined weekly audience of the top three talk show hosts alone stands close to 40 million. Beyond talk radio are other formats that still attract audiences. Radio consultant Bill James took exception to a reference we made to radio being in intensive care: "Radio won't die because it will be the medium of choice for those over 50. Those people don't know... how to download to an iPod." People still listen to the radio as they drive around in their car and some like to have it on while they work.

It is the business model for radio that is in decline. Stations still broadcast and people do still listen—it is just that the audience is graying out of advertiser desirability. James is right when he said "There's still a country audience who wants to hear Waylon Jennings." There are also advertisers who want to reach Waylon Jennings fans, but there are plenty of alternatives available to reach the same consumers. As noted in Chapter 2, radio is struggling to adapt to a new business model. Streaming radio might seem like a great opportunity, as those stations with niche formats could scale up. Internet radio can work for national advertisers but it's irrelevant to those wanting to reach a local audience, the traditional strength of terrestrial radio. As for national advertisers, Internet radio has expanded the number of outlets but more supply means lower CPMs. Bridge Ratings' Dave Van Dyke said in an interview, "Because there is more inventory it's all less valuable." All the advertising executives we spoke with said essentially the same thing: radio ads are cheap.

Rush Limbaugh's $50 million a year salary from Premiere indicates that talk radio is still a good delivery vehicle to reach older white males. And the skyrocketing number of all-talk stations demonstrates that this demographic possesses some discretionary income to spend. Clearly talk radio works for certain advertisers. Yet Limbaugh and the other top hosts are far from representative of the broader business as only a bit lower down the industry food chain are many programs and stations that just get by. As a group the consultants and radio analysts we spoke with pointed toward little or no profit for stations that carried programs with more ordinary ratings.

Despite these problems, talk radio survives because it offers advertisers two valuable qualities. The first is a highly engaged audience. Radio analysts believe the audience for talk radio is a more attentive audience than the audience for music, a boon for advertisers eager to capture the attention of increasingly distracted multitaskers. Says radio consultant Bob Cohen, "It's an active, involved audience. It's a very responsive audience." Cohen added, "The currency is people's attention span." Holland Cooke says that advertisers have found that the talk radio audience "has better retention because [unlike music] it is not on in the background." Consistently the experts we interviewed emphasized that the talk radio audience is engaged in the discussion and its members are more careful listeners than those of other types of programming.

Another highly valued attribute of the talk radio audience is that regular listeners have great trust in the personality hosting the program. Seventy-two percent of listeners talk to their friends about their favorite radio personality and 70 percent follow the hosts they like via social media.[41] Audience self-selection means, of course, that listeners gravitate to those personalities they not only find most interesting but also those they tend to agree with and whose judgment and knowledge they respect. Robin Bertolucci, the program director for talk radio station KFI in Los Angeles, suggested that we "Think about if your brother or sister told you a product was good." The value of the trust in hosts is enhanced when they read the ads themselves rather than using a taped segment. Such "live read" is appealing because it's conversational and seems more authentic than a taped commercial. Live read can command a premium from advertisers. For double his normal going rate Rush Limbaugh will turn an ad into a product placement, threading it into his normal monologue.[42] The trust engendered by the hosts is particularly attractive to sponsors selling products that appeal to those who may be susceptible to anxiety about their personal security. Consider this commercial pitch by popular radio host Michael Savage,

> Look I know you worry about what's going on in Afghanistan, what's going on the Gulf, and what's going on in the White House, but with everything going on you shouldn't have to worry about your computer on top of everything else, so go visit my advertisers at Carbonite.com . . . enter my offer code Savage.[43]

On Glenn Beck's radio program (as well as on his former cable show) his emphasis on the abyss that awaits us fits perfectly with those advertising products relating to personal security. He is like a preacher warning the end is near. With an audience he has primed for catastrophe, he attracts ad dollars from companies selling computer backup systems, identity theft protections, and gold. Perhaps the most bizarre Beck sponsor is the Survival Seed Bank. After Armageddon, one can take out survival seeds that have been put away and grow food for the family.[44] Beck's sponsorship by gold dealers has proven controversial. On his Fox show he stood at a doorway painted in gold and told viewers that when the economic system reaches "the point of insanity," they should buy gold.[45] Yet Beck sponsor Goldline sells its gold in the form of antique coins and other collectibles. Unless a buyer knows a lot about coin collecting, he may not know what the gold he has purchased is truly worth as coins are not a pure play on gold and commissions can be as high as 30 percent.[46] Coins from Goldline might represent a bad investment, but its product is a great fit for Beck's shtick and Beck's audience.

Analysis of profits and advertising may seem rather far removed from more pressing issues in our political system. Revenue, however, is related to whose voice is heard, or heard the most: with more revenue, come bigger platforms, and a louder voice.

GROWING THE BUSINESS

If the revenue stream is a key to being heard by the public, then a critical issue is how to expand revenue so that the voice can be extended beyond its current reach. In many ways we have been discussing the most obvious path of increasing revenue, growing the core business entity. The pursuit of ratings or readers is the most direct route to increasing revenues. An alternative to the basic strategy of internal growth is to extend a brand to new lines of business.

Brand Identity

Given the challenges of a competitive marketplace, a strategy to stand out is to create a clear identity—an identity that communicates product differentiation and product quality. For outrage businesses, establishing a brand identity is just as much a key to success as it is for a retailer, service firm, or other conventional business entity.

The media companies in the Outrage Industry take different routes to creating a brand identity. Talk radio programs are typically named after the host, and the brand equity—the value of that identity in the marketplace—is the value of that host's appeal to an audience.[47] When a new blog entrepreneur begins writing, he or she sometimes bestows a quirky name—*Little Green Footballs, Moonbattery, Crooks and Liars*—to help the blog stand out. If the blogs succeed over the long run, their owners/writers will often become well known as followers come to associate the name with the quality of the political commentary. Those who read *Firedoglake* regularly know it represents Jane Hamsher's vision of current affairs.

When it comes to brand building and brand equity there is no greater success in the Outrage Industry than Fox Cable News. As trade publication *Broadcasting & Cable* put it, Fox has created "a clear and strong brand, and an unwavering commitment to stick with it. Viewers, advertisers and cable operators all know what they're getting."[48] "Unwavering" is apt; no matter how much it is criticized for the ideological nature of its content, Fox remains unbowed. It continues to deliver a strong conservative perspective throughout its programming. To the chagrin of liberals, Fox is the most trusted name in television news. Forty-nine percent of the public reports trusting Fox, a rating ten points higher than the second most trusted network, CNN.[49]

Some conservative media pundits have recently criticized Fox for allegedly moving toward the political center.[50] In the wake of Beck's contract termination, Fox News CEO Roger Ailes said in an interview that there would be a "course correction" at the network.[51] There was certainly push back toward Beck from within the news division as Beck's continuing stream of highly controversial claims was thought to discredit more serious news shows on the network, notably those hosted by Shepard Smith and Bret Baier. Fox also raised eyebrows by hiring some liberal commentators. But over the years Fox has actually moved further to the right, and recent changes appear cosmetic rather than substantive. The most basic principles of business dictate that you don't tamper with a highly successful brand. Fox is sure to protect its image as an icon of conservative commentary.

Extending the Brand

The cable news networks, talk radio stations, and syndicators face the same pressures of other large corporations: the quarterly bottom line. The individual media businesses we've discussed are for the most part subsidiaries of publicly traded companies. The most important are News Corp,[52] Comcast NBC, Clear Channel, CBS radio, Cumulus Media, Entercom, Salem Communications, and a small number of others with talk radio holdings. For the radio syndicators the primary business strategy has been to sell programs from their inventories to more stations, develop new programs, or to buy more stations to play their syndicated programming.

Fox Cable has gone a bit further to extend its brand to a sibling network devoted to the stock market and business news. The Fox Business Network competes directly with two successful and well-entrenched cable competitors, Bloomberg Television and CNBC. What Fox Business offers that is different from them is a conservative point of view on business, building on the reputation of Fox Cable News. Fox Business debuted in 2007 and has been a disappointment to News Corp, drawing an average of only 65,000 viewers a day (one third of CNBC's audience).[53] Clearly Fox was trying to reach beyond the older audience and retirees who follow Fox Cable News (and who are unlikely to be active investors) but this strategy has not yet worked.

Another way of looking at extending the business is to examine hosts rather than the companies that broadcast their shows. People watch or listen to a show because they are drawn to the particular personality. Few listeners have any recognition of Premiere as a brand, even though they may be listening to its stars each day. Fox News stands out for the network brand loyalty it engenders, but even within Fox some personalities are much bigger attractions than others. The personalities are thus brands and in the Outrage Industry when one leaves a show, the mantle falls to no one. It is not like NBC's *Tonight Show* where a new host inherits a venerated legacy.

Top-rated hosts have had great success in extending their personal brand beyond their radio or TV shows. Many of the leading personalities have written books, books that they can hawk on their own shows and then through guest appearances on other like-minded hosts' vehicles. Bill O'Reilly has published eleven books, ten of which made the *New York Times* best-seller list. *Pinheads and Patriots*, debuted at number two on the list. Recently he has turned to American history and his book *Killing Lincoln* was a colossal success, selling well over 2 million copies. His follow-up, *Killing Kennedy*, appears to be equally successful.[54] Others such as Glenn Beck, Michael Savage, Laura Ingraham, and Keith Olbermann have also written books that share their unique perspectives on American politics. Beck and Savage have turned to fiction as well, broadening their literary oeuvre. It's not unusual to find two or three outrage authors on the *New York Times* best-seller list. So strong is his marketing power that when Glenn Beck devoted one of his shows to Friedrich von Hayek, the legendary Austrian free market economist, von Hayek's classic, *The Road to Serfdom*, sold over 60,000 copies in the ensuing week.[55] A few, notably O'Reilly, Beck, and Hannity, have even taken their shows on the road. Beck does comedy in some appearances, and he and O'Reilly toured together in 2010 to eleven cities with their "Fresh and Bold" show. Stephanie Miller went on the road as well with her "Sexy Liberal Comedy Tour." Rush Limbaugh even has his own beverage, Two If by Tea, and radio host Laura Schlessinger has her very own line of jewelry.

Much of the cross-selling comes from hosts driving viewers and listeners to their websites. These sites sell T-shirts, sweatshirts, and various tchotchkes. They also sell insider access, which fans can purchase for a fee. Insiders typically get a newsletter or some other form of extended commentary. For an annual fee of $55 one can become a Glenn Beck "Insider," or for $75 can purchase "Insider Extreme" access, which allows one to watch him do his radio show. As noted earlier, for a fee one can also subscribe to TheBlaze TV. With three hours a day on the radio that is free to listeners, one wonders why even the most fervent Beck fan would want to pay for even more Glenn Beck. But as one marketing analyst told us, these fans "have such identification with Glenn Beck…, with Glenn Beck's anger. All of this is confirming and affirming. They can't get enough."

The extension of the personal brand is not the norm in the industry. Only a modest number of hosts can successfully market their names on coffee cups, much less launch a book backed by a commercial press. The top Fox personalities and a handful of radio hosts like Limbaugh, Savage, and Ingraham have been able to use their shows to sell other products, but they are the exception and not the rule. Scale is, of course, a problem, as local radio hosts and those who have small syndications just do not possess the audience size to generate investments in other products.

Turning from cable and radio hosts to bloggers, their efforts to extend the brand are focused on trying to become a personality beyond the written word. Bloggers want to command influence, and few would see their blog as entirely sufficient. Some may dream of becoming a figure like Arianna Huffington or Markos Moulitsas. Moulitsas, a pioneer in blogging, saw the potential of the Internet to provide sharp but popular political commentary. Quickly the *Daily Kos* became a commanding presence and he became a power broker as his yearly Netroots Nation conference swiftly turned into a must-stop-by venue for aspiring liberal politicians. A more realistic goal for blog impresarios is to appear on either Fox or MSNBC and for conservative bloggers, on a top radio show. Being quoted in the mainstream press is another means of extending their voice, and a call from a reporter with the *New York Times, Washington Post, Politico,* or one of the broadcast network news shows is prized. After explaining the financial woes of his blog, one owner-operator told us that the blog was nevertheless successful because "[we're] quoted in the *Wall Street Journal* and the *New York Times.*" Such recognition does little to improve the bottom line of their blogs, but such appearances validate the effort to maintain a blog that year in, year out, makes little money.

Even for reasonably successful enterprises in the Outrage Industry, extending the brand into new product areas is difficult. The core sectors, TV, radio, and the blogosphere, remain extraordinarily competitive. Even as outrage personalities try to find ways of extending their presence, they must also be concerned that more skillful competitors might take market share away. The financial success of Beck and Limbaugh is startling, but more indicative of the industry are the radio hosts of a weekend show on a single AM station, trying to develop a voice, a style, that might lead to a weekday slot.

COMPETITIVE ADVANTAGE

In many ways outrage businesses seem similar to those in any other industry: they struggle to make a profit, operate in a highly competitive environment, adapt to newly emerging technological advances, and must always be wary of new competitors stealing their customers. As discussed, what stands out most about outrage businesses is that there is little product differentiation. This is puzzling as these are not retail stores where store personnel interact with the customers; thus individual firms are unable to distinguish themselves by the quality of such contact. Nor are there price differences—for the consumer the products are generally free. Cable does require a monthly fee, of course, but Fox Cable and MSNBC are not premium channels and are included in basic packages. In sum, without any means of differentiating themselves through personal service or price, outrage businesses must find a way of standing out so potential new customers can find them, and those who already patronize them continue to do so.

"Be Self-Deprecating, Be Polarizing"

In his magnum opus, *Competitive Advantage*, Harvard Business School professor Michael Porter says that "a firm differentiates itself from its competitors if it can be unique at something that is valuable to buyers."[56] Without price or personal service at issue, what is of unique value to outrage consumers? For the media entities offering political commentary, such unique value must come from either the appeal of the content or the appeal of the host or writer.

The competitive advantage comes from the charismatic personalities at the center of these blogs and programs. Yet the constraints of the formats and the instinct to imitate successful practices push hosts to move beyond just being themselves to emulating the most successful in the industry. When we interviewed Gabe Hobbs, a well-known radio consultant who advises talk hosts on their on-air presence, we asked him what he recommends to clients wanting to expand their audience. He said his message is simple: "Be self-deprecating, be polarizing." Hobbs's essential elements were common themes in other interviews. Although this book centers on what's polarizing, the other part of his answer, "be self-deprecating," speaks to a critical part of a host's appeal. Hosts must convey that they are to be trusted. And to be trusted means being authentic. Part of the speech pattern of hosts is to reference themselves as being ordinary, being just like listeners, and evoking empathy and commonality. We examine this more closely in the next chapter.

For those interested in politics and who prefer thoughtful and intellectual content, there is a wide range of appealing alternatives. But for those hosts interested in competing for people attracted to sharp and opinionated political commentary, there is a fundamental decision to be made on an approach that allows them to stand out. Being analytical, being thorough, being thoughtful all play poorly on these cable and radio shows. Shows rarely mix in anything more than superficial analysis, leaning heavily instead on venting, caustic criticism, and laying into the other side. A few hosts, like liberal Thom Hartmann and conservative Hugh Hewitt make a conspicuous effort to demonstrate more intellect than the competition, but their failure to crack the top echelon of radio may be interpreted as a warning rather than a strategy to emulate. Despite all the compliments that Hewitt, a law professor, gets for being a thinking-man's conservative, he's heard on only 120 stations. By comparison, Sean Hannity is heard on 500.[57] The highest ranked hosts are harsh in their rhetoric and uncompromising in their contempt for those who don't agree with them.

Hosts and bloggers try to gain a competitive advantage through the volume and unique expression of outrage. It is the way that principals try to stand out. As Holland Cooke puts it, cable and talk radio is all about "Notice me! Notice me!" Cooke adds, "There is an outsized, deliberate overstating to rise above the competitive cacophony." Consequently, the full range of outrage appeals pours forth. There's violent imagery: Glenn Beck walking on to his TV set with a baseball bat; old-fashioned name-calling: Alan Colmes telling listeners "It's going to be moron night, isn't it?"; ad hominem attacks: Keith Olbermann opining, "Sean Hannity doesn't understand that because Sean is very dim"; racist appeals: Rush Limbaugh playing the song "Barack the Magic Negro"; homophobia: Mike Gallagher wanting the world to know that "Anderson Cooper...he's the last guy who should go on television and make oral sex references"; and dire warnings: Mark Levin sounding a clarion call because "Nancy Pelosi's politics comes as close to a form of modern-day fascism as I've ever seen."[58]

Political blogs offer a broader range in the amount of outrage, but as we showed in Chapter 2, it's a staple among highly trafficked blogs. Also, many of the blogs that have recently risen to move past the hordes into the rarified realm of celebrity have relied on their own brand of outrage. RedState, Big Government, and Atlas Shrugs all leaped forward through outrage-based commentary. Pamela Geller's Atlas Shrugs is particularly instructive. She began blogging after 9/11 and launched her own site in 2003. Geller's focus is on what she calls "Islamofascism" and her breakthrough came in 2010 when a New York City community board approved construction of a mosque a few blocks from the site of the World Trade Center. She gave readers the impression that the mosque was actually going to be built on the land where the twin towers had stood, asking readers to protest "the 9/11 monster mosque being built on hallowed ground." Geller makes no apologies for her attacks on the religion itself, declaring that "In the war between the savage and the civilized man, you side with the civilized man." Her harsh and insistent denunciations of Islam and the "monster mosque" led to appearances on Fox Cable, Sean Hannity's radio show, and many other outlets.

Those appearances, in turn, drove more people to *Atlas Shrugs*. Geller had gradually been building a following but in the wake of the controversy that surrounded the proposed mosque, she became part of the story. *Atlas Shrugs* now has a readership of close to 200,000 a month. Before the fight over the mosque, it was markedly less. Geller is a marketer of extraordinary talent and *Atlas Shrugs* is a case study in the potential of outrage. Says Geller, "I have an interesting play on words sometimes. If people like it, I think that's great."[59]

When Geller runs out of things to say about what Muslims are trying to do to America she starts in on President Obama, telling readers, for example, that he slept with a "crack whore."[60] Hamas, the Palestinians, and Israel are also favorite topics. Geller aptly illustrates a driving theme of Porter's theory of competitive advantage: "The fundamental basis of above-average performance in the long run is *sustainable competitive advantage*."[61] Maintaining viewer, listener, or reader attention over a sustained period is an enormous challenge. A continuing flow of interesting content is the starting point to sustainable advantage and outrage is an inexpensive and easy way to make content compelling.

Vague Limits

Hosts want to be controversial as programs often benefit when what they have said becomes newsworthy. Such publicity can lead to higher ratings. It is possible, though, to go too far. Because of its sensitivity, race might seem to be the one issue hosts would shy away from.

But far from it. As shown in Chapter 3, many hosts and writers are drawn to race, using it to agitate their listeners and demonstrate their own forthrightness. Fox Cable has repeatedly angered African Americans who feel that the network is especially harsh in its treatment of blacks who have done something a network host disdains. One time Fox

was injured by racially tinged commentary was Glenn Beck's denunciation of President Obama as a racist. In response, an African American
group, Color of Change, called for a boycott of sponsors and had some
success as well-known companies like Wal-Mart, CVS, Best Buy, and
Travelocity pulled their advertisements from Beck's cable show. This
surely contributed to Fox's decision to dump Beck, though there is no
evidence that there's been any long-term damage to Fox Cable. The
reason Fox cares little about offending African Americans is easy to
explain: Nielsen measurements show that only 1.38 percent of Fox
viewers are black.[62] The reality is that race has surely helped conservative
hosts as their criticism of what they regard as reverse racism resonates
with their audiences.

Aside from the boycott against advertisers for Glenn Beck's Fox show,
there had been very little push back against sponsors of outrage programming until Rush Limbaugh attacked Georgetown University Law student
Sandra Fluke. True to form Limbaugh followed the outrage template by initially refusing to apologize to Fluke and, as noted in Chapter 1, continuing
to criticize her again on his show in the days that followed his initial denunciation. This time was different, though. Liberal activists spread the names
of Limbaugh's advertisers across the Internet generating an outpouring of
tweets and messages on the sponsors' corporate Facebook pages. The mainstream press was full of critical articles as well. Within a few days Carbonite,
AOL, Quicken Loans, and virtually all of Limbaugh's other national sponsors abandoned ship and issued apologies.[63] Finally, three days after his
initial remarks and with his program in financial turmoil, Limbaugh half-
heartedly apologized on his website, saying his words "were inappropriate
and uncalled for."[64]

Limbaugh had every right to be shocked by the turn of events. He has
made many equally offensive statements over the years and suffered no
negative repercussions while gaining increased attention from the press
and added respect from his followers. He once told an African American
caller to "take that bone out of your nose and call me back." After a Mexican
won the New York Marathon, Limbaugh joked that "An immigration agent
chased him the last 10 miles." On another show he said that we should let
"stupid and unskilled Mexicans do that work."[65] In these cases and countless others, advertisers stayed with Limbaugh.

What made this episode different? It might seem that gender is more
dangerous than race, though Limbaugh has baited the women's movement
over the years. Fluke came across as an accomplished and modest young
woman who was being bullied by an intensely polarizing figure.[66] Yet individuals are attacked every day in talk radio. Although the answer will

never be fully clear, what is evident is that political activists and interest groups, led by the liberal Media Matters, saw an opportunity and mobilized immediately.[67] Twitter and Facebook were used to take action.[68] Most importantly, activists were blessed with a vulnerable target: advertisers with brands they needed to protect. In an interview with us before this episode, one marketing expert noted the vulnerability of talk radio advertisers: "There's the potential for negative brand equity. If the customer's experience with the brand is poor, then there can be negative equity."

As the episode metastasized, Limbaugh's corporate parents, Premiere and Clear Channel, were helpless to effectively defend him as they couldn't say that his description of Fluke was justified. They could only cite his right to free speech, which seemed to make hardly a ripple in news coverage of the controversy.[69] Since Clear Channel and Premiere have many other talk radio properties, they were sensitive to advertiser demands that they no longer be associated with Limbaugh. Premiere sent a memorandum to its managers ten days after the controversy erupted indicating that 98 sponsors had asked "that you schedule their commercials in dayparts or programs free of content that you know are deemed to be offensive or controversial (for example, Mark Levin, Rush Limbaugh, Tom Leykis, Michael Savage, Glenn Beck, Sean Hannity)."[70]

The Limbaugh backlash spread across talk radio; revenues and earnings are down across the sector. Eight months after Limbaugh's attack on Fluke, Spencer Brown, an executive with Dial Global, a major player in the industry, told *Radio Ink* that the "news-talk sector for us has materially slowed down in terms of billing." Brown added, "we started to experience the slow down the day after [Limbaugh] made the comments."[71] The CEO of Cumulus, Lew Dickey, said his company was losing millions because of the weakness of advertising for the Limbaugh show on the thirty-eight company-owned stations that carry the program.[72] Clear Channel CEO Bob Pittman dismissed the problem, however, saying the controversy was just "part of the normal day-to-day of talk radio."[73] Although Limbaugh's advertising has diminished, his huge following stayed with him—at least in the short run. Arbitron ratings in the period following the Fluke episode showed that his aggregate rating was approximately the same as it was in the prior period.[74]

Our own interpretation of these developments is that talk radio revenues were vulnerable independent of Limbaugh's problems. The expansion of talk radio over the years has been stratospheric (recall the sharply ascending trend line in Figure 3.2). There is some limit to the number of stations that can divide up the audience for talk radio and still make money. It seems likely that the sector will shrink at least some until the number of stations comes into equilibrium with what ad revenues will support. Two high-profile contract disputes in 2012 also suggest that the economics of the industry may be deteriorating. Both Michael Savage and Laura Ingraham quit their syndicators and signed with new companies. For a radio host to quit his or her syndicator has very serious financial consequences as they lose the stations that carry them and they must then slowly re-create a national lineup.[75]

The adverse reaction by advertisers to Limbaugh's attack on Fluke may result in the bottom line dipping into the red for some weak stations. Yet Limbaugh remains unbowed. Six months after his initial attack Limbaugh ridiculed Fluke again because of her support of Barack Obama's reelection. "I don't know if they give out condoms at Obama's fundraisers," said Limbaugh of Fluke's endorsement.[76] In the years to follow it may be possible to look back at the Limbaugh-Fluke controversy and conclude that it finally established some limits on what can be said on talk radio. In the immediate aftermath of the controversy, those limits remain ambiguous as ever, as it is difficult to articulate what was truly distinctive about what Limbaugh said about Fluke compared to what we heard in our content analysis of talk radio (Chapter 2).

COMPETITION AND SUCCESS

The business model for the Outrage Industry supports an enormous array of individual firms offering provocative political commentary. The perfect storm of deregulation and technological change opened the doors to the growth of the industry but did nothing to assure that it would remain viable and vibrant. Today it is certainly both. Collectively, the scale of these three business sectors is impressive.

What we have found, however, is that the business model for each sector is rather different. Each sector is succeeding for very different business-related reasons. The two point-of-view cable networks are extremely profitable as the networks facilitate highly efficient advertising while, at the same time, the companies incur only modest costs to produce the programming. As we discussed in the previous chapter, talk radio's business model has emerged out of the cost cutting and format switching necessitated by the migration of music to other platforms. Talk radio is profitable at the top of the ratings but marginal at lower levels of popularity. Nevertheless, this modestly profitable segment of the industry is enormous. Most blogs are supported by free or discounted labor as readers have no incentive to pay for access and advertising revenues are very low.

In the end, the general business model for the Outrage Industry is easy to describe. Advertisers are attracted to cable and radio (and to a lesser extent blogs) because they draw audiences of varying appeal to marketers. In their hyper-competitive environment the individual businesses work to maintain and expand their audiences by offering compelling content. As Michael Porter points out, a business must *sustain* quality to retain a competitive advantage. Every day, new compelling content must be generated. And each day much of that content is outrage, which is inexpensive to produce, dramatic enough to cut through the clutter of alternatives, resonant with our current cultural milieu, and, as we will show in the next chapter, comforting for fans.

NOTES

1. The TV Neilsen ratings are posted daily at http://tvbythenumbers.zap2it.com/. These figures are for May, 2013.
2. See Dana Milbank, *Tears of a Clown* (New York: Doubleday, 2010).
3. Jeremy W. Peters, "Dueling Bitterness on Cable News," *New York Times*, November 5, 2012, http://www.nytimes.com/2012/11/06/us/politics/on-cable-news-networks-a-battle-of-bitterness.html?pagewanted=all&_r=0, as of December 20, 2012.
4. Mackenzie Weinger, "Clinton: MSNBC 'Our Version of Fox,'" *Politico*, January 18, 2012, http://www.politico.com/news/stories/0112/71601.html, as of December 20, 2012.
5. "Both Candidates Received More Negative than Positive Coverage in Mainstream News, but Social Media Was Even Harsher," Pew Research Center's Project for Excellence in Journalism, November 2, 2012, http://www.journalism.org/analysis_report/winning_media_campaign_2012, as of December 20, 2012.
6. Brian Stelter, "Seeking More Viewers, MSNBC Turns Left," *New York Times*, August 22, 2008.
7. Brian Stelter, "Liberal Radio, Even without Air America," *New York Times*, January 24, 2010.
8. Mike Kinosian, "Progressive Talk: Not Dead Yet!" *Talkers Magazine*, April, 2011, 1ff.
9. *Black Radio Today* 2010, Arbitron 2010, http://www.arbitron.com/downloads/BlackRadioToday_2010.pdf, March 23, 2012 (site discontinued); *Hispanic Radio Today* 2010, Arbitron 2010, http://www.arbitron.com/downloads/hisp_radio_today_10.pdf, as of March 23, 2012 (site discontinued).
10. Of those surveyed who listen to NPR, 36 percent identify as liberal, 39 percent as moderate, and 21 percent as conservative. If party identification is used, the difference expands further. See *In Changing News Landscape, Even Television Is Vulnerable*, Pew Research Center for People and the Press, September 27, 2012, http://www.people-press.org/2012/09/27/section-4-demographics-and-political-views-of-news-audiences/, as of February 2, 2013.
11. Kara Swisher, "Why Online Won't Kill the Radio Star," *Wall Street Journal*, June 7, 2010.
12. William Mayer, "Why Talk Radio Is Conservative," *Public Interest* 156 (2004): 86–103; Jonathan M. Ladd, *Why Americans Hate the Media and How It Matters* (Princeton,

NJ: Princeton University Press, 2012); and "Many Americans Remain Distrusting of News Media," Gallup Poll, October 1, 2009, http://www.gallup.com/poll/123365/americans-remain-distrusting-news-media.aspx, as of March 23, 2012.

13. Matthew Gentzkow and Jesse M. Shapiro find that some media properties will bias their presentation because it actually conveys a sense among their target audiences that they are receiving a higher quality product. "Media Bias and Reputation," *Journal of Political Economy* 114 (2006): 280–316.

14. Marc J. Hetherington and Jonathan D. Weiler, *Authoritarianism and Polarization in American Politics* (New York: Cambridge University Press, 2009), 65.

15. Hetherington and Weiler, *Authoritarianism and Polarization in American Politics*. See also, Jonathan Haidt, *The Righteous Mind* (New York: Pantheon, 2012).

16. Zev Chafets, *Rush Limbaugh: An Army of One* (New York: Sentinel, 2010), 112–113.

17. Theodore Hamm, *New Blue Media: How Michael Moore, MoveOn.org, Jon Stewart and Company Are Transforming Progressive Politics* (New York: New Press, 2008).

18. See, though, Matthew Hindman, *The Myth of Digital Democracy* (Princeton, NJ: Princeton University Press, 2009).

19. The site subsequently reemerged but then went silent again. http://dneiwert.blogspot.com/, as of June 6, 2012.

20. The *Huffington Post* also changed in terms of content. It was already far more than a blog when we initially conducted the content analysis but in addition to its stable of political bloggers it now offers greater news aggregation and many other features, including a recently added page for divorced readers. Its expansion into many attractive areas led to its purchase by AOL in early 2011 for $315 million.

21. Richard Davis, *Typing Politics* (New York: Oxford University Press, 2009), 187.

22. Davis, *Typing Politics*, 25.

23. A survey by Technorati shows that 60 percent of bloggers are "hobbyists." Full- or part-time professionals (18 percent) mostly blog about technology or personal musings. Bloggers working for corporations are 8 percent of the sample and entrepreneurs in the business world are 13 percent. *State of the Blogosphere 2011: Introduction and Methodology*, http://technorati.com/social-media/article/state-of-the-blogosphere-2011-introduction/, as of July 5, 2012.

24. Chafets, *Rush Limbaugh*, 122–123.

25. Lacey Ross, "Glenn Beck Inc," *Forbes*, April 26, 2010, http://www.forbes.com/forbes/2010/0426/entertainment-fox-news-simon-schuster-glenn-beck-inc.html, as of March 23, 2012.

26. Brian Stelter, "Beck Is Taking His Conservative Internet Shows to the Dish Network," *New York Times*, September 12, 2012, http://www.nytimes.com/2012/09/12/business/media/glenn-becks-show-heads-to-dish-network.html?pagewanted=all, as of December 20, 2012.

27. Janko Roettgers, "How Profitable Is Glenn Beck's New Web TV Venture?," GIGAOM, September 12, 2011, http://gigaom.com/video/gbtv-subscriber-numbers/, as of March 23, 2012.

28. "*Newsweek's* Power 50: The List," *Newsweek*, November 1, 2010, http://www.the-dailybeast.com/newsweek/2010/11/01/power-list.html, as of March 23, 2012.

29. "The Economics of Cable News," Pew Project for Excellence in Journalism, http://www.stateofthemedia.org/2010/cable_tv_economics.php, as of March 23, 2012.

30. "The Economics of Cable News."

31. This calculation was made by veteran television analyst Steve Sternberg. James Hibberd, "Fox News Has Oldest Audience on Cable," Reuters, http://www.reuters.

com/article/2010/08/11/industry-us-foxnews-idUSTRE67A08W20100811, as of March 23, 2012.

32. *In Changing News Landscape, Even Television Is Vulnerable*, Pew Research Center for the People and the Press, September 27, 2012, http://www.people-press.org/files/legacy-pdf/2012%20News%20Consumption%20Report.pdf, as of February 2, 2013. See also, http://tvbythenumbers.zap2it.com for December 17, 2012; and *Cable Leads the Pack as Campaign News Source*, Pew Research Center for the People and the Press, February 7, 2012, http://www.people-press.org/2012/02/07/cable-leads-the-pack-as-campaign-news-source/, as of January 21, 2013.

33. See Andrew Hampp, "Fox News: We're an Upscale Buy on Par with Mainstream Nets," *AdAge*, March 22, 2010, http://adage.com/article/mediaworks/fox-news-upscale-buy-par-mainstream-nets/142900/, as of March 23, 2012.

34. Bharat Anand and Dmitri Byzalov, "Spatial Competition in Cable News," Working Paper, Harvard Business School, April, 2008.

35. David Goetzl, "ESPN Trumps All Cable Fees, CPMs," *MediaDailyNews*, January 27, 2012, http://www.mediapost.com/publications/article/166754/espn-trumps-all-cable-fees-cpms.html, as of March 23, 2012.

36. These figures are from Blogads, a middleman linking blogs with advertisers, at http://web.blogads.com/adspotgroups/, as of November 16, 2010.

37. This cursory examination was on November 16, 2010, but we have examined our top twenty blogs repeatedly and find the same thing no matter what day we look.

38. http://www.intermarkets.net/assets/pdf/kits/MichelleMalkin.pdf, as of June 6, 2012.

39. Kenny Olmstead, Amy Mitchell, and Tom Rosenstiel, *Navigating News Online: Where People Go, How They Get There and What Lures Them Away*, Pew Research Center, May 9, 2011, http://www.journalism.org/analysis_report/navigating_news_online, as of June 1, 2011.

40. Edmund Lee, "Social Networks Sink Online-Ad Pricing," *AdAge*, July 12, 2010, dage.com/article/digital/social-networks-sink-online-ad-pricing/144884/, as of March 23, 2012.

41. "Nearly Half of Respondents Considered or Purchased Products Recommended by Their Favorite Radio Personalities," Katz Media Group, June 28, 2012, http://www.katz-media.com/newsroom/Lists/Newsroom/DispForm.aspx?ID=115&ContentTypeId=0x0104001CC469D696FE464A8A8D4A5554FA03A2, as of July 6, 2012.

42. Chafets, *Rush Limbaugh*, 123.

43. *Savage Nation*, June 24, 2010.

44. Milbank, *Tears of a Clown*, 69.

45. Mark Leibovich, "Being Glenn Beck," *New York Times Magazine*, September 20, 2010, http://www.nytimes.com/2010/10/03/magazine/03beck-t.html?pagewanted=all, as of January 9, 2013.

46. Kenneth P. Vogel, "Beck Mocks Gold Controversy," *Politico*, December 17, 2009, http://www.politico.com/news/stories/1209/30755.html, as of March 23, 2012; Kenneth P. Vogel, "Weiner Targets Beck and Gold Retailer," *Politico*, May 18, 2010, http://www.politico.com/news/stories/0510/37413.html, as of March 23, 2012; and Will Bunch, *The Backlash* (New York: Harper, 2010), 234–235. The industry's point of view is expressed in Mike Kinosian, "War on Words Targets Media Economics Lifeline," *Talkers Magazine*, November, 2010, 1ff.

47. See Philip Kotler and Kevin Keller, *Marketing Management*, 13th ed. (Upper Saddle River, NJ: Prentice-Hall, 2009), 238–241.

48. Ben Grossman, "Why You Should Learn from Fox News," *Broadcasting & Cable*, February 8, 2010, http://www.broadcastingcable.com/article/448009-Why_You_Should_Learn_From_Fox_News.php, as of March 23, 2012.

49. Andy Barr, "Poll: Fox Most Trusted Name in News," *Politico*, January 26, 2010, http://www.politico.com/news/stories/0110/32039.html, as of March 23, 2012.

50. Keach Hagey, "Fox 'Course Correction' Rankles Some," *Politico*, February 14, 2012, http://www.politico.com/news/stories/0212/72825.html, as of March 23, 2012.

51. Howard Kurtz, "Roger's Reality Show," *Newsweek* and the *Daily Beast,* September 25, 2011, http://www.thedailybeast.com/newsweek/2011/09/25/roger-ailes-repositions-fox-news.html, as of March 23, 2012.

52. In the wake of the hacking scandal at a News Corp newspaper in Great Britain, the company responded to pressure from shareholders by dividing its properties into two new corporations. A publication division, embracing many newspapers as well as book publishers, will maintain the name "News Corp." The entertainment assets, including Fox Cable, will be known as "21st Century Fox" when the reorganization is formally put into place. See Jennifer Saba, "Murdoch Keeps News Corp Name, Thomson Becomes Publishing CEO," Reuters, December 3, 2012, http://www.reuters.com/article/2012/12/03/us-news-corp-ceo-idUSBRE-8B20JP20121203, as of December 21, 2012.

53. D. M. Levine, "Four Years In, Fox Business Network Still Treading Water," *Adweek*, November 11, 2011, http://www.adweek.com/news/television/four-years-fox-business-network-still-treading-water-136307, as of March 23, 2012; "Fox Business Network Receives Orders to Differentiate from Fox News Channel," *Talkers.com*, October 20, 2011, http://www.talkers.com/tag/phil-griffin/, as of March 23, 2012; and Matt Pressman, "Is Fox Business Network a Lost Cause?," *Vanity Fair*, November 13, 2009, http://www.vanityfair.com/online/daily/2009/11/is-fox-business-network-a-lost-cause, as of March 23, 2012. The only bright spot for the business channel is Lou Dobbs, who has attracted a modest but growing audience since he was given a time slot. Dobbs and his previous show on CNN are discussed at length in Chapter 7.

54. Bill O'Reilly, *Pinheads and Patriots* (New York: Morrow, 2010); Bill O'Reilly and Martin Dugard, *Killing Lincoln* (New York: Henry Holt, 2011); and Bill O'Reilly and Martin Dugard, *Killing Kennedy* (New York: Henry Holt, 2012).

55. Jennifer Schuessler, "Beck Bump," *New York Times Book Review*, June 27, 2010, http://www.nytimes.com/2010/06/27/books/review/InsideList-t.html?_r=0, as of January 9, 2013.

56. Michael Porter, *Competitive Advantage* (New York: Free Press, 1985), 119.

57. www.hughhewitt.com/pages/about_hugh; and http://radiotime.com/options/|p_20631/The_Sean_Hannity_Show.aspx.

58. The direct quotations come from our content analysis of programs. "Moron night," from the *Alan Colmes Show,* March 25, 2009; "Sean is dim," from *Countdown with Keith Olbermann,* April 7, 2009; "Anderson Cooper," from the *Mike Gallagher Show,* April 16, 2009; and "Nancy Pelosi," from the *Mark Levin Show,* March 16, 2009.

59. Anne Barnard and Alan Feuer, "Outraged, and Outrageous," *New York Times*, October 8 2010, http://www.nytimes.com/2010/10/10/nyregion/10geller.html?pagewanted=all, as of March 23, 2012; and Michelle Boorstein, "In Ground Zero Mosque Controversy, Conservative Writers Have Growing Influence," *Washington Post*, August 18, 2010, http://www.washingtonpost.com/wp-dyn/content/article/2010/08/18/AR2010081802582.html, as of March 23, 2012.

60. Barnard and Feuer, "Outraged, and Outrageous."

61. Porter, *Competitive Advantage*, 11. Emphasis in the original.

62. Danny Shea, "Fox News Audience Just 1.38% Black," *Huffington Post*, June 26, 2010, http://www.huffingtonpost.com/2010/07/26/fox-news-audience-just-13_n_659800.html, as of March 22, 2012.

63. As we discuss in Chapter 8, some companies, such as Ford Motors, claimed that it didn't know that it sponsored the Limbaugh show. It may seem to stretch credulity that a sophisticated company wouldn't know where its advertisements are placed but it reflects the nature of radio advertising. A significant amount of commercial time is purchased by ad agencies, which buy remnant time and plug in clients to available slots where the demographics are right.

64. Paul Farhi, "Rush Limbaugh Apologizes Again, but Advertisers Continue to Sever Ties," *Washington Post*, March 5, 2012, http://www.washingtonpost.com/lifestyle/style/rush-limbaugh-apologizes-again-but-advertisers-continue-to-sever-ties/2012/03/05/gIQAmM3WtR_story.html, as of March 6, 2012.

65. Derrick Z. Jackson, "Limbaugh Baggage with His ESPN Blabber," *Boston Globe*, July 16, 2003, as of March 22, 2012.

66. According to a survey by Harris Interactive, Rush Limbaugh is the most disliked news personality in America with 46 percent of respondents identifying him as their least favorite among the twenty-six news figures offered to subjects. Bill O'Reilly finished second, with 31 percent deeming him most objectionable. "Diane Sawyer, Anderson Cooper and Brian Williams Are America's Favorite News Personalities," http://www.harrisinteractive.com/NewsRoom/HarrisPolls/tabid/447/mid/1508/articleId/971/ctl/ReadCustom%20Default/Default.aspx, as of June 4, 2012.

67. Dylan Byers and Keach Hagey, "The Left's War on Rush's Advertisers," *Politico*, March 14, 2012, http://www.politico.com/news/stories/0312/73998.html; Lee, "Limbaugh Clash Has Advertisers Recalculating"; and "Activists Planning for a Protracted Fight against Limbaugh, and Provoking 1 Themselves," Associate Press wire, March 22, 2012, http://www.washingtonpost.com/entertainment/activists-planning-for-a-protracted-fight-against-limbaugh-and-provoking-one-themselves/2012/03/22/gIQAMOKSTS_story.html, all as of March 22, 2012.

68. Edmund Lee, "Limbaugh Clash Has Advertisers Recalculating Web's Power: Tech," *Bloomberg*, March 15, 2012, http://www.bloomberg.com/news/2012-03-15/limbaugh-clash-has-advertisers-recalculating-web-s-power-tech.html, as of March 22, 2012.

69. Suzanne Vranica and Christopher S. Stewart, "Show Distributor Defends Limbaugh," *Wall Street Journal*, March 6, 2012.

70. "It's Not Just Rush," *Taylor on Radio-Info*, March 9, 2012, http://www.radio-info.com/news/when-it-comes-to-advertisers-avoiding-controversial-shows-its-not-just-rush, as of March 22, 2012. Determining the overall number of Limbaugh sponsors is not realistically possible as much of the advertising comes from local sponsors who buy time only from one station. Unlike many talk radio shows, the Limbaugh program requires substantial payment from individual stations to run the show. In return, those local stations receive more of the commercial time available to run their own sponsor ads. Complicating matters further, as noted in note 63, is that many companies are indirectly purchasing remnant time through ad agencies. They may appear on the show only here and there.

71. "Dial Global-Moving Forward," *Radio Ink Magazine*, November 19, 2012, http://www.radioink.com/article.asp?id=2576718&spid=24698, as of December 21, 2012.

72. Dylan Byers, "Cumulus: Limbaugh Boycott Cost 'Millions,'" *Politico*, May 8, 2012, http://www.politico.com/blogs/media/2012/05/cumulus-ceo-limbaugh-boycott-hit-pretty-hard-122847.html, as of December 21, 2012. See also, Jack Mirikinson, "Cumulus: Nearly All Top Advertisers Have 'Exclude Rush Limbaugh' Orders," *Huffington Post*, May 8, 2013, http://www.huffingtonpost.com/2013/05/08/rush-limbaugh-advertisers-cumulus_n_3237496.html, as of May 29, 2013.

73. "Clear Channel's Bob Pittman Addresses Limbaugh Case in AP Interview," *Talkers*, March 28, 2012, http://www.talkers.com/tag/bob-clark/.

74. Limbaugh was at 14.75 million listeners a week. This compares to 15 million before the Fluke controversy, the difference between the two times is smaller than the error term in Arbitron ratings. "The Top Talk Radio Audiences," *Talkers*, August 17, 2012, http://www.talkers.com/top-talk-radio-audiences/, as of December 21, 2012.

75. After a protracted legal battle with his syndicator, Talk Radio Network, Savage won a decision in 2012 freeing him to take his services elsewhere. He signed with Cumulus but his broadcast is now at 9:00 to 12:00 pm, which suggests that even when his program enlists a full array of stations to carry him, it will attract a smaller audience than before. Ingraham also left the Talk Radio Network in late 2012. She signed with Courtside Entertainment to offer the same basic show and, like Savage, she will have to reconstruct a lineup of radio stations to carry her program. Jim Meyers, "Michael Savage Returns to Talk Radio Oct. 23," *Newsmax*, October 17, 2012, http://www.newsmax.com/Newsfront/Savage-Returns-Talk-Radio/2012/10/17/id/460395; and "It's Official: Laura Ingraham Joins Norm Pattiz's Courtside Entertainment Group and Launchpad Digital Media," *Talkers*, December 13, 2012, http://www.talkers.com/tag/laura-ingraham/, both as of December 24, 2012.

76. Kevin Robillard, "Rush Limbaugh: I Deserve Finder's Fee for Sandra Fluke," *Politico*, August 8, 2012, http://www.politico.com/news/stories/0812/79492.html, as of December 21, 2012.

CHAPTER 5

Political Anxiety and Outrage Fandom

Many of you have been hoodwinked into believing that we are a multicultural nation which we are not. We're a nation of many races and many cultures that is true, it has been true from the beginning, but in the past people would come over and become Americans. Now they come over and they want you to become them. They want you to speak Spanish. They want you to act Muslim....We're going to have a revolution in this country if this keeps up. These people are pushing the wrong people around. Just watch extreme fighting and you'll see what the white male is capable of. That's all I can say to you. Just understand why extreme fighting is becoming popular in this country—because the rage has reached a boil. If they keep pushing us around and if we keep having these schmucks running for office, catering to the multicultural people who are destroying the culture in this country, guaranteed the people, the white male in particular—let me talk specifically—the white male in particular, the one without connections, the one without money has nothing to lose and you haven't seen him yet. You haven't seen him explode in this country. And he's still the majority by the way, in case you don't know it. He is still the majority and no one speaks for him, everyone craps on him...and he has no voice whatsoever...so he goes to these extreme fighting events. Take a look at them and you'll see what the white male is capable of. And you're going to find out that if you keep pushing this country around you'll find out that there's an ugly side to the white male.

— *conservative radio host* Michael Savage[1]

This excerpt is unusually outrageous, brimming with rage that is nearly palpable when heard live as the bitterness in Savage's voice reverberates off the microphone. It is racist, xenophobic, and ethnocentric. Yet such talk by leading radio hosts draws remarkably large audiences.

The preceding chapters have addressed the structural factors that make outrage content profitable, but we know far more about why a network or syndicator might benefit from this type of content than why audiences find it appealing. The existing research suggests that we gravitate toward media sources that support our preexisting beliefs, but the explanations as to *why* we do this dwell on psychological processes or perceptions of information quality. We find such explanations unsatisfying for this unique genre and use this chapter to explore the audience experience with a more sociological lens. In doing so, we find that outrage-based political opinion programs create safe political spaces for fans. In these contexts, fans experience none of the discomfort we associate with face-to-face political conversation. Instead, they feel included in a like-minded community, have their lifestyles and viewpoints validated, and walk away armed with ammunition for any who might challenge them. We end by showing how shifts in the broader political climate have left conservative audiences unusually hungry for such content.

SELECTIVE EXPOSURE AND OUTRAGE

Why would anyone enjoy Michael Savage? One possibility is that tuning into outrage programming is simply an extension of the partisan selective exposure that has been well documented in recent years.[2] Perhaps one might conclude that watching Sean Hannity or Rachel Maddow is akin to choosing Fox or MSNBC for your evening news—an act that allows users to avoid information that might challenge their preexisting assumptions. We are concerned that the emphasis on individuals and information misses important dimensions of the social value audiences find in this kind of programming.

Most frequently cited work on selective exposure implicitly conceptualizes media choices as psychological processes, decisions made by individuals without attention to the social context they navigate. We see this in Festinger's (1957) theory of cognitive dissonance, which, while not about political media, serves as one of the classic texts in the selective exposure literature. Festinger finds that we prefer information that supports our preexisting beliefs and he attributes this preference to our desire to avoid psychological discomfort, or dissonance.[3] Through this lens we might understand a preference for outrage-based content as a search to find information that will allow us to engage in dissonance reduction. Inspired by Festinger, the body of work on motivated reasoning takes a similarly psychological approach, with an added a layer of nuance. Motivated reasoning suggests that people seeking information are frequently caught in a bind, as a tension may exist between reaching an accurate conclusion and reaching a conclusion that allows them to feel correct, whether or not that conclusion is accurate. These motivations guide what information we seek and how critically we evaluate the information we find.[4] Related research suggests that selective exposure is driven by our perceptions of information quality, which are themselves informed by our propensity to find affirming information more credible.[5]

Generally speaking, these psychological accounts and others like them seem plausible for news, but outrage-based programming has two attributes that complicate matters. First, its misrepresentative exaggerations, conspiracy theories, and caricature-like images that vilify or valorize political figures make the notion that these sources are seen as credible somewhat less plausible. Why, for example, would conservatives turn to Sean Hannity instead of turning to the *Weekly Standard* if they want to have their conservative political views supported by sources of information they believe to be credible? Second, if users' motivation is to avoid psychological discomfort, outrage-based shows seem an unlikely choice given their propensity for fear-mongering and their routine efforts to stoke anger and moral indignation. It is not impossible that outrage might feel comforting—indeed, we will show that it does—but if the goal is to minimize dissonance, we would expect audiences to avoid programming that suggests our way of life is under siege.

To fully understand these particular political media preferences, we argue that it is critical to look beyond what kinds of *information* audience members are seeking and ask about the *experiences* they desire. What do they find valuable? What's more, we argue that the experiences they value from political media (as in all realms of media) have as much to do with what is happening in the social world that audience members inhabit as they do with psychological drives. The popularity of outrage content makes sense only in the context of the broader landscape of real-life political dialogue in the United States, supporting Jamieson and Cappella's (2008) assertion that an analysis of the echo chamber must simultaneously "[capture] the interrelations of text, context, and audience."[6]

SEEING WHAT FANS SEE

To learn about the value fans find in outrage-based content, we combined two original data sets. The first is a six-week qualitative content analysis of ten outrage-based radio and television programs conducted during summer

2010 for the purpose of examining the techniques the most successful hosts use to connect with members of the audience. We used the Nielsen Media Cable News Ratings to select five of the most-watched conservative and liberal television programs, and chose to include the *Glenn Beck Program*, the *Sean Hannity Show*, the *O'Reilly Factor*, and then passed over several more highly rated conservative television programs so that we could include the top two liberal programs on the air at that time: *Countdown with Keith Olbermann* and the *Rachel Maddow Show*. Our five radio programs were selected using Arbitron popularity estimates for Talk Radio and included the *Rush Limbaugh Show*, the *Sean Hannity Show*, the *Glenn Beck Program*, *Savage Nation* (hosted by Michael Savage), and the *Mark Levin Show*. We examined these shows over a six-week period during summer 2010. Since we are trying to understand how the most successful hosts communicate with their audiences, we chose not to include any liberal radio programs. There is simply no Rush Limbaugh equivalent on the left. And, as we noted in Chapter 4, *none* of the top talk radio programs are liberal in orientation.[7] Liberal talk radio exists—Alan Colmes, Thom Hartmann, Stephanie Miller, and Ed Schultz are the most successful national hosts— but progressive talk tends to be local and has far smaller audiences. Liberal hosts contain no shortage of outrage, but they lack the conservatives' audience. Mike Malloy, who is every bit as outrageous as Mark Levin or Michael Savage, is carried on only thirteen stations across the country, a far cry from the likes of a Rush Limbaugh who can be found on over 600. In other words, the bias in the sample reflects the bias in the genre. As a result, we will not be able to compare liberal and conservative hosts, but that is not the goal of this inquiry.

We used observations made by the coding team that gathered the quantitative content analysis data from Chapter 2 as a jumping-off point to generate a series of themes, which we used to focus our analysis of this new data set. We set out to observe how hosts relate to their audience by focusing on key dimensions such as establishing credibility and authority, the construction of in-groups and out-groups, displays of authenticity, building community, and flattery.[8] The patterns we identified emerged from our close reading of the data relevant to these themes.

The data from the content analysis are revealing in their own right, but become even more meaningful when we combine them with information about how these programs are experienced by the audience. As a result, we have wedded the content analysis to twenty-four in-depth interviews with self-identified fans of outrage-based television and radio programming. The majority of the fans (n = 21) were recruited via

Internet postings in unofficial fan clubs and meet-up groups as well as through subsequent snowball sampling. The remaining respondents were recruited via personal referrals elicited through our social networks. The sample is composed of an equal number of liberals and conservatives and men and women, with a disproportionate number of male conservatives and female liberals (9 individuals in both cases). The respondents are overwhelmingly though not entirely, white and middle aged (roughly 30–60).[9] Respondents were asked open-ended questions about their viewing habits, their favorite programs and hosts, and the role of political talk in their lives more broadly. All respondents' names have been changed, and, due to the intimacy of some of the social groups from which the respondents emerge, identifying information such as geographical area and age are not linked with the responses shared here.[10]

THE AVERSION TO POLITICAL CONVERSATION

When we think about the literature on (unmediated) political discussion in the United States, what comes to mind is the assertion that political discussion among citizens is vital to healthy democracy,[11] as well as the significant body of empirical work demonstrating that public political conversation is a relatively intimidating proposition. Political communications scholars Hayes, Scheufele, and Huge describe public political activities, including discussion, as presenting potential interpersonal dangers, and research suggests we are acutely aware of these risks.[12] Conover, Searing, and Crewe uncovered some of the fears around political talk through focus group research, where respondents explained why they choose to avoid political discussion. They described many fears including social rejection/isolation, looking uneducated/uninformed, being unable to defend their positions, and social conflict.[13] Wyatt, Katz, Levinsohn, and Al-Haj's comparative analysis of political expression showed respondents' fear of hurting others as a particularly powerful inhibiting force. Of course, not all political talk provokes the same level of anxiety.[14] Political scientist Elisabeth Noelle-Neumann's spiral of silence theory captures this uneven reticence, arguing that we are less likely to voice an opinion on issues when we sense we are in the minority because we believe (consciously or unconsciously) that sharing unpopular opinions will lead to negative consequences.[15]

In light of these anxieties, it comes as little surprise that most of us avoid political conversations with others whose views are known to be different from our own or whose views are unknown (and hence may differ from our own). Such "cross-cutting" political conversations can be extremely uncomfortable, and Diana Mutz describes Americans as "unusually adept" at avoiding them.[16] Indeed, she shows that our social networks are remarkably homogeneous; less than 25 percent of her survey respondents were able to identify one person with differing views with whom they interact. As a result, political conversations today are generally saved for our most intimate circles of friends and family, usually taking place in the home, with like-minded peers, as documented by a preponderance of research.[17] As a result of these evasive measures, research shows that Americans are more likely to come into contact with political views that differ from their own through mass media than through their social networks,[18] a sobering conclusion in light of the recent work on selective exposure.[19]

SAFE POLITICAL TALK

We argue that this anxiety around everyday political conversation shapes our relationship to outrage-based political programming. More specifically, we contend that these two aspects of American political culture—anxiety around political talk and the related tendency to reserve such talk for intimate spaces—create a situation in which a new kind of political "dialogue" between political opinion program hosts and their loyal followers offers a safe and comfortable alternative to other kinds of political discussion. Our inspection of outrage-based programs and interviews with fans reveal that the programs are structured so that they systematically diffuse the most common fears evoked by political conversation and create a safe space for audience members. In the pages that follow we combine fans' accounts with information culled during content analysis to address three of these fears and highlight those elements of the programs that ameliorate them.

It is not that these shows replace informal political conversations—we believe they inform them rather than erase them—but listening closely to our respondents makes clear that outrage-based programs provide a risk-free option for political companionship that is often missing in our face-to-face encounters. For example, when asked if he enjoys talking about politics, Gabriel, a Glenn Beck fan shared this:

My girlfriend doesn't like talking about politics and I don't like talking politics with her. She doesn't want to talk about it, she gets mad if I push it...so I just don't bother. I'll go and I'll do something, I'll check out something, some kind of show or something.

The shows Gabriel turns to are those of his favorite outrageous political opinion hosts. When fans like Gabriel turn to Glenn Beck they not only avoid the social risks that come with face-to-face political conversation— Gabriel's TV won't get mad at him—they also reap benefits: social connections, a sense of being well informed, and the reassurance that they are right.

We detail our findings in two waves. First, we show the way that the programs eliminate fears surrounding political talk, examining three in particular: the fear of social rejection, the fear of looking uneducated, and the fear of social conflict. Then we explore the differences between liberal and conservative fans, to shed light on why conservatives might seek out such fear-free zones more eagerly than liberals.

Social Connection, Not Social Exclusion

As we have described, prior research points to several distinct fears churned up by political conversations outside our inner circles of like-minded friends. One key fear is of social exclusion or rejection. Such anxiety is unnecessary in the context of the camaraderie engendered by the charismatic hosts of political opinion media, who construct a welcoming political environment that makes audience members feel as though they are at home, among friends. Each time they turn on their show, it is as if they have walked into a local coffee shop where they are a regular; people recognize them and know how they take their coffee. Although it may sound counterintuitive, we find that fans are attracted to outrage-based programs because they offer social connections to those on their side of who share their worldview.

One way the programs offer social connections is by building a sense of intimacy, creating what feels distinctly like a one-on-one relationship between the individual fan and the host. Gene, a Bill O'Reilly fan, distinguishes this intimacy from the distant professionalism doled out by anchors on the evening news:

It's clear that they're not like in the old days, like Walter Cronkite who is just serious reading the news. These hosts are all talking to their audience directly. It's a very different style from a straight newsperson.

But what do you mean by that? Cronkite looked into the camera just like O'Reilly looks into the camera. What do you mean when you say he's talking to his audience directly?

Cronkite was reporting to his audience. He was looking into the camera, but O'Reilly and Maddow, they are having a conversation, even though obviously it's one way, it's conversational and it's not a presentation. They're talking to me.

They're talking to you?

Yeah.

Whereas political conversation generates fears of social exclusion, outrage programs incorporate and include viewers and listeners. The host presents as a kindred spirit who "gets you" even when other folks don't. Ben, a Maddow fan, says: "That's why I watch these shows.... I'm like 'Yes! There's someone out there who agrees with me...somebody who understands what's going on.'" Rachel Maddow is, for him, like a surrogate friend. He continues, "She is down to earth and like somebody you'd like to sit in a coffee house and have a conversation with about the news."

The affective attachments shared by our respondents are not entirely surprising. In 1956, Horton and Wohl suggested that although mass media (usually) involved one-way communication, broadcast media gave the audience the feeling that they are having a one-on-one relationship with media figures in a way print media could not. They describe these connections as "parasocial," in that viewers and listeners can come to feel as though they know the celebrities, much in the way they know their friends.[20] Meyrowitz has also explored this phenomenon ("media friends" in his parlance) more deeply. Meyrowitz writes, "as with real-life friends, one feels bound to the person not simply because of what they can do, but based on a more personal set of feelings about who they are—and how their "presence" makes one feel."[21] The fans we interviewed spoke about their favorite hosts in this way, as if they know something about who the hosts are as people, just as Meyrowitz indicates. Describing Glenn Beck and Sean Hannity, for example, Richard says, "They're honest people. They're human people. They're not arrogant." He comments here not on their political insights or their wit, but on their character.

One reason fans feel they know their favorite hosts is because the hosts present themselves (and are presented as) relatable, reliable friends. Richard got this message: "They want to talk to regular folk, and they present themselves as regular folk." Maddow, Beck, and Hannity feel relatable to Ben and Richard because the hosts work to minimize the difference in status between themselves and their audience. Rhetorically, they level the playing field between by characterizing themselves as an "average Joe" or in some way imperfect, making clear that their credentials and celebrity status do not separate them from their viewers and listeners. Glenn Beck often reminds his audience that he's not perfect, referring to his history of personal mistakes and battles with alcoholism, and Ed Schultz frequently talks about his passion for hunting and describes himself as a "meat and potatoes" kind of guy, posting photos of himself fishing on his website. The message is that these are regular, fallible people with whom fans can identify. In discussing the BP oil spill, conservative radio host Mark Levin communicates this by assuring listeners, "You know, I just think about these things the way you do," and Rachel Maddow modestly requested that viewers "Forgive the speed at which I absorb these things, I'm not a scientist."[22] Gabe Hobbs, the radio consultant quoted in the last chapter, is apparently not the only person who thinks being self-deprecating wins over audiences. This leveling works to create a peer-like commonality between hosts and fans.

Roderick Hart attributed the sense of intimacy that people feel with political figures to television, particularly its focus on personality politics, but we find winks of intimacy are extended across media platforms and they sometimes offer not only the sense of closeness, but actual (if not substantive) access to the attention and lives of their favorite hosts. With most talk radio programs, calling in is an option. The chances of being "put through" are relatively slim, but this is not the only avenue available to fans wanting to reach out. For example, members of BillOReilly.com are rewarded with "backstage conversations," in which O'Reilly takes questions from premium members (all members are actually "premium" members) and answers them in a private webcast. They are also told: "Premium Members can email Bill using BillOReilly.com. Your message will not be shuffled in with the massive amounts of emails delivered each day, but will receive priority treatment and guaranteed review." Rush Limbaugh 24/7 members are given access to "Rush's super-secret e-mail address" and a member-only "DittoCam" (Limbaugh fans are called "dittoheads"), with exclusive live video of Rush's broadcast.[23] Perhaps Ed Schultz offers the most intimate access; he owns a fishing lodge where $3,500 per person will buy visitors three days of fishing and an opportunity to brush shoulders with Schultz and his family. His website says, "This is where I go on the weekends and for summer vacation. Come join us ... *Ed and Wendy!*"[24] It is no coincidence that many fans describe having friend-like feelings about their favorite hosts; the hosts present themselves as such.

In addition to offering social connections through pseudo-friendships with charismatic hosts, outrage-based programs also dissolve the fear of social isolation by connecting fans to like-minded others in an imagined community. In this social space, fans fit in, are valued, and understood. Hosts create this community in a variety of ways. Much like non-outrage-based talk show hosts, the hosts we studied regularly use inclusive language such as "us," "we," and "our" to bring the audience into the fold. In the outrage context this brand of in-grouping takes on added significance because the insider/outsider distinction is such a prevalent theme in the genre. Although there is variation in intensity across the programs, insiders are constructed as wise, noble, and rational teammates (we'll discus validation momentarily), juxtaposed with outsiders who are not simply people with different perspectives or priorities, but rather are dangerous and misguided opponents who pose a threat to insiders' most cherished values.[25] Linguistically, then, these techniques offer the audience admittance into a morally righteous social circle.

Some hosts build a sense of community more concretely through the construction of special events, online spaces, and meet-up groups. Virtual connections play a particularly big role. For example, the Hannity website includes a discussion forum; O'Reilly Factor "premium members" gain access to members-only message boards: "The BillOReilly.com Message Boards hold a wealth of opinions and information from people just like you. Exchange thoughts, ideas and insights of your own, or simply tune in and follow exchanges," as well as access to member mail: "Our 'Member Mail' system makes the exchange of ideas easy, and it's the best way to keep in touch with your fellow Premium Members worldwide!"[26] A few sites, such as Mark Levin's, link to fan pages where interaction can take place. Some fans described immersing themselves in these virtual networks. Listen to Elizabeth:

> There's the Maddow Fan website and then there's the website for her TV show, there's a bunch of us who hang out on Twitter . . . a lot of Maddow fans use Twitter to communicate with each other and sort of talk about stuff and have fun and joke around, it's a great sort of tool.

Maddow has 2.5 million followers on twitter, and while she is no Lady Gaga, she outshines her conventional peers such as Brian Williams, John King, or Bob Scheiffer, who hover around 100,000 followers.[27]

These online connections are not always initiated by the hosts. A few respondents described making virtual links to like-minded others after being inspired by their favorite political talk media. Trent, a Limbaugh fan, took it upon himself to use Meetup.com to find other fans. These virtual introductions quickly led to a face-to-face discussion group.

Some hosts attempt to foster face-to-face connections among fans by planning events and encouraging audience members to participate. Listen, for example, to Sean Hannity promote his 2010 Freedom Summer Concerts. Hannity's on-air promotion of the series involved very little emphasis on performers, instead highlighting the experience of being immersed in the Hannity community—the emotionality, patriotism, and camaraderie experienced by attendees:

> I think this will be the best show we've ever put on.... We get to celebrate free-dom and fun because of the sacrifice of people like your sons.... Isn't it amaz-ing? Isn't it great to see, I mean this is what makes this thing so unique, I try and explain to people the range of emotions that you feel during the concert, look, I'm feeling, and I'm telling you, there are moments you wanna cry, there are moments you just couldn't be happier, you're rocking out having a good time, and on your feet and dancing and laughing and me singing, and all of this stuff, it's just, and you see patriotism on display, it makes you literally leave there with the feeling that you just, you love your country even more, and you're grateful to see that there are so many other like-minded people out there.[28]

The concert, as per his pitch, is not about the performances but about sharing a group experience undergirded by common conservative values. Hannity's concert series was profit-driven, but not all communal efforts are, as best illustrated by Glenn Beck's 9/12 Project. This effort attempted to foster local connections among Beck fans who committed to a series of nine principles and twelve values. Gabriel, the Beck fan, described real-life social connections fostered by his connections stemming from the *Glenn Beck Show*:

> He's [Beck is] telling us to meet others, not to just be that one person that "damn I know, I'm surrounded by all these crazy goons trying to do one thing or another, and I'm by myself I don't have a voice"—he wanted us to meet others, to know there are other people out there who have the same opinion.... For me [the 9/12 project] is all about meeting people who think like me and want to gather up and maybe have a say in some of the matters that are happening out there.... I belong to the [local] 9/12 project, and we do get-togethers. We have a constitution club and a book club. We did rallies. I've been to several rallies.

So, while political conversations with neighbors, friends, and colleagues are fraught with the risk of social rejection, the comfort zones provided by the shows we studied present no such risk, and in fact, offer imagined and in some cases tangible social connections. Communities build around many "media friends," but being part of the group in the outrage context is unique. Participants have not only shared affinities but also shared aversions, and unlike video gaming communities, Justin Bieber's "beliebers," or sports fans, these loyalties are actively constructed as a reflection of personal attributes such as morality, intelligence, and character rather than more idiosyncratic tastes and preferences.

Feeling Educated Rather than Ill-Informed

For some people, the thought of talking politics with those holding different political views creates performance anxiety and the possibility of appearing uneducated. Outrage hosts buffer against that by helping audience members feel as though they are informed. Richard, a Beck fan, and Trent, the Limbaugh fan, illustrate:

> I like anything that increases my knowledge so that I can form valid opinions. And I think that Fox News [the network, not the nightly news] more than any other of the visual media, increases my knowledge....I downloaded the [health care] legislation on my computer from the government sites. I don't know if you've ever looked at the actual verbiage of congressional legislation but, it is not readily understood, ok....What I am interested in is having people whom I trust, with their knowledge, interpret the laws that I can't understand. (Richard)

> Rush is breaking it down and saying, "this is why things are happening this way." That's what I think makes a good show because he's got everybody going, "ah, I understand that, that's much better now." (Trent)

And although she reports avoiding political conversations, Roberta, a Schultz fan, links feeling informed directly to helping her should she become involved in a challenging political encounter:

> I love facts. I'm going to call it ammunition, I love ammunition. When you can have facts to back up your opinion, and then if somebody says something to you, you got the ammunition to say: no, these are the facts."...This isn't just opinion, I'm not just making this up in the air, this is what really is the case.

She wants to avoid feeling foolish should she find herself confronted with one of the uncomfortable political conversations she fears. Importantly, "facts," which Roberta says she values, can be found in many venues. Why not turn to *Roll Call* or *Congressional Quarterly* for "facts" or to *National Review* or *The Nation* for analysis? Because Roberta wants to feel informed for strategic reasons, and for many, the stories and pithy one-liners offered by entertainment-based opinion shows are more portable than in-depth policy analysis. Her interest in ammunition reveals an orientation toward accessibility; she wants information she can readily deploy.

In some situations, production techniques work to support the transmission of key pieces of information (or "ammunition"). This is the case on the *O'Reilly Factor* during a segment of the program called "talking points" in which a box on the side of the screen summarizes O'Reilly's arguments, abridging them into neatly packaged tidbits, in keeping with the title of the segment. On *The Last Word with Lawrence O'Donnell*, during the "rewrite" segment, he reviews remarks made by prominent figures and inserts "corrections," presented as facts as he goes (these might be graphs, data, contradictory text, or incriminating video evidence, etc.). The *Ed Show* has a similar segment called "psycho talk." Segments like these offer both rebuttal training and certainty; the favored position is correct (there are facts to support it!) and the opposing view is presented as "psycho talk."

Hosts also diffuse the fear of feeling dumb by contrasting fans with political opponents who are depicted as childish or stupid. Here is Keith Olbermann:

> These [Tea Party members] are essentially people who have never been out in the real world before, at least in the political world, and…have not hit that moment all the rest of us have that our own personal views that we developed when we were six and half years old are not in fact the exact identical views of everybody else in the world, and we may need to control the id a little bit.[29]

Listen also to Mark Levin, as he assures listeners that it is *others* who are ill-informed:

> Listen to me, listen to me, we call them drones. Don't waste your time with the drones. There are other people out there who are just full of shit or misinformed, or whatever, but do not waste your time with the drones, because they are not people to be persuaded.[30]

In the world of the show, fans are more intelligent than the idiotic others who don't "get it." Those whose views differ from the norms of the group are routinely vilified (e.g., political opponents, journalists, people at the other end of the ideological spectrum), elevating insiders in contrast.

Fans want to become informed, prepared in the event they find themselves in political conversations, and hosts position their programs as trustworthy sources of information—the place to get the *real* story—casting doubt on the reliability of the "mainstream" media, which is described as awash in liberal (or corporate) bias, depending on their political view. In an impressive sleight of hand, the hosts regularly present opinion media as the place to come for news and dismiss the news media as manipulative opinion-mongers with hidden agendas. Only in the outrage cocoon can respondents be safe from bias.

While this is an especially common tactic for conservative opinion hosts, who reserve particular venom for NPR, the *New York Times,* and the *Washington Post,* progressive hosts are relentless in their demonization of Fox and periodically present the broader news media as inadequate as well.[31] This is in keeping with the "hostile media phenomenon," in which audiences interpret the media as biased against their particular viewpoints, even when those on opposing sides are shown the same content.[32] Still, the perception of bias is not distributed evenly. A 2012 study by Pew Research Center for People and the Press found that while 32 percent of Democrats say there is a "great deal of media bias," 49 percent of Republicans feel this way, and among conservative Republicans, the agreement is even higher, with 57 percent seeing a great deal of bias.[33]

The fans we interviewed report a much higher degree of trust in their favorite outrage-based programming than they do in conventional news sources. David, an O'Reilly fan, feels that his favorite conservative programs on Fox set themselves apart from the liberal mainstream media by being "meticulous about making sure the liberal viewpoint is heard." In terms of other sources, he says:

> If you read the *New York Times,* what you're reading on the front page really should belong on the editorial page.... I basically have given up on subscribing to newspapers because of the bias that is so evident. It should be editorial comment. It is actually slanted toward opinion even though they call it news.... [I used to] watch CNN when I was on the treadmill and it was a bad idea, bad experience, bad trip, because I could see how they were presenting me poor news and they had such a bias—that would increase my adrenaline.

Throughout the interview, David repeatedly describes the *O'Reilly Factor* as unbiased, especially in contrast to the news: "Network news gives you their opinions, but they call it news. N.E.W.S. That's different. Big time." Because of this intense frustration, David described finding the *O'Reilly Factor* as "a great revelation." He shared his first impressions of the program:

> When you watch something that you're not familiar with and don't know what to expect you're, you're pretty cautious, and so my first impressions

were really positive as a result of my concerns about reporting bias which were somewhat allayed by having seen the first several episodes.

O'Reilly offers a respite from the bias he perceives in sources like the *New York Times* and CNN. And Richard explains that the news offends him, while his favorite opinion hosts educate him:

> We've shifted away from, let's say the mainstream media because a lot of what they put out is offensive and biased. Offensive because of the bias. I do like Rush Limbaugh...my opinion on Rush is that he's pretty knowledge-able...he's very erudite ...what impresses me about Glenn Beck is also his knowledge....To me it's like going to a college lecture...he reminds me of a teaching assistant or grad assistant at MIT teaching.

Catherine, a Beck fan, is concerned about bias but also believes conventional news sources to be riddled with errors in a way the *Glenn Beck Show* is not:

> You can't, you know, go to *Yahoo News* without getting the liberal presentation. The *Boston Globe* has it, all the local TV stations have it, including the local Fox although they're not quite as bad. So you really have to search out and pay attention to find a non-liberal perspective.... [I] have never found [Beck] to be factually in error. There have certainly been opinions he has stated with which I have disagreed. But I have never found a factual error in anything he has presented. So that means a hell of a lot....I wish I could say the same thing for the mainstream media because, you know, they have glaring factual errors all the time that they never bother to correct.

It appears, then, that while political conversations in everyday life leave participants fearing they will look ill-informed, outrage-based opinion programs help fans feel knowledgeable. Not only because they are up to date with pressing current events but also because they know what is "really" going on without relying on the mainstream media, which can't be trusted to cover the news fairly, or in depth, or, in some minds, even correctly.[34]

Validated Instead of Challenged

Outrage-based programs reassure and embolden the audience members rather than leaving them fearful. They do this in a variety of ways, but most notably by valorizing their audience, celebrating their strong character, and allowing the audience to position themselves in the role of the victor—capable of handily dominating naysayers in imaginary political jousts.

The hosts function as supportive cheerleaders for and defenders of the values that fans hold dear. Our respondents sound almost elated as they describe how it feels to hear their favorite host talk about the issues they care about in ways that are consistent with their own perspectives and beliefs. Roberta, whom we met earlier, described it as validating:

> Usually my husband and I sit there, listening [to Schultz], being like, "Yeah, you go!" That's what usually happens.... There's so much right wing media, there's so much right wing talk...and after a while of turning off most of the media, it's just so nice to have some people you can listen to and that validate your feelings, not only validate your opinions, but also validate it with fact.

And Mary, a Maddow fan, explained what draws her to the show:

> [Maddow] aligns with my own political views, and so I think I recognize that she is entertainment and that she is presenting a certain perspective, but I tend to agree with her perspective so I appreciate hearing her say—It's that what she says resonates with my own values...she aligns with my own values.

Tuning into these programs brings no risk of social conflict, instead it brings reassurance that fans' insights are astute and their priorities are in order.

Hosts not only affirm the political views held by members of the audience but they also tell them in many subtle and not so subtle ways that they *themselves* are valued. Flattery abounds in outrage. Sometimes it takes the form of direct compliments as we have here from Glenn Beck and Rachel Maddow:

> I've tried to package these things for general consumption as much as I can, and you are doing such an amazing job, boy I hear from 9/12 people all the time, you're doing amazing things in restoring our own history.[35]

> But the *Rachel Maddow Show* viewers are not just plain old regular awesome. You are THE Awesome. We know this because one of you went online and made a little what's called a de-motivator out of the viral photo of that gas station in Ohio...de-motivators are a cinch to make but great ones, they take genius, like these, sent by you.[36]

And sometimes the flattery is indirect, bolstering the audience member by making that person the center of attention, as in these examples from Mark Levin and Rush Limbaugh:

You see ladies and gentlemen, now that they've destroyed the treasury, now they're coming more and more for you. How many times have I had to say? This isn't about the rich it's about you. Healthcare: you. Cap and Trade: you. Illegal aliens: you. Diminishing your citizenship, stealing your private property, stealing your liberty. It's about you.[37]

I hate writing all these *I* sentences, I almost sound like Obama, so let's make this about you. What are *you* gonna do about this? What do *you* want to see happen? How much do you care about your country and your community? It's not everybody asking themselves these things.[38]

In still other cases, the audience is praised indirectly through celebrations of "the little people" or "hardworking Americans" in a way that ennobles those who may feel devalued or disrespected in other settings. Here is Sean Hannity:

Well, let me tell you something, the people that make this country great are the so-called little people! It's the people that get up every single day, they take care of their kids, that are responsible for their lives, that go to work and shovel coffee down their throat and they take their kids to school, those are the great people in this country. And they don't complain and they don't have big, fat egos and they just wanna have good lives for their kids and grandkids.[39]

"The little people" Hannity describes may not have "fat egos," but there is little question that tuning in offers regular viewers positive feedback that they do not associate with political conversations.

Fans tune in to hear the charismatic hosts articulate the very things they feel most strongly about in ways they find persuasive. Some respondents seem to live vicariously through the host—imagining that they are as witty, clever, and confident as their favorite personality. Catherine says,

[Glenn Beck] has an amazing ability to take widely diverging facts, pieces of information, and put them together in a coherent picture. He sees connections better than just about anyone else I have ever come across. I have always been good at seeing connections myself... but Glenn does it way better than I do.

And talking about O'Reilly, Gene says,

I just think he's obnoxious. I guess I wish I could be obnoxious like that sometimes... there's some appeal in watching somebody who's obnoxious in a way generally you can't be.... In your day-to-day interactions at least, you sort of have to be polite and every once in a while you'd like to just say what you really think. And these guys do.

By identifying with the host, fans imagine themselves deploying the same skills, defending their views against critics with a magical combination of intellectual acumen, fervor, humor, and dismissiveness. Although, admittedly, it takes a certain je ne sais quoi to master such style, as one liberal fan reflected: "I get enough information to be able to sometimes carry on a conversation...but could I be as eloquent in presenting those ideas as Rachel Maddow or Keith Olbermann? Not necessarily." (Joan)

Taken as a whole, we find that outrage programs create a comfortable space that offers the fans something more akin to collusion than conflict. They are empowerment zones that bolster viewers' and listeners' self-assuredness rather than challenging their beliefs. Fans can tune in without fear of being uncomfortable. They need not fear confrontation, nor do the guests on the shows. Although these programs have a reputation for hostility, conflict on set is quite low. Chris Matthews often interrupts and badgers his guests, and Mark Levin sometimes insults his callers, but the majority of hosts serve up less social tension than an episode of The View, by incorporating guests and callers with whom they agree or those who tend to dissent softly and then acquiesce politely. The tough questions, insults, and accusations are generally made at a safe distance from their targets.

THE COMFORT ZONE

Recognizing these shows as safe havens leads us to wonder if this comfort is part of the reason that conservative outrage programming is so much more prevalent and successful than liberal outrage. While it certainly is not the only reason, differential levels of cultural anxiety around political discussion may be an important part of this story.[40] We suspect this is relevant because our research suggests that conservatives take a greater social risk (or perceive that they do) when engaging in public political discussion than moderates or progressives. Liberals may be criticized as unrealistic or even immoral, but the most loaded term they are called is usually "unpatriotic" or "socialist." These labels have been damning at certain historical moments—"unpatriotic" carried weight immediately post 9/11 and "socialist" was a weighty accusation in the 1950s—today they feel more eye-roll-worthy than threatening to most recipients, even if the terms are deeply derogatory in the minds of those levying them.

Conservatives, however, feel more vulnerable in the current cultural climate, as we will show.

The 1990s were marked by heightened American sensitivity to cultural difference, which took center stage through debates over Eurocentrism and multiculturalism on college campuses, talk of inclusion and tolerance in political rhetoric, and increased attention to diversity in the workplace.[41] This sea change places conservatives, particularly social conservatives, in a precarious position, because the rhetorical (if not political) triumph of multiculturalism has given discourses of tolerance growing currency and simultaneously stigmatized talk that can be read as intolerant.[42] In contrast, rhetoric of tolerance and equality used by progressives is socially acceptable, often valued, even if policies that support social justice are less widely supported. We do not mean to imply that the multiculturalist movement is complete or that it has gone unchallenged. The turn toward embracing diversity faced and continues to receive considerable hostility, particularly around curricular changes on college campuses (e.g., introducing ethnic studies departments and diminishing the centrality of the study of Western civilization) and the entrance of affirmative action policies in admissions and hiring. Furthermore, legislation that might translate "valuing difference" talk into tangible support of and for marginalized social groups has had mixed outcomes, but the stigma against perceived intolerance has remained a lasting legacy.[43]

For conservatives, this means that articulating political opinions around political issues such as immigration policy, affirmative action, and LGBT rights can be thorny, opening them to accusations that are more socially damaging than labeling someone a socialist. In other words, we suspect conservatives feel that they are in a more precarious position than liberals when it comes to political talk, an activity that is strenuously avoided by many to begin with. If this is the case, we might expect to find that conservatives have fewer conversations with those whose perspectives differ from their own. Indeed this is the case; Mutz (2006) found that conservatives engage in significantly fewer cross-cutting political conversations than do liberals, with the effect getting stronger at the end of the spectrum. The same pattern appears for party identification, with "strong" Republicans having fewer cross-cutting exposures than "strong" Democrats. Intensity of party identification also matters: "strong" Republicans have the fewest cross-cutting exposures, and "not very strong" Republicans have more than those who only "lean" Republican. Democrats exhibit the same pattern, although they have more cross-cutting exposures as a whole than do Republicans.[44] Whether this difference is attributable to conservatives' greater perception of social risk is unknown, but the pattern

Mutz identifies is consistent with our emergent sense that the cultural climate for conservatives and liberals is different. In a context of perceived social threat, it makes sense that conservatives might gravitate inward—toward homogeneous conversation partners in everyday life and the sanctuary provided by outrage-based content.[45]

What's so different? Well, presumably no one likes to be called sexist or homophobic, but being called a racist carries particular cultural force. Bonilla-Silva's (2010) revealing qualitative excerpts highlight the way that this shapes whites' speech by illustrating the linguistic cartwheels used by white respondents when race is the topic of conversation. He argues that these awkward fumblings are "the result of talking about racially sensitive matters in a period in which certain things can not be uttered in public" (p. 54).[46] Social psychology offers us a wealth of evidence that white respondents (regardless of political perspective) are so fearful of being perceived as racist that they regularly adopt "strategic colorblindness" during interracial interactions, going out of their way to avoid mentioning race, even when experimental conditions make it exceedingly difficult to do so.[47] Taken together, these studies suggest that white anxiety about being perceived as racist is powerful even in nonpolitical contexts.

All but one of our conservative respondents are white and likely carry such anxiety in nonpolitical conversations, but when asked about discussing politics, it was clear that these fears had been realized in ways not described by our liberal respondents. Conservatives routinely shared stories about being called racist, as illustrated by these two accounts:

I wrote something [on Facebook] about the mosque being built [near the 9/11 site] and it ended up a *huge* thing—I think 156 comments were made. Everybody—people I haven't talked to in a very long time were even writing on it. There were people saying it wasn't right where it was so close to the 9/11 site because they felt that the terrorists were able to win that way. Other people were saying who cares, because it's across the street or down the block. People got very offended. My point of view on that was, you know, there are 7 or 8 other mosques in that area so I thought, you know, you can have your mosque and that's fine I don't care ...but where it is so close to home where that particular religion ended up hurting people and it was kind of like a sensitive thing ...move it somewhere else. And people got very offended with that and wrote, you know, not all Muslims are terrorists and that's where people lost sight of what the conversation was and what my particular point of view was, they didn't listen. It was just, you know, "You're racist," and it went on from there.... Well, you have no idea why I feel this way. Being called a racist is a really powerful insult. (Missy)

What [my brother] said that really got me worked up was that the Tea Party was a racist thing. The only reason why the Tea Party existed was because they hated Obama because he was black, and that to me gets into the realm of ridiculous nonsense. The reason the Tea Party exists was because we are spending too much money in America: our children and grandchildren are being robbed of money because we are spending it today. That's why the Tea Party exists—it has absolutely nothing to do with the color of our president's skin. But he bought that whole cause.... "Well, if Obama's saving this country and is doing great things, you know, you just must not like him because you're a racist," and that's bullcrap. And this is my younger brother and he knows that I'm not a racist! I really get offended by that....So to hear my younger brother saying, "the Tea Party's racist," and he knows I helped organize one, I said "that's nonsense, no we're not," they're not racist, that's not why it's happening, and yet he would not back down from it. So that got into some heated exchange ... but because he was obstinate and would not back down from it, I said, "I just can't talk about this with you anymore. We just need to avoid politics." Now, I told him, I said, "you have to understand that the political parties each have one big trump card that they like to pull out." Republicans, when they're backed into a corner, will accuse Democrats of being unpatriotic....When Democrats get backed into a corner, they need to say, "well you must be a racist." (Trent)

The experience of being perceived as racist loomed large in the minds of conservative fans. In fact, every conservative respondent asked how he or she feels about talking politics raised the issue of being called racist *without even being asked*, revealing the social power of such accusations. The impact of being labeled racist was also visible in the level of detail that marked the accounts respondents offered. Over the course of the interviews, these experiences, even those dating back several years, seemed close to the surface. Fans shared lengthy, concrete accounts, animated with emotion, as if the interactions had just transpired.

What makes accusations of racism so upsetting for respondents is that racism is socially stigmatized, but also that they feel powerless to defend themselves once the specter is raised. For example, Gabriel, the one conservative fan of color in our sample, complained that even his Puerto Rican heritage was inadequate to convince others that his political views are not grounded in racist ideology. And Trent, who had the disagreement with his brother, described arguing with an accuser as an unwinnable war. We asked what he says when someone calls him racist, and he replied:

Well, you strongly dispute it in no uncertain terms. You end up looking like a blithering idiot though when you do it. That's why it works.... It's one of those questions where once that's thrown out there there's not a whole lot that you can do. Because if that person just said that to you, they're not going to believe you, whatever you happen to say, you know what I'm saying? So sometimes it's better just to simply refute it and not really go into a lot about it unless they keep calling you it, and then it gets a little bit more difficult. But I might simply say something like, "I am not a racist. I have never espoused any views like that, you know my family has always been very tolerant, you know I'll always tell you to shut up if you're trying to tell a racist joke," or whatever, something like that. I'll mention the friends that I have. But when you're doing all that, it's, "the lady doth protest too much," you know what I'm saying? It's hard. It's really hard.... Because when you start to have to convince someone that you're not a racist, that doesn't bode well for you. It makes it sound like you're defensive because maybe you actually do have that problem.

Liberal respondents shared no such horror stories. This imbalance is something that our conservative respondents are attuned to in a way our liberal respondents are not. We asked respondents whether it is harder to be liberal or conservative when it comes to talking politics. Every conservative respondent said it was harder to be conservative, even those who live in overwhelmingly conservative communities. Listen to Gabriel:

It's just harder to be conservative because it's easy to call someone a racist. It's easy to think, "Well, you just want people to starve." It's easy to think, "Well, you just want to keep people poor." Well I know all my views on all those topics, I can tell you exactly what they are, and some people will sit there and go, "You're just wrong, you're conservative, you just hate people. You just hate Black people or poor people or gay people, or whatever." It is very easy to be liberal and just say, "Someone else just hates [people of color, poor people, gay people]. They hate whatever."

Although we might expect liberal respondents to have analogous answers, it appears this is not a simple case of in-group defensiveness. Liberal reactions to the question were very different, with each respondent indicating that the burden depends on social context. When asked whether she thinks talking politics with those whose political views differ from their own is harder for liberals or conservatives, Alexandra, a Chris Matthews fan, offers one such response:

Ummm...I don't think it matters. I think the only thing that matters is whether you're outnumbered and feel you can say what you want to say, because when I'm running in conservative circles, I temper my words more than if I were surrounded by liberals and I think conservatives feel the same way.

Every one of the liberal respondents offered a version of this "it depends" answer. For liberals, what makes political talk uncomfortable is feeling bullied or alone. This is quite different from conservative respondents who feel they can be shut down in any context by virtue of the social stigma of perceived intolerance, particularly racial intolerance. Talking politics during the leadership of the first nation's black president only heightens this tension for conservatives. Supporting or opposing Barack Obama's candidacies and/or policies might be interpreted by others as an indication of racial attitudes rather than of political preferences—a perk for white liberals concerned with embracing (or appearing to embrace) diversity, and a challenge for white conservatives put in the position of defending a political choice that needs more explanation than if the president were white.

While all respondents are guarded when it comes to talking politics, describing certain spaces (e.g., work, dinner parties) as taboo and indicating a strong preference for talking with like-minded others, there is a difference that appears when we compare the responses of our liberal and conservative respondents. All respondents allude implicitly or explicitly to wanting to avoid offending others or engaging in awkward social exchanges, but conservative respondents alone describe feeling wary of being judged negatively *as people* because of their views.

> There are friends that I don't feel comfortable talking about stuff like that with who I've known a long, long while. The people that I do feel comfortable with, they usually see the way I see. They feel the same way I do politically. There's a few who don't feel the same way and I'm still able to talk to them because they're not the type of people who are going to get upset or they already know the type of person I am so *they're not going to think differently of me for the way I feel*. I tend not to when I'm first meeting someone I don't, you know, bring up political things. If I hear people speaking politically and I don't agree with them, I won't jump into the conversation right away ...if I'm in an online forum, they don't know me so it doesn't bother me. I'll say whatever. (Missy)

It is not that Missy doesn't have political opinions or that she dislikes sharing them. Indeed, she doesn't even seem particularly rattled by social conflict, as she is comfortable being politically contrarian under the cloak of anonymity. It is not criticism of her *views* that concerns her. Instead, Missy's account suggests that she is afraid that people will think differently of her *as a person* because of her political views.

Conservatives do have higher levels of racial resentment, as we will show in the chapters that follow, and perhaps some of these respondents have racist beliefs. But whether Missy or any of the respondents are racist is less significant to understanding their fan experience than the way the *fear of being perceived as racist* looms over the conservative respondents in the sample. They feel afraid to speak. We suspect that this heightened social risk increases the appeal of the safe political environs provided by outrage programs and may partially explain the large audience for outrage-based political talk media. Many will argue that conservative views are far from marginalized, but again, this is not what is salient here; fans' feelings of marginalization are shaping their choices.

COMPLICATING POLITICAL TALK

These findings raise a host of questions. Some key works on political media and public opinion stress the pivotal role of the media (through mechanisms such as transmission of elite discourses, and news selection and framing processes) in determining what the audience will find important and how they will understand the information that they encounter.[48] Yet other research suggests that the way people interpret political information and events is heavily shaped by their personal experiences, social contexts, and conversations with others.[49] Walsh, for example, shows that members of cohesive groups use identity-based perspectives to transform the frames they encounter in the news, and even circumvent them, substituting their own interpretations for the frames proffered by the media through their discursive practices.[50]

These programs complicate the implicit dichotomy between news and conversation. Outrage offers an experience that is not-quite-news (yet news-like), and not-quite-conversation (yet conversation-like), presenting a hybrid: news analysis that feels to sympathetic audience members remarkably similar to Moose Lodge chat. We want to take seriously the possibility that for fans, this brand of programming provides a new type of political "discussion." Some may argue that this cannot be discussion because the fans are not participating; we disagree. We see participation, interaction, and connection emerging in behaviors that we think must be understood as discursive practices. Some practices, such as tweeting or participating in meet-up groups, are interactive in the traditional sense. Others, such as becoming a premium member of a website or feeling "understood" or "validated" by a host, are more challenging to our sense of what qualifies as interaction, yet these fans feel involved in the shows, feel connected to the host and/or to an imagined community of fans, rendering the relationships real in their consequences. These are not traditional conversations, but that is precisely our point. To understand the role of political talk in democratic processes, we need to find the conversations, and finding them may require recognizing new types of talk, as scholars have identified our aversion to the political conversations with which we are most familiar.

Whether the relationship between hosts and fans can be reasonably conceptualized as conversant is a question open for analysis, but what we can say with certainty is that this growing genre of political media defies several familiar concepts examined by social scientists attending to political culture—news, civility, discourse—and begs us to add nuance to our ongoing discussions in these areas. For example, this information/conversation hybrid requires reevaluation of the implicit conceptualization of group talk as a variable that interacts with individual interpretation to make sense of news content. In other words, do fans interact with the shows as they do with conventional *news*: drawing on the host's frame, but also bringing their personal experiences and outside political conversations to bear, ready to reshape, or reject the interpretation offered? Or, might we expect that fans relate to the host's ideas and interpretations as those of a *friend*, united with the viewer/listener in their shared interpretation of conventional news which remains the point of reference, even though it is filtered through the program? Perhaps it is both or neither, depending on the fan and the use context. This is an empirical question in need of examination.

What we are reporting here is inductive research, and as such, rather than test hypotheses, we offer them. Rather than going to Bill O'Reilly or Ed Schultz for information that confirms preexisting beliefs or that minimized cognitive dissonance, our data suggest to us that outrage offers fans a satisfying social and political experience. It provides flattering, reassuring environments that make audience members feel good. Fans experience them as safe havens from the tense exchanges they associate with cross-cutting political talk they may encounter with neighbors, colleagues, and community members. We also believe that audience sizes for conservative shows are more robust than liberal audiences in part because the perceived social risk posed by cross-cutting political talk is higher for conservatives whose views may be read as intolerant at a moment when intolerance is stigmatized in most social circles.

If our hypotheses are correct, outrage-based programs have important social implications. Cross-cutting political conversations have been shown to have benefits such as increased tolerance and better understanding of others' points of view.[51] If outrage programs offer an escape from these conversations, we might expect to see a decrease in intersubjectivity and tolerance. At the same time, Mutz also found a correlation between social network homogeneity and political participation. Increases in political participation are traditionally thought to be beneficial, yet increased involvement of an intolerant and ill-informed citizenry may not serve us well.

Indeed, we must also ask if host-fan and fan-fan relationships press participants further toward political extremes as suggested by Cass Sunstein in his compelling discussion of group polarization. While the political talk we examine may seem implausibly far from the deliberative activity that interests Sunstein, we see powerful linkages; hosts actively produce contexts that he argues increase polarization, such as a sense of intragroup similarity, a "common fate," a sense of solidarity, and the introduction of rival outgroups. This polarization effect might be heightened for conservative fans who express greater fear of cross-cutting political conversations. Of "enclave deliberation," Sunstein writes, "Excluded by choice or coercion from discussion with others, such groups may become polarized in quite extreme directions."[52] In considering this possibility, we presume not that the audience is passive and vulnerable, but question what will emerge from the involvement fans seek in these new real and imagined "conversations."

NOTES

1. *Savage Nation*, August 20, 2009.
2. See, for example, Seth K. Goldman and Diana Mutz, "The Friendly Media Phenomenon: A Cross-National Analysis or Cross-National Exposure," *Political Communication* 28 (January 2011): 42–68; Shanto Iyengar and Kyu S. Hahn, "Red Media, Blue Media: Evidence of Ideological Selectivity in Media Use," *Journal of Communication* 59 (March 2009): 19–39; Silvia Knobloch-Westerwick and Jingbo Meng, "Reinforcement of the Political Self through Selective Exposure to Political Messages," *Journal of Communication* 61 (April 2011): 349–368; Natalie Jomini Stroud, "Media Use and Political Predispositions: Revisiting the Concept of Selective Exposure," *Political Behavior* 30 (September 2008): 341–366; Natalie Jomini Stroud, *Niche News: The Politics of News Choice* (New York: Oxford University Press, 2011). Selective exposure had fallen out of favor in political communications, based largely on a history of inconsistent findings and distaste for the term "exposure," but these recent studies show consistently and convincingly that partisan selective exposure is prevalent. See Diana C. Mutz and Paul S. Martin, "Facilitating Political Communication across Lines of Political Difference: The Role of Mass Media," *American Political Science Review* 95 (March 2001): 97–114. Importantly, though, there is also evidence to suggest that even people who prefer opinion-reinforcing information may seek out this information without systematically avoiding opinion-challenging information. In other words, the propensity to seek out supportive information appears stronger than the desire to avoid contradictory evidence. Jamieson, Kathleen Hall and Joseph Cappella, *Echo Chamber* (New York: Oxford University Press, 2009) suggest encounters with challenging information may not be particularly significant, as their research finds that immersion in supportive contexts serves to bolster resistance to challenging ideas.

3. Leon Festinger, *A Theory of Cognitive Dissonance* (Stanford, CA: Stanford University Press, 1957).

4. See Ziva Kunda, "The Case for Motivated Reasoning," *Psychological Bulletin* 108 (November 1990): 480–498 and two pieces by Milton Lodge and Charles S. Taber: "Three Steps toward a Theory of Motivated Political Reasoning," in Arthur Lupia, Mathew D. McCubbins, and Samuel L. Popkin, eds., *Elements of Reason: Understanding and Expanding the Limits of Political Rationality* (London: Cambridge University Press, 2000), 183–212. And Charles S. Taber and Milton Lodge, "Motivated Skepticism in Evaluating Political Information," *American Political Science Review* 50 (July 2006): 755–769.

5. Peter Fischer, Stefan Schulz-Hardt, and Dieter Frey, "Selective Exposure to Information: The Impact of Information Limits," *European Journal of Social Psychology* 35 (July/August 2005): 465–492; Peter Fischer, Eva Jonas, Dieter Frey, and Stefan Schulz-Hardt, "Selective Exposure and Information Quantity: How Different Information Quantities Moderate Decision Makers' Preference for Consistent and Inconsistent Information," *Journal of Personality and Social Psychology* 94 (February 2008): 231–244.

6. Kathleen Jamieson Hall and Joseph Cappella, *Echo Chamber* (New York: Oxford University Press, 2009), 75.

7. See Table 4.1.

8. See the Appendix for additional information on methods.

9. All but two respondents (one Latino man and one black woman) were white, and two of the respondents, both women, were in their twenties.

10. We wish to thank former students Amy Connors, Sara DeForest, Matt McGrath, Brittany Robbins, and Charlotte Steinway whose pilot interviews were an important part of the foundation for the research discussed in this chapter.

11. Though there is a difference in opinion about what form this discussion should take. See Michael Schudson, "Why Conversation Is not the Soul of Democracy," *Critical Studies in Mass Communication* 14 (December 1997): 297–309, for an account that makes a distinction between casual conversation about politics and structured, goal-driven political talk and portrays everyday political exchanges as less central to democratic processes than most.

12. Andrew F. Hayes, Dietram A. Scheufele, and Michael Huge, "Nonparticipation as Self-Censorship: Publicly-Observable Political Activity in a Polarized Opinion Climate," *Political Behavior* 28 (September 2006): 259–283.

13. Pamela Johnston Conover, Donald D. Searing, and Ivor Crewe, "The Deliberative Potential of Political Discussion," *British Journal of Political Science* 32 (January 2002): 21–62.

14. Robert O. Wyatt, Elihu Katz, Hanna Levinsohn, and Majid Al-Haj, "The Dimensions of Inhibition: Perceptions of Obstacles to Free Speech in Three Cultures," *International Journal of Public Opinion Research* 8 (Fall 1996): 229–247.

15. Elisabeth Noelle-Neumann, *The Spiral of Silence: Public Opinion—Our Social Skin* (Chicago: University of Chicago Press, 1984).

16. Diana C. Mutz, *Hearing the Other Side* (New York: Cambridge University Press, 2006), 141.

17. See Paul Allen Beck, "Voters' Intermediation Environments in the 1988 Presidential Contest," *Public Opinion Quarterly* 55 (Fall 1991): 371–394; Bernard Berelson, Paul Lazarsfeld, and William N. McPhee, *Voting: A Study of Opinion Formation in a Presidential Campaign* (Chicago: University of Chicago Press, 1954); Nina Eliasoph, *Avoiding Politics: How Americans Produce Apathy in Everyday Life* (New York:

Cambridge University Press, 1998); Robert Huckfeldt and John Sprague, "Networks in Context: The Social Flow of Political Information," *American Political Science Review* 81 (December 1987): 1197–1216; Robert Huckfeldt and John Sprague, *Citizens, Politics, and Social Communication: Information and Influence in an Election Campaign* (New York: Cambridge University Press, 1995); Paul Lazarsfeld, Bernard Berelson, and Hazel Gaudet, *The People's Choice: How the Voter Makes Up His Mind in a Presidential Campaign* (New York: Columbia University Press, 1944); Peter V. Marsden, "Core Discussion Networks of Americans," *American Sociological Review* 52 (February 1987): 122–131; Mutz, *Hearing the Other Side*; Diana C. Mutz and Paul S. Martin, "Facilitating Political Communication across Lines of Political Difference: The Role of Mass Media," *American Political Science Review* 95 (March 2001): 97–114; Robert O. Wyatt, Elihu Katz, and Joohan Kim, "Bridging the Spheres: Political and Personal Conversation in Public and Private Spaces," *Journal of Communication* 50 (March 2000): 71–92.

18. Mutz and Martin, "Facilitating Political Communication across Lines of Political Difference."

19. Seth K. Goldman and Diana C. Mutz, "The Friendly Media Phenomenon: A Cross-National Analysis of Cross-Cutting Exposure," *Political Communication* 28 (February 2011): 42–66; Natalie Jomini Stroud, *Niche News: The Politics of News Choice* (New York: Oxford University Press, 2011).

20. Donald Horton and R. Richard Wohl, "Mass Communication and Para-Social Interaction: Observations on Intimacy at a Distance," *Psychiatry* 19 (1956): 215–229.

21. Joshua Meyrowitz, *No Sense of Place: The Impact of Electronic Media on Social Behavior* (New York: Oxford University Press, 1985).

22. *Mark Levin Show*, June 14, 2011; *Rachel Maddow Show*, June 9, 2011.

23. http://www.rushlimbaugh.com/home/Rush247.guest.html, as of April 25, 2011.

24. http://wegoted.com/lodge/, as of June 10, 2013.

25. Insider/outsider caricatures are found in all the shows we studied but are less central to the work of hosts such as Sean Hannity and Rachel Maddow than they are to Ed Schultz and Michael Savage, who dwell more intensely and venomously on the vilification of outsiders.

26. http://www.billoreilly.com/membership, as of April 25, 2011.

27. As of January 15, 2013.

28. *Sean Hannity Show*, June 23, 2010.

29. *Countdown with Keith Olbermann*, June 23, 2010.

30. *Mark Levin Show*, June 11, 2010.

31. Liberal hosts' critiques of mainstream news focus on their lack of in-depth reporting or coverage of issues they find important, which is constructed as an implicit bias.

32. Robert P. Vallone, Lee Ross, and Mark R. Lepper, "The Hostile Media Phenomenon: Biased Perception and Perceptions of Media Bias in Coverage of the Beirut Massacre," *Journal of Personality and Social Psychology* 49 (September 1985): 577–585.

33. Pew Center for People & the Press, Campaign News Survey, http://www.people-press.org/2012/02/07/section-3-perceptions-of-bias-news-knowledge/, as of June 14, 2013.

34. It is not only conventional news that comes under fire. Liberal and conservative hosts regularly ridicule the information offered by the other side and in rare instances even suggest their peers are suspect. Michael Savage went on one such

tirade: "Yet, although Andrew [Breitbart] defended himself from attacks by the mainstream media, and he took direct questions from callers on the *Savage Nation*, not a single media outlet mentioned this interview, not a website, no radio show, no cable news program. Nobody...the Limbaughs, the Hannitys, the O'Reillys. Every last member of the self-proclaimed conservative media has placed themselves in the same camp as the Obama Administration, by refusing to mention this important interview. It has become worse in America than the ex-Soviet Union...here in America, the government-media complex has a tighter seal on information than Stalin's regime" *Savage Nation*, July 27, 2011.

35. *Glenn Beck Program,* June 9, 2010.
36. *Rachel Maddow Show,* June 16, 2010.
37. *Mark Levin Show,* June 22, 2011.
38. *Rush Limbaugh Show,* July 29, 2011.
39. *Sean Hannity Show,* June 23, 2011.
40. There are certainly other contributing factors ranging from supply side influences such as attempts to capitalize on the success of key conservative talkers to other demand side influences such as lower levels of mainstream news media dissatisfaction on the left.
41. Ron Becker, *Gay TV and Straight America* (New Brunswick, NJ: Rutgers University Press, 2006).
42. This stigma is in no way universal; many places exist where racist, xenophobic, sexist, and homophobic speech can be worn as a badge of honor, but there are far more settings where overt intolerance is met with formal and/or informal (negative) social sanctions than existed in the 1980s.
43. This is not to say that people do not make offensive, intolerant remarks, but rather that such comments are usually uttered privately among friends or in carefully vetted venues where those who congregate are of similar minds.
44. Mutz, *Hearing the Other Side*. Importantly though, Mutz explains that cross-cutting exposures may be a product of social environment (the degree to which your workplace is politically homogeneous, for example), rather than of choice.
45. We also suspect that conservatives exhibit a greater preference for like-minded partisan content that is not outrage-based, but we have not explored that here.
46. Eduardo Bonilla-Silva, *Racism without Racists: Color-Blind Racism and Racial Inequality in Contemporary America* (Lanham, MD: Rowman & Littlefield, 2010).
47. Evan P. Apfelbaum, Kristin Pauker, Nalini Ambady, Samuel R. Sommers, and Michael I. Norton, "Learning (Not) to Talk about Race: When Older Children Underperform in Social Categorization," *Developmental Psychology* 44 (September 2008): 1513–1518; Evan P. Apfelbaum, Samuel R. Sommers, and Michael I. Norton, "Seeing Race and Seeming Racist? Evaluating Strategic Colorblindness in Social Interaction," *Journal of Personality and Social Psychology* 95 (October 2008): 918–932; Michael I. Norton, Samuel R. Sommers, Evan P. Apfelbaum, Natassia Pura, and Dan Ariely, "Color Blindness and Interracial Interaction: Playing the Political Correctness Game," *Psychological Science* 17 (November 2006): 949–953; Sophie Trawalter and Jennifer A. Richeson, "Let's Talk about Race, Baby! When Whites' and Blacks' Interracial Contact Experiences Diverge," *Journal of Experimental Psychology* 44 (July 2008): 1214–1217.
48. See John R. Zaller, *The Nature and Origins of Mass Opinion* (Cambridge, UK: Cambridge University Press, 1992), although Zaller's "Monica Lewinsky's Contribution to Political Science," *PS: Political Science and Politics* 31 (June 1998): 182–189 argues that Clinton's high approval ratings in the face of intense media

criticism during the Lewinsky scandal is evidence that his 1992 book overstated the role of elite influence on public opinion. Also see Shanto Iyengar and Donald R. Kinder, *News That Matters: Television and American Opinion* (Chicago: University of Chicago Press, 1987).

49. William A. Gamson, *Talking Politics* (New York: Cambridge University Press, 1992); Doris A. Graber, *Processing the News: How People Tame the Information Tide* (London: Longman Group, 1988); Marion Just, Ann Crigler, Dean Alger, Timothy Cook, Montague Kern, and Darrell West, *Crosstalk: Citizens, Candidates, and the Media in a Presidential Campaign* (Chicago: University of Chicago Press, 1996); Andrew J. Perrin, *Citizen Speak: The Democratic Imagination in American Life* (Chicago: University of Chicago Press, 2006); Katherine Cramer Walsh, *Talking about Politics: Informal Groups and Social Identity in American Life* (Chicago: University of Chicago Press, 2004).

50. Walsh, *Talking about Politics*.

51. Mutz, *Hearing the Other Side*.

52. Cass R. Sunstein, "The Law of Group Polarization," *Journal of Political Philosophy* 10 (June 2002): 175–195, p. 184.

CHAPTER 6

Mobilizing Outrage

W hen we asked a Tea Party leader from Idaho how he came to be involved in the Tea Party he replied, "Michael Savage." He added, "He just gets my blood boiling. He's the reason I investigated the Tea Party." We heard many similar stories from Tea Party leaders we interviewed, including several who cited the Tax Day demonstrations in 2009 so heavily promoted by Fox Cable. Yet the relationship between the outrage media and the Tea Party is more complex than this simple cause-and-effect.

Here we examine this broader relationship in an effort to shed light on what linkages, if any, are developing between outrage media, advocacy groups, and political parties. Does what's seen in the living room or heard on the car radio carry over into electoral politics? In detail we show how the Outrage Industry has provided a communications network for the Tea Party insurgency. We also document the ways in which content from outrage sources has served as an information base for Tea Party advocacy. Looking closely inside local chapters, we analyze how outrage media have influenced the course of action by this national movement, showing that the Outrage Industry was instrumental in aiding the Tea Party in its success in the 2010 Republican congressional primaries. Overall, we build a case in this chapter, as well as in the one that follows, that a complicated synergy has emerged among conservative media outlets, the Tea Party and other conservative advocacy organizations, and the Republican Party.

This chapter draws largely on two databases. First is a set of twenty-eight in-depth interviews with Tea Party leaders from around the country conducted between 2010 and 2012. They offer a broad sense of how the party is organized and operates. Second, we assembled a 2010 Congressional

Primary Database based upon monitoring political coverage of contested primary races for both House and Senate. A unique feature of this data set is that it incorporates a sample of both conventional and blog coverage of each race.

STEEPING

Although the Tea Party has been in existence for only a few years, there is already dramatic folklore that tells the tale of its birth. As this quickly established legend has it, the fuse was lit at 7:11 (Chicago time) on February 19, 2009, when CNBC reporter Rick Santelli exploded into a rant about the Obama administration's efforts to rescue homeowners behind on their mortgages. Santelli reports on fixed income investments from the floor of the Chicago Mercantile Exchange and can get excited about the movement of five basis points in German bonds. But on this day Santelli became apoplectic, shouting to the traders working behind him "How many of you people want to pay for your neighbor's mortgage that has an extra bathroom and can't pay their bills? Raise their hand!" He added, "We're thinking of having a Chicago Tea Party in July."[1]

Mad as Hell

Santelli's rant may seem a rather suspect beginning of such a powerful movement. CNBC is a specialty cable channel focused on the stock market and its average audience during the day is a mere 200,000 viewers.[2] Although the finance professionals and day traders that make up the channel's audience may skew conservatively in their politics, they are hardly fertile soil for transformation into activists who want to take to the street. Yet the Santelli rant had a second life on YouTube where a million viewers watched it and, more significantly, it was picked up by Fox personalities Sean Hannity and Glenn Beck who, in turn, began to promote organizing to oppose Obama administration initiatives.[3] This amplification gave the Santelli rant far more than its fifteen minutes of fame.

Santelli may have bequeathed to the movement its name but just as there would have been a civil rights movement without Rosa Parks, there would have been an anti-Obama movement without Rick Santelli. (And Rick Santelli is no Rosa Parks.) Strong opposition was inevitable because in a democracy the primary goal of the opposition party is not to support the president in solving the nation's ills but to attack his vulnerabilities so that it can win the next election. The sharp attack on the Obama administration began just a month into his term in office. But if spirited opposition is a constant, the form it takes varies with context as the political culture evolves over time.

The opposition to the previous Democratic president, Bill Clinton, offers a striking contrast to Tea Party mobilization against President Obama. The centerpiece of the Republican counteroffensive then was the attack on the Clinton health care plan and the proposed expansion of bureaucracy to regulate the new system. Congressional Republicans were at the center of this challenge. A second front in the effort to diminish Clinton came from attacks on his character, and early in his presidency a concerted campaign emerged to try to convince Americans that he and his wife had exerted undue influence in aiding the principal investors in a land development deal known as Whitewater. This line of attack came from a small group of conservative activists funded by wealthy Republican patrons. The ongoing campaign against President Clinton's character led Hillary Clinton to insist that accusations against Clinton were part of a "vast right-wing conspiracy."[4]

In contrast, the main thrust of the conservative offensive against Obama came not from Washington, congressional Republicans, or secret funders. Rather, the charge rose from the grassroots. Instrumental to this effort was conservative outrage hosts on Fox and talk radio, and several conservative blogs, all championing the activists, giving them visibility, and cheering the righteousness of their actions against an administration they regarded as dangerous. Indeed, they held out the activism itself as evidence of Obama's failure. During the Clinton period, Fox was in its infancy and not yet a political force, talk radio was smaller in scope and more ideologically diverse, and blogs hadn't yet emerged.[5] Throughout this time conservatives were still dependent on the *Washington Post*, the *New York Times*, the broadcast television networks, and the rest of a mainstream press they distrusted to disseminate their message. In 2009, however, conservatives were navigating a new media landscape.

Journalistic accounts of the Tea Party point toward a movement built around amateurs who, like the iconic Howard Beale in the movie *Network*, were "mad as hell and [weren't] going to take this anymore." The *Wall Street Journal* profiled Stacy Mott, a stay-at-home mom whose Howard Beale moment came when George W. Bush defended the bank bailout just before he left office. She began blogging and started Smart Girl Politics, a website designed to provide conservative women with a social networking capacity.[6] Jennifer Stefano, frustrated with the local Bucks County (Pennsylvania) Republican establishment that didn't seem to want her help, moved to organize local Tea Party activists. Awaiting the birth of a child, Stefano used this time to become a political organizer, pushing Tea Party sympathizers into running for state party committee positions. They were attempting a takeover of the Republican Party from the bottom up.[7] Some of the Tea Party members we interviewed indicated that these efforts were their first step into politics. A California leader told us, "I'm not an activist [but] last year, when the Tea Party gained some support, I got together with some friends and formed the [local] Patriots. Now our group has 2,000 people."

Like the Rick Santelli narrative, the early journalistic history of the Tea Party is a little overly romantic, with martyrs rising up to save the country. Research suggests that the movement did involve a Herculean effort on the part of amateurs, but that the party is actually a mix of experienced and inexperienced activists. A 2009 study of the Massachusetts Tea Party showed that the organizing there included many who had been previously active in national politics. A national survey revealed that 43 percent of Tea Party identifiers had previously worked for or contributed money to a candidate.[8] And the Tea Party Express, one of the leading organizations, was founded by Republican consultants.[9] In his study of rank-and-file Tea Party participation, Alan Abramowitz notes that over more than three decades Republican identifiers have become increasingly conservative and the most conservative of those have become increasingly active in politics. Thus, the Tea Party markets opportunities to participate to a cohort that has become more interested in being involved.[10]

The journalistic version of the Tea Party's history also glosses over the link between outrage media and the movement's origins. In particular, our interviews revealed that a number of chapters grew out of Glenn Beck's 9/12 Project. The 9/12 philosophy reflects Beck's larger conspiratorial view of an American society manipulated by a liberal establishment. Beck's effort ran parallel to the emergence of the Tea Party and he was trying to accomplish the same goal of creating a national grassroots movement based around local organizing. One California leader told us that "I started my [Tea Party chapter] as a 9/12 group affiliated with Glenn Beck." A Minnesota leader said that Beck's influence on his chapter was profound because "a lot of our members [were] in D.C. with him at the 9/12 [rally]."Another leader complained that her vision of what her Tea Party chapter should stand for had been compromised by members who were also part of the 9/12 Project. She wanted to stick to fiscal issues but her 9/12'ers forced the chapter to expand its agenda to include some of Beck's moral issues.

The importance of the early cheerleading by conservative figures in the Outrage Industry cannot be underestimated. In the early part of 2009, before the congressional town hall meetings galvanized national attention, outrage hosts validated the movement with their coverage and lavish praise. The leader of a northern California chapter recalled her group's birth: "By and large, in February of 2009, you heard nothing about the Tea Party [from the mainstream media]. Had it not been for Fox, conservative talk radio, or the blogosphere, people would have had a hard time learning about the Tea Party movement. That's how I got so many of my initial members." As she reflected on the current state of her organization in June of 2012 she said that the same conservative media were still responsible for generating new memberships. After hearing about the organization from outrage hosts and bloggers, the curious "go online, find out about us, and email us."

Tea Drinking White Elephants

Who got involved? A group of people bearing much in common with outrage audiences. Gallup found that 83 percent of Tea Party supporters were Republican or Republican leaners while just 4 percent were pure Independents.[11] Polling by CNN shows that only 5 percent of Tea Partiers voted for a Democratic congressional candidate in the previous election.[12] In short, Tea Party supporters are Republicans and not some newly engaged movement of Independents. In terms of demographics, Tea Party supporters are not terribly distinctive from Republican identifiers. Most conspicuously, perhaps, is that Tea Party identifiers are almost exclusively non-Hispanic whites. A poll by CNN found that a minuscule 2 percent of Tea Party identifiers are African American and just 10 percent are Hispanic.[13] A *New York Times* poll puts the Hispanic percentage lower, at only 3 percent.[14] The larger Republican Party does better with Hispanics, though only a tiny bit better with blacks. The Tea Party is disproportionately male (60 percent or so) while the GOP is closer to even along gender lines. Comparisons to the population at large reveal significant differences: Tea Party supporters are more educated and more affluent than Americans in general and they are more likely to be religious. These differences with the American population are also reflected among Republican identifiers. Tea Party volunteerism is aided by a large cohort within the movement that is not working. The study of Massachusetts Tea Partiers found that a third were either students, unemployed, or retired.[15]

Although some of the rhetoric in the early days of the Tea Party movement suggested a strong libertarian focus among followers, the broadest concerns have related to the economy.[16] The issues emphasized at early rallies and in the disruptions of the congressional town halls were the federal deficit, the Obama health care reform, the stimulus package, the Troubled Asset Relief Program (TARP), and a claim that Washington was ignoring what the people really wanted. Less visible were the social issues like abortion and same-sex marriage, matters that animate the Christian Right and which are so central in Republican Party politics. Polling, however, indicates that Tea Party supporters and social value conservatives are largely one and the same. A Pew survey found that only 4 percent of those who identified with the conservative Christian movement said they disagreed with the Tea Party. Sixty-nine percent agreed with the Tea Party's goals. On abortion and same sex marriage, Tea Party supporters are about as likely to say that religion is the most important influence on their views as are all Republicans.[17]

Attitudinally, the New York Times poll also called attention to Tea Partiers' anger: "while most Republicans say they are 'dissatisfied' with Washington, Tea Party supporters are more likely to classify themselves as 'angry.'"[18] Tea Party messaging suggests that Republicans abandoned their core beliefs for eight years during the Bush administration, only then to have someone they regard as a socialist (Barack Obama) elected president. What's more, they claim that they represent the views of the broad mainstream of the American public—fully 84 percent of Tea Partiers believe their views are in the majority.[19] They gravitate toward Fox News—close to two thirds of Tea Party adherents say that they get most of their news from the cable network.[20]

When we asked Tea Party leaders about Fox News they revealed something of a love-hate relationship with the network. On the one hand they were deeply appreciative of the coverage that Fox has given to the movement over its short life span. "They cover us, and they're the only ones who do cover us," said a chapter president from Illinois." A leader from Arkansas used Rush Limbaugh's language to express his frustration: "The drive-by media doesn't get us. But Fox and conservative radio hosts get us. They get us." We were told repeatedly that Fox had succeeded because it was a source of objective news. A southern leader said that he and other activists gravitated to Fox because they had "become frustrated with the 'lamestream' media.... They're shaping, not reporting the news." A New Mexico chapter head explained: "Fox is successful because Americans want stuff without spin and just want news." These respondents' voices and concerns sound so similar to the conservative fans of outrage media we met in the last chapter that it warrants mention that they are not the same respondents. We recruited fans and Tea Party leaders separately and the interviews were conducted by different members of our research team.

Some fans interviewed mentioned involvement with the Tea Party (they were not asked specifically about the party) and many Tea Party leaders described themselves as fans, an overlap that while unintentional is not coincidental.

Yet while they were regular viewers and listeners, more often than not, respondents expressed frustration with Fox and even with some of the most popular radio hosts. A Michigan chapter head said that Fox is "not a voice for freedom. I view guys like Rush and Hannity as mouthpieces for the establishment and they put forth only the ideas of the Republican Party." Fox's most popular host, Bill O'Reilly, was not mentioned at all by respondents. Among Fox hosts, only Glenn Beck (still on Fox during our early interviews) received positive marks. It's possible that Fox's unceremonious dumping of Beck may have contributed to the negative comments on the network we heard in our second round of interviews.

Respondents were more consistent in citing that which they found most valuable in outrage programming. To echo a theme in the previous chapter, those who listen, watch, and read believe they are being educated. Audiences learn what's in the news in a straightforward fashion. A North Carolina leader praised talk radio because it went behind the headlines to convey what really goes on. Limbaugh and other radio hosts were his chapter's "source of news." Again, Glenn Beck is at the head of this class. A California leader told us that "Glenn Beck has done more for this country than any other talk show host. He's visionary, proactive. Rush and Hannity, those guys are reactive. Glenn Beck sees things two years ahead and that gives us time.... I listen to Glenn Beck every morning."

Respondents felt they were smart enough to figure out that they had been misled for many years by mainstream newspapers and broadcast television. They were passionate in denouncing these media as tools of liberals. As we reviewed the hundreds of pages of interview transcripts from Tea Party leaders, no theme emerged more clearly than how conservative media hosts and bloggers have succeeded in creating a comfortable cocoon of "news" that affirms the values and direction of the movement.

A Whiter Shade of Pale

Initial impressions of Tea Party sentiments on race were surely influenced by media accounts of racist signs held by protesters at early rallies. Photos revealed signs with racist images of President Obama, such as those portraying him as Adolf Hitler, with excessively large lips, or with a bone through his nose. Some had slogans that made reference to his African heritage and raised the question of where he was born. "Somewhere in Kenya a Village is Missing its Idiot" and "Go back to Kenya" were among the signs at various rallies. The homemade, racially tinged signs were perfect photo opportunities for journalists. Over time Tea Party leaders began to walk through their rallies and ask those holding up offensive signs to put them down.[21]

With the polls showing that somewhere around nine of ten Tea Partiers are non-Hispanic whites, one would not expect that race and equality would have any significant place on the movement's agenda. But the matter is not simply one of omission. Rather, poll after poll shows evidence of resentment toward minority groups. The *New York Times* found that 52 percent of Tea Party supporters believe that too much has been made of problems facing blacks (almost twice the percentage of all adults).[22] A Ford Foundation–sponsored study by the nonpartisan Public Religion Research Institute revealed that 62 percent of white Tea Partiers believe that discrimination against whites has become as much a problem as discrimination against blacks and other minorities. Overall, 48 percent of all whites agree with the statement, so the views of the Tea Party are moderately higher on this dimension than the views of all whites.[23] In a revealing study using multivariate analysis to estimate the distinctive impact of identification with the Tea Party, University of Washington political scientist Christopher Parker found that after controlling for the impact of conservative ideology and party identification, those who regard themselves as Tea Party supporters are "25 percent *more* likely to be racially resentful."[24] This is perhaps most visible in the passionate stance taken against immigration by the Tea Party.[25] This bitterness is mirrored in the work of many conservative outrage hosts, creating a media space that is compatible with, and supportive of, racial resentment.

In our interviews with Tea Party activists we asked why the movement hadn't been more successful in attracting minorities. The most common answer we got was, in effect, denial. "We have lots of minorities, but we just consider them freedom-minded Americans," said one activist. Another answered similarly, "We've got some great African American leaders out there for the Tea Party." One activist blamed the lack of minorities on intimidation: "I'll tell you about an African American woman at one of our town hall events recently. She stood up and spoke so eloquently and in such a well informed manner that I approached her afterwards and asked her to work with us. She declined and told me that she was afraid to put her name out there, afraid of the reaction of her own family." Others acknowledged that they didn't do well with minorities but offered no convincing strategy to change that. "The Democrats do a great job in attracting them," explained one Midwest activist. Another interviewee said simply, "We haven't been able to get our message across."

LOOSELY STRUCTURED

The Tea Party is striking in its degree of decentralization as it operates without direction from any one national Tea Party organization.[26] National Tea Party organizations do exist; five organizations emerged out of the burst of local organizing that gave life to community-based Tea Parties across the country. Most local Tea Parties have come to identify with one of three Tea Party brands: Tea Party Nation, Tea Party Express, and Tea Party Patriots. We refer to these as brands because the formal structure of these federations is rather loose. Local groups are not chapters in the classic sense as the relationship with other local groups and coordinators at the national level is rather casual. Two other organizations, Freedom Works and the National Tea Party Federation, have tried to act as coordinating bodies for any and all local Tea Parties but have experienced limited success. The national organizations have provided some resources and coordination for events, but they have yet to build a national structure of like-minded chapters.[27] One local Tea Party Patriot leader we spoke with said simply, "there's no national network…there's no formal organization." In Iowa there are more than fifty groups around the state that call themselves a Tea Party but no statewide unifying structure.[28] The more than fifty Tea Parties in South Carolina have warred openly with each other.[29]

Although there are conference calls and online communication, the Tea Party movement is not much more centralized today than in the early months of organizing in 2009. On the surface this may seem to be a shortcoming, with the enormous base of activists failing to come together to push forward in a unified manner. It may be just the opposite though: a real strength of the Tea Party appears to be that it has so many local organizations, all of which are independent of any larger authority structure. Surely a major appeal of the Tea Parties to their followers is that they are volunteer organizations that are controlled by the activists of each chapter. These local structures offer many channels for participation.

What has emerged is a "wiki" structure composed of a headless but energetic set of ideologically compatible organizations.[30] The differences among the three grassroots confederations are not ideological in nature. They have clashed at times, but these local and state rivalries have to do with territoriality and ego rather than substantive ideological differences. In its own way, the wiki organizational structure has helped the party, accentuating its image as a genuine grassroots movement. One important consequence of its informal structure is that the Tea Party can't be persuaded to compromise on matters before Congress because there is no one who is empowered to negotiate on its behalf.

By avoiding formal organization within larger federated structures, local Tea Parties have minimized organizational maintenance costs. Little effort or time is spent on fundraising, as without an office, paid employees, or dues to pay to a national organization, the financial resources necessary to keep a local Tea Party afloat are modest. The leader from Idaho told us proudly, "We take an offering at every meeting and currently our budget is about $350. [That's what is] in our bank account." For voluntary organizations, fundraising can become a preoccupation. The flip side of this, of course, is that without a paid staff, these organizations are subject to the inconsistencies of key volunteers' lives.

Despite the grassroots nature of the movement and the lack of strong national leadership, the Tea Parties around the country have had little difficulty in staying "on message." As we show in Chapter 7, outrage media stick closely to current events, and emphatic stands on those issues emanate clearly from all these various sources. Talk radio in particular seems especially influential in shaping party priorities. One North Carolina leader explained that radio hosts like Glenn Beck "define what people [in the party] are thinking and feeling." Talk radio is the de facto communications link among Tea Party chapters and is one more way in which chapters keep organizational maintenance costs to a minimum. Individual chapters forgo media staff and depend on the forceful messaging that emanates from the key conservative media figures.

Our research suggests that a combination of digital tools, community organizing, and support of outrage-based media were critical to the success of the movement.[31] For example, web-based conference calls helped geographically dispersed activists "meet." During the early throes of intense Tea Party organizing, "The weekly conference calls grew so large, phones sometimes crashed."[32] One of the organizers we interviewed said she relied on "Smart Girl Politics, #tcot [Top Conservatives on Twitter], and ResistNet." A reporter for the *National Journal* recounted one conference call among 200 leaders prior to the 2010 election where a "coordinator gives an update on an iPhone app for Tea Partiers who will be going door to door this fall to talk to voters. (It will use Global Positioning System [GPS] technology to download walking lists and upload voter data in real time.)"[33]

Nevertheless, the tools that have received the most use tend to be less sophisticated than GPS apps for mobile phones. Email has been the workhorse as it is the easiest way for organizers to get the word out quickly.

As we'll discuss later in this chapter, blogs were critical communication networks during the 2010 congressional campaign. In contrast, social networking has played a limited role. Even though some Tea Party leaders use social networking, only 11 percent of all Tea Party supporters have used Twitter or Facebook.[34] In the last analysis, though, the Internet lowered the barriers to entry for those who wanted to organize and those who wanted to be involved in some way in the political process.[35]

The effectiveness of old-fashioned community organizing and personal interaction is also evident. What might seem most improbable is the role demonstrations played in the early days of the movement. Demonstrations have been a tool of liberals, the young, and organized labor. The older conservatives who are the core constituency of the Tea Parties hardly seem apt to use this tactic. And yet the early demonstrations drew supporters and played a critical role in building the Tea Party's credibility. Tax day demonstrations on April 15, 2009, were held in hundreds of cities and the Taxpayer March on Washington on September 12 of that year drew tens of thousands of protesters. These were not massive outpourings, but they gave journalists a concrete manifestation of movement politics and produced intriguing photos and video supplements for the stories that followed.

Demonstrations are demanding forms of participation, requiring time, physical stamina, and often less-than-luxurious bus travel. But demonstrations energize those who participate, particularly when they are large and morale is high, as was the case with these early efforts. The great value to participants is that demonstrations build social solidarity with "rewards arising out of the act of associating."[36] Meeting others who share your political views and engaging along with them in political action not only creates an opportunity to build social networks but also offers affective benefits as seeing that one's personal values and priorities are widely shared is validating and invigorating. The extensive press coverage of these early rallies was also a reward as it gave participants a sense of collective identity and efficacy.[37]

Because demonstrations require a considerable commitment of time and energy by participants, the number and size of a movement's protests generally diminish over time. Not surprisingly, therefore, over time the Tea Party protests in Washington have dwindled. A few weeks before the ultimate vote on the federal budget in March, 2011, which was broadly seen as the first real legislative test of the movement's prowess since the 2010 elections, a Tea Party rally at the Capitol in Washington attracted a group of fewer than 200 participants.[38] The issue attention cycle can shift sharply and that is always a threat to a protest movement.[39]

Protests are far from the only means of building the Tea Party. At the local level there are open meetings for those who are interested. More imaginatively, the local groups have utilized a range of activities designed to engage followers. One of our interviewees noted, "We've had constitutional classes, book study classes, [and] street protests." Another interviewee emphasized the regularity of their interactions: "We're having fun. We enjoy being together [and we have] events at least twice a week."

THE EXPLOSION

The disruptive behavior of Tea Party and other conservative activists at town hall meetings held by congressional Democrats during the summer of 2009 grabbed the nation's attention and conveyed a startling amount of anger and resentment toward President Obama. The rudeness at these open meetings was regarded as justifiable by most conservatives, believing that the stakes were so grave that shouting down members of Congress was acceptable behavior. As one Tea Party activist we spoke with put it, "This will be seen as the turning point in history. Just keep that in mind."

Legislators are used to tough questioning; it goes with the territory of serving in Congress. Democratic incumbents had already been questioned aggressively by the spring of 2009 as the outlines of President Obama's proposal on health care emerged in the media. As spring turned to summer, however, the town halls became unruly in a number of locations across the country. In his Long Island district, Tim Bishop found his June meeting different from the other 100 or so he had held over his career in Congress. The shouting and hostility of the crowd was such that police were called in to escort him safely to his car. Eighty-three-year-old Michigan Representative John Dingell was shouted down at a health care town hall meeting by demonstrators yelling "shame on you." A fight broke out at a town hall meeting hosted by Pennsylvania Senator Arlen Specter when a critic started to shout at Specter and another attendee, angered at the conservative protester, began to shove him. A local chapter of Glenn Beck's 9/12 Project overwhelmed a town hall in Moss, Mississippi, and incumbent Gene Taylor was escorted out of the meeting by "a protective phalanx of eight uniformed Jackson County Sheriffs." As this turbulent political summer wore on, Obama supporters started to show up in significant numbers at these meetings to try to counter the impression that the whole country was against the president's health care proposal. This strategy misfired as it simply made crowds more unruly when the two sides taunted each other. In Reston, Virginia, a town hall meeting hosted by Representative James Moran and Democratic National Party Chair Howard Dean took on the character of a sporting event. Thirty minutes before Dean and Moran arrived, "hundreds of people on one side of the gym began chanting: 'We can't afford it!' Hundreds more on opposite bleachers began their own chant: 'Yes, we can!' deploying Mr. Obama's campaign slogan. 'No, we can't! No, we can't!' people chanted back from the first side of the bleachers." When a local rabbi offered an opening prayer, he was booed.[40]

The town hall meetings were extraordinary political theater. It was a striking breach of civility for participants to speak out of turn, ignore requests to follow a line of speakers, and yell at incumbent members of Congress. No matter how much we disagree with those on the other side, Americans traditionally abide by common rules of courtesy at such events. These scenes were also compelling because many of those yelling were visibly enraged and some appeared out of control. The legislators on stage seemed helpless to stop the disruption since those shouting at them wanted to attract attention with their aggressive behavior. When Gallup asked Americans about the town halls and whether "making angry attacks," "booing members of Congress they disagreed with," and "shouting down" opponents were examples of "democracy in action" or an "abuse of democracy," only shouting down opponents was frowned upon by a solid majority (see Table 6.1).

Those who participated believed that the urgency of the nation's problems warranted such behavior. Yet participants' fury also seemed driven

Table 6.1 PUBLIC OPINION ON TEA PARTY TOWN HALL DISRUPTIONS

	Total Sample	Dems.	Ind.	GOP
Making angry attacks				
Democracy in Action	51%	39	55	64
Abuse of Democracy	41	53	37	32
Booing Congressmen				
Democracy in Action	44	33	47	54
Abuse of Democracy	47	56	42	43
Shouting down opponents				
Democracy in Action	33	25	38	38
Abuse of Democracy	59	69	54	58

Questions:
Generally speaking, do you consider each of the following actions at town hall meetings to be an example of democracy in action (or) an example of abuse of democracy?
Individuals making angry attacks against a healthcare bill and what it might do
Booing when members of Congress make statements that the opponents disagree with
Shouting down supporters when they speak in favor of a healthcare bill.
Source: Gallup Poll, "Town Hall Meetings Generate Interest, Some Sympathy," August 12, 2009.

by a sense of being marginalized, being ignored by those in Washington. A northern California Tea Party organizer said that whenever she attends a town hall meeting "the condescension [is] palpable and the stonewalling frustrating.... They lie to you, BS you." In another interview a Tennessee leader justified the shouting down at the meetings this way:

> When it comes to the federal government, citizens' access has gradually disintegrated to the point of standardized emails and robo calls. This disengagement from the Republicans and Democrats has created a tremendous gulf between local citizens and those in the ivory towers. That access is completely opposite to what I think of in a constitutional republic. The Tennessee constitution says that citizens should instruct their representatives. Think about that: instruct their representatives. And I've seen it at Democratic and Republican meetings, and the response was [due to] frustration at not being heard.... You go to a meeting and a representative speaks the whole time while citizens sit in stalls like animals and are forced to listen.

Unfortunately for the Obama administration, coverage of the town hall meeting disruptions were of enormous interest to the broad public. Gallup found that fully two thirds of respondents said that they were watching the news about the town halls either "very closely" or "somewhat closely" (see Figure 6.1). This level of attention compares favorably to the percentage of people following the health care debate itself.[41] It was relatively easy for citizens to follow the town halls as media coverage was ubiquitous. Skocpol and Williamson found an interesting pattern in TV coverage. Fox Cable

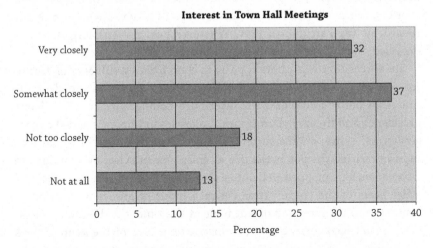

Figure 6.1
Source: Gallup Poll, "Town Hall Meetings Generate Interest, Some Sympathy," August 12, 2009.

News gave the Tea Party generous coverage throughout the spring and summer of 2009 while most weeks CNN generally ignored the movement. When the town hall meeting disruptions exploded during the August congressional recess, CNN provided extensive coverage.[42]

Newspaper reporting was extensive, too, and many websites linked dramatic video clips of the angry outbursts to their written stories. Democrats were truly flummoxed as no matter how often they noted that it was only a small number of people who were behaving in this way (most town hall meetings were conducted without disruption), it made little difference; the events came to represent strong opposition to the president's health care proposal. It is hard to know the precise effect of the town halls on public opinion on health care. Prior to the these meetings, opposition was rising sharply. In their wake, it climbed more.[43]

Liberal critics also tried to debunk the idea that the town hall protests represented authentic grassroots activism. The liberal blog *Talking Points Memo* noted sarcastically, the Tea Party protests are "just a spontaneous groundswell of populist opposition to health care reform. Right? Riiiight."[44] Freedom Works and business-oriented lobbies like Conservatives for Patient Rights were certainly active in disseminating advice and encouragement to local Tea Parties. The Tea Party Patriots carried a set of instructions on its website encouraging its followers to "Pack the hall. Yell out and challenge the Rep's statements early. Get him off his prepared script and agenda. Stand up and shout and sit right back down."[45] Yet it's hard to make the case that the disruptions followed a nationally coordinated plan of attack. The template for disruption was showcased by heavy coverage of the first protests. The town hall protests that followed needed little coordination or direction, just small groups of activists who were easily roused by Tea Party email lists. Whatever help national organizations provided, the initial protests were grassroots actions.

The success of the protests appears to stem from a confluence of events. An economy that had fallen off the precipice soured the mood of the American public and worked to legitimize boiling outrage. The Obama presidency and the large Democratic majorities in Congress added to conservatives' sense of alienation and disenfranchisement. The Outrage Industry stirred the pot as the tale of grassroots activists overcoming the Obama machine mapped well onto a David and Goliath storyline. Fox and other parts of the conservative Outrage Industry always need gripping content, and the most important issue at the time, the deepening recession, wasn't ideological enough to fit the templates of the genre. It was much too early to blame the Obama administration for the economy as the president inherited its weakened condition from his Republican predecessor.

But "Obamacare" was clearly his fault and the protests made for great TV. The outrage coverage helped to build fervor among conservatives, and in this case outrage rhetoric led to incensed mobilization. The mobilization did not merely result in protest but also in startling confrontation between members of Congress and apoplectic constituents who combined boorish manners with vitriolic language.

The success of the town hall protests left progressive activists scratching their heads; many left-leaning groups have summoned large numbers of people, staged remarkably creative events, and at times been disruptive with precious little attention from the mainstream news media. Sobieraj's research on the relationship between movements and the news media offers some insight into this selectivity. She demonstrates that journalists have an appetite for activist stories, but that they have a very clear idea about what makes activism newsworthy: authenticity.[46] Authenticity can be communicated to journalists in a variety of ways including emotionality, spontaneity, and originality, all of which the town hall meetings possessed in excess. The breaching of social norms around decorum fueled by frustration and rage, the seeming unpredictability of the scenes, and the novelty of a very unfamiliar breed of activist all worked to make these meetings perfect fodder for the twenty-four-hour news cycle.

Perhaps it was inevitable, but by the next Congress liberals used the same tactics at town hall meetings hosted by Republican legislators. After the Republican-controlled House of Representatives passed a budget resolution incorporating a proposed conversion of Medicare from a federal entitlement to a block grant to the states, seniors and liberals attacked. The Medicare proposal was broadly unpopular and Republican legislators were immediately put on the defensive during their spring recess in 2011. New York freshman Michael Grimm was repeatedly shouted down by angry constituents. "My town halls are being disrupted by Democrats," complained Pennsylvania Republican Lou Barletta. Liberal groups like MoveOn.org and Americans United for Change actively tried to mobilize liberals for the Republican town hall gatherings, though it's unclear how many of the disruptions they were responsible for. The attacks attracted widespread (if short-lived) media attention.[47] By the summer recess in August, most members of the House decided not to hold any open town halls during that period.[48]

SPEAK HARSHLY AND CARRY A BIG STICK

With the town hall meetings ended, the various Tea Parties faced an uncertain agenda as to what to do next. This decision was influenced by three significant factors. First, the local Tea Parties continued to resist scaling up into real national federations.[49] This worked against the development of a unified Tea Party lobby in Washington, as even a strong grassroots network requires a national infrastructure. Second, the success of the Tea Parties' disruptions suggested that drama is an effective strategy. Harsh rhetoric, in-your-face activism, and an uncompromising stance attracted attention to their concerns. Third, a strategy of having activists act out and scream at congressmen at events or to continue to come to marches and rallies was not sustainable. Only under the most critical conditions are activists going to engage in protests over the long term. Thus, with the cycle of town halls completed, the local groups needed appropriate opportunities where the resources at hand could be effectively applied. The upcoming 2010 congressional elections fit the Tea Parties' needs perfectly. Surprisingly, perhaps, the targets chosen weren't Democrat officeholders but Republican incumbents running in their party's primaries. With a few notable exceptions, it wasn't moderate Republicans that the Tea Party went after. Rather, the wrath of the Tea Party was visited upon conservative Republicans.

Primary Structure

The primaries worked to the Tea Parties' strengths for a variety of reasons. At its core, the early Tea Party was a rebellion against the status quo, which included the Republican establishment. As noted, many Tea Party activists had experience in Republican politics but were not empowered within the party at the time they joined the movement. The structure of the American electoral system effectively limits the number of parties, and the duopoly of the Republicans and Democrats has ruled since the Civil War era. But just as general elections are inhospitable to new parties, primaries are open to all who can meet their state ballot requirements. As a practical matter, what is required of viable candidates is money, volunteers, and name recognition. Local Tea Parties were a good fit for primary candidates who could not rely on the GOP establishment or its large donors. These groups offered a communications network, including their own email lists and websites. In addition, local and statewide political blogs spread the word among a small but highly motivated circle of conservative activists. Fundraising potential varied widely across local Tea Parties, but their mailing lists offered insurgent candidates at least the possibility of quickly building a donor base.

The Tea Party electoral uprising went against the long-term historical trend of a decline in the number of competitive party primaries. In some recent election years there have been fewer than twenty primaries in which the incumbent received less than 75 percent of the vote.[50] It seems likely that the increasing costs of campaigns coupled with the incumbents' greater ease in raising money has deterred many would-be challengers. We monitored their efforts by constructing the 2010 Congressional Primary Database, systematically examining every House and Senate race in which an incumbent was being challenged from within his or her own party, as well as all primaries in districts with open seats. Research also focused on amassing a representative sample of both conventional news coverage and blog postings about each of these races. (Additional information about the Congressional Primary Database can be found in the Appendix.)

This database shows that the number of competitive primaries for the House surged, with fifty-seven incumbents receiving less than 75 percent of the vote in their primary. This is higher than any congressional primary season since 1970 save one (1992).[51] Given the fury on the right it is somewhat surprising that there were only a few more Republican than Democratic cases where the incumbent was held to below 75 percent (see Table 6.2). We follow political scientist Robert Boatright's classification of primary challengers to examine how many were motivated by ideological or issue-based concerns.[52] Depending on their ideology, incumbents may be challenged from the left, right, or moderate center. Alternatively, challenges can also arise for reasons having nothing to do with ideology. Incumbents may have ethical problems, be viewed as too old, have had a close call in the last election, or have been redistricted in a way that significantly alters the composition of their district. Tea Party candidates in 2010 emphasized their overall political orientation and contrasted it to that of the incumbent. As Table 6.2 demonstrates, most House challengers, Republican and Democrat, were motivated by ideology.[53]

Table 6.2 2010 CONGRESSIONAL PRIMARY CHALLENGES
Primaries where the incumbent received less than 75 percent of the aggregate vote

Reason for Challenge	Ideology/Issues	Other	Unclear
House			
GOP Primaries	18	10	2 (n=30)
Democratic Primaries	14	10	3 (27)
Senate			
GOP Primaries	4	0	0 (4)
Democratic Primaries	2	1	0 (3)

Source: 2010 data from the Outrage Industry project, data assembled by Suzanne Schlossberg of Tufts University.

Democratic challenges typically came from the left of incumbents. In Massachusetts' 9th congressional district, incumbent Stephen Lynch had angered liberals in his district by voting against the president's health care proposal. Liberal Mac D'Alessandro, the political director for the labor union, SEIU, ran against Lynch but lost in a two-person race with 35 percent of the vote. In this sense, the ideological Democrat challenges were mirror images of those faced by the Republicans with the opposition coming from the left of the spectrum and not the center. Just two Democratic incumbents lost and only one, Pennsylvania senator Arlen Specter, arguably, lost for ideological reasons. Specter, a longtime Republican, who seemed sure to lose a Republican primary against announced candidate Pat Toomey, made a deathbed conversion to the Democratic Party before his state's primaries. Democratic challenger Joe Sestak ran to the left of Specter but the reason for Specter's change of political identity was so transparent that the party switch in and of itself may have cost him the election.

Despite the large number of challenges on the Democratic side, they did not emerge from a national-level movement against incumbents who had strayed from orthodoxy. There was nothing comparable to the Tea Party insurgency and no widespread dissatisfaction with the Obama administration. Even though there were almost as many challenges to Democratic incumbents as to Republicans, they largely flew under the radar of the national media, which focused more heavily on the Tea Party.

Given the enormous news coverage of the Tea Party challenge to Republican incumbents, it may seem as though there was a wholesale sweep in the GOP primaries, but only four Republican incumbents actually lost, two in each house. On the House side, Parker Griffith of Alabama (another party switcher) lost as did South Carolina's Bob Inglis. Incumbent senators Bob Bennett of Utah and Lisa Murkowski of Alaska lost as well, though Murkowski came back to win, running as an independent in the general election. The most shocking primary defeat on the Republican side came in Delaware where there was an open Senate seat. Mike Castle was not technically the incumbent but had been the sole Delaware representative in the House for eighteen years. In the GOP primary he lost to Tea Party upstart Christine O'Donnell by 6 percent.

Outrage as Signaling

With a mere four defeats despite the surge in challengers, 2010 seems to fit neatly into the sleepy historical pattern of party primary outcomes. As Stephen Ansolabehere and his colleagues noted in 2006, "If elections are like single-elimination tournaments, then almost all incumbents draw a bye in the first round. Given the utter lack of competition in primary elections it seems unlikely that incumbents are 'running scared' that they might lose the next primary."[54] Nevertheless, these electoral defeats shook the foundation of the Republican Party. The fates of Bennett, Murkowski, and Castle signaled a shifting electoral landscape. The three were widely viewed as responsible, hard-working, and attentive to their states. None were seen as in trouble until the Tea Party rebellion emerged. What was truly startling was that Bennett and Murkowski were conservatives beaten by candidates who ran at them from the right. Castle was widely seen as a moderate, though in a state where the GOP is thought to be moderate. Tea Party–backed nominees in Alaska (Joe Miller) and Delaware (O'Donnell) were by any standard, weak candidates. Miller, endorsed by Sarah Palin, self-destructed in the general election. At one point he refused to answer questions by journalists about his past (he had been disciplined in his work as a government attorney). O'Donnell became a national laughingstock for running a television commercial where she declared "I am not a witch." She had little in the way of a work record, had experienced serious financial problems (including defaulting on her mortgage), and showed an unusually weak command of the issues. In a debate with her Democratic opponent, O'Donnell said she doubted that the Constitution provided for separation of church and state. She then expressed surprise when her Democratic opponent said that the First Amendment is the source of that principle.

Every election has its share of weak candidates and it's not clear that 2010 had any more than the normal distribution. Miller and O'Donnell weren't perceived so much as oddballs as a reflection of the strength of the Tea Party undertow. What stood out about the Republican Party in 2010 was the breadth and ferocity of the Tea Party electoral involvement. Other Tea Party–identified candidates, including Marco Rubio in Florida, Sharron Angle in Nevada, Ken Buck in Colorado, and Rand Paul in Kentucky, defeated strong conventional Republican opponents in open Senate primaries. Many Republican gubernatorial candidates in open primaries who identified themselves as Tea Party supporters, such as Rick Scott in Florida, Nikki Haley in South Carolina, and Carl Paladino in New York, won their GOP nomination fights. It is difficult to count accurately how many Tea Party candidates ran in 2010 because the vast majority of challengers to incumbents presented themselves as affiliated with the movement (even if they had no formal support from one of the Tea Party organizations). If it was an open seat, then all candidates typically claimed to be the most conservative and most committed to Tea Party principles.

Instrumental in the distinctiveness of the 2010 primaries was the coverage by Outrage Industry media. For some of the challengers, large national outrage-based venues brought favorable coverage to their campaigns. Glenn Beck ridiculed South Carolina incumbent Bob Inglis for using a phrase Beck associates with African Americans (Inglis is white). While speaking on his radio show with one of Inglis's challengers, Beck said "Everybody from Washington's black. So Bob Inglis, I guess the latest addition to the African-American community, is speaking here and saying that we tea partygoers, we racists, I guess, need to stop listening to Glenn Beck."[55] During the primary season the popular blogger Michelle Malkin hammered away at those she regarded as Republican apostates, including Mike Castle and Mary Bono Mack from California. After their vote in support of cap-and-trade legislation, Malkin wrote "Congrats, congresspeople, you helped the Democrats pass a junk science-based, massive national energy tax. Headed to Disney World now?" She added, "We still want to know: What were your payoffs/earmarks?"[56]

For challengers whose campaigns didn't attract the attention of leading conservative media figures, state and local political blogs often stepped in. Our extensive monitoring of the blogging related to congressional races with primaries revealed some common patterns in the attacks on incumbents. Most conspicuously, the attacks focused on a select vote or two, as illustrated by the Michelle Malkin passage cited earlier. The blog *Seeing Red AZ* took Arizona incumbent Jeff Flake to task for working "on behalf of the costliest of measures ...granting tuition and other benefits, while extending amnesty for illegal aliens living in our country."[57] Another readily apparent pattern was a rejection of the pragmatism that argued that it was better to elect a not-absolutely-perfect Republican than to endanger the seat by nominating a more conservative challenger who might give the Democrats an opening to capture the seat. A blogger writing on *Big Government* told readers about his California district: "And for all of the practical political types who want to stick by a Republican like Gary Miller because it's one more seat to add to our majority so we can remove Nancy Pelosi, let me just point out one more thing: Republican Gary Miller voted with Nancy Pelosi and Barney Frank" [on Fannie Mae and Freddie Mac].[58] For those who worried that nominating Christine O'Donnell could give the seat to the Democrats, the Delaware blog *Politically Frank* said there was something much larger at stake: "If the GOP does not cleanse itself of these moderates, it will doom itself to history and will have no future."[59] In classic outrage style, it wasn't about Christine O'Donnell but the entire future of the Republican party.

Round Two: 2012

Clearly apprehensive about antagonizing the Tea Party and hewing to their conservative moorings, Republicans in both the House and Senate positioned themselves sharply to the right in the 112th Congress, each vote a testament to their stalwart commitment to conservatism. This left few incumbents vulnerable as the 2012 election approached. Only two challenges to Republican incumbents attracted much attention. Both Senator Richard Lugar of Indiana and Orrin Hatch of Utah drew viable challengers. Hatch faced Utah state senator Dan Liljenquist who was the Tea Party favorite. Freedom Works spent heavily to defeat Hatch who was seemingly vulnerable because of his reputation of bipartisan work with the late Senator Edward Kennedy. Hatch helped himself in the 112th Congress by accruing a 100 percent voting score from the American Conservative Union and ultimately prevailed, but Lugar fell to Tea Party candidate Richard Mourdock. Mourdock's promise not to go to Washington and compromise struck a chord with Indiana conservatives.

An open Senate seat in Texas gave the Tea Party another clear victory. There Republican Senate candidate Ted Cruz won a 2012 party runoff against Lieutenant Governor David Dewhurst in a race that developed into a now-familiar narrative of the Tea Party versus the establishment. Dewhurst entered the primary race with the whole state party hierarchy in his camp, including Governor Rick Perry, and outspent Cruz by a margin of three to one. There were no ideological differences between the two candidates—both are highly conservative. Dewhurst won 45 percent of the vote in a nine-person field in the May primary but was crushed by Cruz in the late July runoff. The only difference between the initial primary and the runoff was that Cruz became increasingly identified across the state as the Tea Party candidate.

An identity for Cruz as a virtuous conservative man of the people and of Dewhurst as a tool of the establishment was forged by outrage media. For example, the well-known conservative blogger and CNN commentator Erick Erickson, advocated on behalf of Cruz aggressively on his widely followed *RedState*. His passionate blog posts followed a common script in these fights, with David standing up to Goliath despite the seemingly insurmountable odds. Although Sarah Palin and South Carolina Senator Jim DeMint would eventually come to Texas to campaign for Cruz, they did so after the race had narrowed. Erickson had been on the case for months, deriding Dewhurst as a "squishy moderate."[60] He portrayed Cruz in heroic terms, claiming he would give the GOP some "testicular fortitude" in the Congress.[61] Local talk radio also favored Cruz. When he appeared on the

Janine Turner Show, she quickly informed the audience that she favored Cruz and then proceeded to lob softballs for him to swat out of the park. Cruz emphasized that America's problems were the result of "career politicians," a less than subtle reference to Dewhurst.[62]

Although some of the local Texas Tea Parties may have formally endorsed Cruz, it was public awareness of his Tea Party affiliation, not any particular endorsement, that was most crucial to his success. The localism of the Tea Party made it impossible for a true endorsement process to proceed statewide. Most of the Tea Party leaders we spoke with said their organizations did not endorse candidates. Nevertheless, the work of blogs like *RedState* and the local conservative radio stations got the word out that Cruz was the Tea Party's candidate. By the time the state's newspapers began to draw the runoff in terms of the Tea Party versus the establishment, Cruz was already anointed.

The 2012 general election was sobering for the Tea Party as its nemesis, Barack Obama, won a decisive victory in the presidential race. More surprising was that the Republicans lost two seats in the Senate, even though the vast majority of seats that were up were held by Democrats. The Tea Party came in for considerable blame in the case of Mourdock's loss in Indiana as well as Todd Akin's defeat in Missouri. In the context of debates about abortion, both Mourdock and Akin made profoundly insensitive and ill-informed remarks about rape, which came to define them. While the Senate results were a bitter pill, the Republicans and the large cohort of Tea Party incumbents did very well in the 2012 House races. Having swept the House in 2010 there was little realistic opportunity for Republicans to increase their majority in 2012. Democrats had hoped that many Tea Party types elected in districts that were not strictly conservative would fall in an electoral climate more hospitable to the Democratic Party. The GOP lost only eight seats, with most incumbent defeats a byproduct of redistricting. Only two incumbents with strong Tea Party identities, Allen West of Florida and Joe Walsh of Illinois, were defeated, again both hurt by redistricting.

Post-election, the *New York Times*, the *Washington Post*, and many others concluded that the Tea Party had been weakened by the losses.[63] The failure of the Tea Party to become involved in the fiscal cliff drama at the end of 2012 was held to be an example of its ebbing strength. But lobbying has never been a central focus of the parties' efforts. Their real influence comes from signaling who is a Tea Party favorite and, in the case of selected incumbents, who is a conservative apostate. As they face the 2014 congressional elections, we doubt that many Republican incumbents feel that they can safely ignore the Tea Party. Abramowitz has calculated that by 2012 many Republican primaries on the state and congressional level were composed of electorates with a majority of Tea Party supporters.[64] Looking over their shoulders at Tea Party voters, Republican members of Congress don't need to be actively lobbied by the organization. It's easy enough for them to acknowledge Tea Party preferences.

ELECTIONS IN AN OUTRAGEOUS ENVIRONMENT

The Outrage Industry represents more than a new twist on the ubiquity of attack politics in election campaigns.[65] What we observed in both 2010 and 2012 is that outrage media served as a communications link, the central nervous system for an insurgency within the Republican Party. Messaging was reinforced by a constant drumbeat across platforms and across national and local outrage outlets. Local Tea Parties could resist the entreaties of Freedom Works and other Washington-based interest groups to centralize because outrage media provided enough of a unifying force to nationalize the movement. The relationships between the Tea Party, conservative outrage outlets, and the Republican Party have proven mutually beneficial in many ways.

• The barriers to entry for insurgent campaigns are lower today. Internet tools can be used by any candidate or faction, but a strong movement like the Tea Party with its many volunteers is well positioned to take maximum advantage of the opportunities offered by the Internet. Mobilization of volunteers for campaigns and fundraising can be enabled by even a modest, low-cost web presence. However, the amount of money needed to actually win a campaign, particularly against an incumbent, remains high.

• Once a candidate is in office, outrage continues to be a path to career advancement. Research shows that members of Congress who are more extreme in their politics receive more coverage in the mainstream press.[66] For those impatient with their progress or blocked from advancement, becoming an outspoken leader of the ideological wing of their party is an alternative. Such a path likely lies with outrage media who help to raise the visibility of relatively obscure members, typically those who are low in seniority. Elected in the Republican landslide of 2010, the aforementioned Republican Allen West of Florida quickly became a darling of Fox and other conservative outrage outlets. The mainstream press soon followed suit and began covering him, albeit in smaller doses. His McCarthyish claim that as many as eighty Democratic members of the House of Representatives were communists drew noteworthy press coverage, both outrage and mainstream, that followed over the next two weeks.[67]

• Abundant political commentary and political coverage of local campaigns can now be found in outrage outlets. Media outlets are far from equal in terms of audience, but as we've demonstrated, the aggregate outrage audience is very large. Such coverage comes from local advocacy groups, independent bloggers, political websites, and local talk radio. Our canvassing of sources of news and commentary on congressional races turned up rather modest conventional journalistic coverage, whether in a newspaper or newspaper website or (infrequently) an independent and nonideological website.[68] In contrast, the appetite for campaign commentary in local outrage media appears to be substantial.

• Outrage outlets provide an important "signaling" function to party faithful. For those interested, how does one come to understand whether a challenger is a significantly better candidate than the incumbent? Or if there is an open seat, who of the five or six candidates running is the one who most deeply represents one's own political philosophy? Signaling can come from many sources—talking to friends, for example—but outrage outlets offer relevant information in a quick and easily accessible format. Even though these sites may not attract large numbers of readers, activists who are interested in commentary on local or statewide races monitor them. And activists in their local communities are opinion leaders who, in turn, also play a signaling role to the larger primary electorate.

• The development of outrage as a genre and the ascent of the Tea Party have taken place during a time of increasing partisanship in Congress and state legislatures, a trend we expand on in the chapter that follows. This long-term trend of party-line voting has placed more and more pressure on legislators to toe the line on key votes. The Outrage Industry affixes a microscope on them as they cast their votes, and deviation from the conservative line is rehashed and often ridiculed by local outrage outlets. In 2011 many Republican members of Congress voted for Budget Committee Chair Paul Ryan's budget with its controversial plan to transform Medicare into a voucher program, knowing full well that the Democrats would use the vote against them in the 2012 elections. For those with safe seats, it wasn't a difficult decision to vote "yea," but for those in more marginal districts, the decision may have come down to a choice between a primary fight and a general election fight. The outrage era of party politics is very much a toe-the-party-line era.

• Outrage outlets provide a virtual community for the politically active. In primary season, the blogs, websites, and email lists not only offer channels for politically charged views but also an opportunity for affirmation of those views. As we point out in Chapter 5, this is especially important for conservatives, many of whom believe that the mainstream media and mainstream culture is biased against them. There have always been those with passionate and polarizing views, but outrage media gives them an inexpensive distribution system, an electronic megaphone of sorts.

• The Outrage Industry worked to enhance the nationalization of congressional elections.[69] The midterm congressional elections have always been considered a rough referendum on the performance of the president and an indicator of the direction of American politics, but outrage outlets have added extensive coverage. Talk radio, with its enormous audience, focused heavily on the 2010 election, and the daily monitoring of program content by *Talkers Magazine* showed that it was often the most frequently discussed topic as the general election approached.[70] In 2012 the presidential race overshadowed the congressional elections, but there was still substantial coverage of competitive House and Senate races.

Still, issues of impact are hard to tease out. The Tea Party helped to swell enthusiasm among conservatives and brought volunteers into local campaigns. The various Tea Parties endorsed 282 Republican candidates for the House in the aggregate while 156 of those candidates were endorsed by only a single Tea Party organization.[71] Three separate statistical analyses of the 2010 election by political scientists revealed no independent electoral impact of these endorsements. Gary Jacobson concluded that for Tea Party–endorsed candidates "neither their vote share nor probability of victory differed significantly from that of other Republican challengers."[72] Although this careful research by political scientists suggests caution in interpreting the election as an affirmation of the Tea Party, the popular perception is that the Tea Party was instrumental in accentuating the nationalization of the election and delivering a devastating defeat to the Democrats.

PARTNERS

There is a reciprocal relationship as outrage media and the Tea Party are informal partners pursuing complementary goals. For conservative outrage media, the Tea Party has offered great content: People organizing at the grassroots ostensibly demonstrates that the dire warnings emanating from shows and posts are valid. Beyond such validation, though, is an energized and engaged constituency interested in, if not completely satisfied by, the content of outrage media. In a hypercompetitive media environment, they are an audience to be pursued. Over and over in our interviews we heard that Glenn Beck or Michael Savage or Michelle Malkin or some other media figure had said something that became a source of discussion at a meeting.

The Tea Party has gained enormously from its coverage in the conventional press but also from the heavy focus on it from outrage media. The outrage media has covered it on a more ongoing basis than the conventional media, which decreased its reporting after the 2010 election. For Tea Partiers outrage media have offered a powerful validation of their efforts. When the media figures they respect praise their efforts as having an effect on the country, it's heady confirmation that their hard work is paying off. As noted, outrage media also act as a communications hub to link the disparate Tea Parties around the country, a major reason that local Tea Parties have not had to scale up into a centralized, national organization.

This synergy extends to the Republican Party as well. Although it has targeted Republican incumbents in primaries, the Tea Party remains aligned with the Republican Party. The GOP has benefited from a built-in set of activists whose harsh language vilifies the Democrats and constantly discredits them. Through the outrage media and the Tea Party, the GOP's messaging is amplified and extended. Still, its relationship with the Tea Party is not without its costs. In the chapter that follows we extend an argument begun here: that the Tea Party is making it more difficult for the GOP to adapt to the changing demographics of the country. As such, it hurts the party as well as helps it.

NOTES

1. "CNBC Rick Santelli Goes Ballistic," http://www.youtube.com/watch?v=fQQfzX-Q6UjA&NR=1, as of May 31, 2011.
2. http://tvbythenumbers.zap2it.com/2011/03/17/cable-news-ratings-for-wednes-day-march-16-2011/86120, as of March 21, 2011.
3. Kate Zernike, *Boiling Mad* (New York: Times Books, 2010), 21–24; and Ben McGrath, "The Movement," *New Yorker*, February 1, 2010, 42–43.
4. See Jeffrey Toobin, *A Vast Conspiracy* (New York: Touchstone, 1999).
5. Andrew Kohut, *The Vocal Minority in American Politics* (Washington, DC: Times Mirror Center for People and the Press, 1993).
6. Douglas A. Blackmon, Jennifer Levitz, Alexandra Berzon, and Lauren Etter, "Birth of a Movement," *Wall Street Journal*, October 29, 2010.
7. Zernike, *Boiling Mad*, 99–119.
8. Vanessa Williamson, Theda Skocpol, and John Coggin, "The Tea Party and the Remaking of Republican Conservatism," *Perspectives on Politics* 9 (March 2011), 27–28.
9. Kate Zernike, "For Tea Party, Power Brings Policy Splits," *New York Times*, June 29, 2011.
10. Alan Abramowitz, "Grand Old Tea Party," in *Steep: The Precipitous Rise of the Tea Party*, ed. Lawrence Rosenthal and Christine Trost (Berkeley: University of California Press, 2012), 199.
11. Mark Blumenthal, "A Teacup 80% (or More) Full," Pollster.com, April 6, 2010, http://www.pollster.com/blogs/a_teacup_80_or_more_full.php?nr=1, as of April

10, 2012. See also David E. Campbell and Robert D. Putnam, "Crashing the Tea Party," *New York Times*, August 17, 2011. Importantly, though, party identification figures for Tea Party adherents varies based on the way a given survey is constructed. For example, some pollsters press those who initially say they are independents to indicate which of the two parties they are at least closest to. Other pollsters accept the Independent as an answer. With no follow-up on a party ID question, as many as half of those who say they are Tea Party supporters will say they are Independents rather than Republicans or Democrats. When pollsters probe, though, the results are dramatically different.

12. "CNN Opinion Research Poll," *CNN.com*. February 17, 2010, at http://i2.cdn. turner.com/cnn/2010/images/02/17/rel4b.pdf, as of May 19, 2011.

13. "CNN Opinion Research Poll."

14. *New York Times*/CBS News Poll: National Survey of Tea Party Supporters, April 5–12, at http://documents.nytimes.com/new-york-timescbs-news-poll-national-survey-of-tea-party-supporters?ref=politics, as of May 31, 2011.

15. Williamson et al., "The Tea Party and the Remaking of Republican Conservatism," 33; and Theda Skocpol and Vanessa Williamson, *The Tea Party and the Remaking of Republican Conservatism* (New York: Oxford University Press, 2012), 19–44. Among Tea Party supporters in the population at large and all adults, there are no differences in terms of employment status or percentage retired. See Lydia Saad, "Tea Partiers Are Fairly Mainstream in Their Demographics," Gallup Poll, April 5, 2010, http://www.gallup.com/poll/127181/tea-partiers-fairly-mainstream-demographics.aspx, as of April 10, 2012.

16. On the libertarian sentiments, see Ronald P. Formisano, *The Tea Party* (Baltimore: Johns Hopkins University Press, 2012): 87–96. In contrast Lisa Disch argues that the Tea Party was catalyzed by its followers' concerns about protecting their share of "the liberal welfare state," "The Tea Party," in *Steep: The Precipitous Rise of the Tea Party*, ed. Lawrence Rosenthal and Christine Trost (Berkeley: University of California Press, 2012), 33–151.

17. Scott Clement and John C. Green, "The Tea Party, Religion and Social Issues," Pew Research Center, February 23, 2011, http://pewresearch.org/pubs/1903/tea-party-movement-religion-social-issues-conservative-christian, as of April 10, 2012. For an analysis of the various strains of thinking that characterize Tea Party sympathizers, see Andrew J. Perrin, Steven J. Tepper, Neal Caren, and Sally Morris, "Cultures of the Tea Party," paper delivered at the annual meeting of the American Sociological Association, Las Vegas, August, 2011.

18. Kate Zernike and Megan Thee-Brenan, "Discontent's Demography: Who Backs the Tea Party," *New York Times*, April 15, 2010.

19. Scott Lehigh, "Inside Tea Party Lines," *Boston Globe*, August 25, 2010.

20. Zernike and Thee-Brenan, "Discontent's Demography."

21. Amy Gardner and Krissah Thompson, "Tea Party Groups Battling Perceptions of Racism," *Washington Post*, May 5, 2010, http://www.washingtonpost.com/wp-dyn/content/article/2010/05/04/AR2010050405168.html, as of April 10, 2012; and Amy Gardner, "Few Signs at Tea Party Rally Expressed Racially Charged Anti-Obama Themes," *Washington Post*, October 13, 2010, http://www.washingtonpost.com/wp-dyn/content/article/2010/10/13/AR2010101303634.html, as of April 10, 2012. Research by Emily Ekins, a UCLA graduate student, suggests that either the visible racism was exaggerated or that the efforts of leaders to rid the rallies of racist signs had some impact. She walked around a Tea Party rally in Washington and photographed 250 different signs held up by participants. Only a small

percentage of the signs were patently racist. Elkins's survey was taken in September of 2010, months after the large Tea Party rallies that were widely covered by the press. Unfortunately there are no comparable data from earlier rallies available and the degree of change, if any, cannot be determined.

22. Zernike and Thee-Brenan, "Discontent's Demography."

23. Charles M. Blow, "Let's Rescue the Race Debate," *New York Times*, November 20, 2010.

24. Christopher Parker, "2010 Multi-state Survey on Race & Politics," University of Washington Institute for the Study of Ethnicity, Race, & Sexuality," http://depts. washington.edu/uwiser/racepolitics.html, as of June 3, 2013.

25. This campaign against undocumented immigrants has had negative consequences for the GOP, something addressed in depth in the next chapter.

26. On the impact of local control on the larger Tea Party movement, see Jeffrey M. Berry, Sarah Sobieraj, and Suzanne Schlossberg, "Tea Party Mobilization," paper delivered at the annual meeting of the American Political Science Association, New Orleans, August, 2012.

27. Chris Good, "A Guide to the Six Major Tea Party Groups," *National Journal*, September 11, 2010, http://www.nationaljournal.com/njmagazine/nj_20100911_ 8295.php, as of April 10, 2012. Good includes Americans for Prosperity as a national Tea Party organization. This organization funded by the wealthy conservative activist, David Koch, has not emerged as a Tea Party coordinating body and it's unclear why the *National Journal* included it. The Koch brothers have actually distanced themselves from the Tea Party movement. See Kenneth Vogel, "The Tea Party's Growing Money Problem," *Politico*, August 9, 2010, http://www.politico. com/news/stories/0810/40800.html, as of April 10, 2012.

28. Christopher Rowland, "Tea Party Fragmented but Still a Force," *Boston Globe*, September 3, 2011.

29. Matt Bai, "The Tea Party's Not-So-Civil-War," *New York Times Magazine*, January 12, 2012, 36.

30. Jonathan Rauch, "How the Tea Party Organizes without Leaders," *National Journal*, September 11, 2010, http://www.freerepublic.com/focus/f-bloggers/2591379/ posts, as of April 10, 2012.

31. There was a great deal of optimism among progressives that they were initially better suited to take advantage of the Internet than were conservatives. See Matthew R. Kerbel, *Netroots* (Boulder, CO: Paradigm, 2009).

32. Blackmon et al., "Birth of a Movement."

33. Rauch, "How the Tea Party Organizes without Leaders."

34. Zernike, *Boiling Mad*, 219.

35. Although the Internet reduces the barriers to entry, a large-scale survey demonstrates that it has done little to ameliorate inequality of participation. Rather, it reinforces the relationship of socioeconomic status to acts of political participation. Kay Lehman Schlozman, Sidney Verba, and Henry E. Brady, *The Unheavenly Chorus: Unequal Political Voice and the Broken Promise of American Democracy* (Princeton, NJ: Princeton University Press, 2012), 483–533.

36. James Q. Wilson, *Political Organizations* (New York: Basic Books, 1973), 33.

37. Francesca Polletta and James M. Jasper, "Collective Identity and Social Movements," *Annual Review of Sociology* 27 (2001): 283–305.

38. Amy Gardner, "Tea Party Activists Rally for Deeper Spending Cuts at Capitol," *Washington Post*, March 31, 2011, http://www.washingtonpost.com/politics/tea-party-activists-rally-for-deeper-spending-cuts-at-capitol/2011/03/31/AFKBGoBC_story. html, as of August 2, 2012.

39. See Christian Joppke, "Social Movements during Cycles of Issue Attention: The Decline of the Anti-Nuclear Energy Movements in West Germany and the USA," *British Journal of Sociology* 42 (March 1991): 43–60; and Jo Freeman and Victoria Johnson, eds., *Waves of Protest* (Lanham, MD: Rowman and Littlefield, 1999), 303–364.

40. Alex Isenstadt, "Town Halls Gone Wild," *Politico*, July 31, 2009, http://www. politico.com/news/stories/0709/25646.html, April 10, 2012; Ian Urbina, "Beyond Beltway, Health Debate Turns Hostile," *New York Times*, August 8, 2009, http:// seiumonitor.com/wp-content/uploads/New-York-Times-8-8-09.pdf; "Specter Faces Hostile Audience at Health Care Forum," *CNN.com*. http://www.cnn.com/ 2009/POLITICS/08/11/specter.town.hall/index.html?iref=allsearch; Kathy Kiely and John Fritze, "Town Hall Meetings Stir More Conservatives to Action," *USA Today*, August 22, 2009, http://www.usatoday.com/news/washington/2009-08-19-townhall_N.htm; "Boos Reign at Reston Health Care Event, *Washington Times*, August 26, 2009, http://www.washingtontimes.com/news/2009/aug/26/connolly-faces-seniors-doubts-about-reform/print/?FORM=ZZNR9. All articles as of May 11, 2011.

41. Around 40 percent of the US population said that they were following the debate over the president's health care debate "very closely." See "Public Closely Tracking Health Care Debate," Pew Research Center, December 16, 2009, http://people-press.org/2009/12/16/public-closely-tracking-health-care-debate/, as of June 2, 2011; and "Health Care Debate Dominates Interest and Coverage," Pew Research Center, March 17, 2010, http://people-press.org/2010/03/17/health-care-debate-dominates-interest-and-coverage/, as of June 2, 2011.

42. CNN also gave substantial coverage to the April 15, 2009 tax day rallies. Skocpol and Williamson, *The Tea Party and the Remaking of Republican Conservatism*, 132 and 141.

43. "Health Care Favor/Oppose," *Pollster.com*, http://www.huffingtonpost.com/2009/07/30/ healthplan_n_725503.html, as of May 11, 2011.

44. "Inside the Tea Partiers Anti-Health Care Organizing Campaign," *TalkingPointsMemo*, August 3, 2009, http://tpmdc.talkingpointsmemo.com/2009/08/inside-the-tea-partiers-anti-health-care-organizing-campaign.php, as of May 11, 2011 (site discontinued).

45. Urbina, "Beyond Beltway," as cited in Christine Trost and Lawrence Rosenthal, "The Rise of the Tea Party," in *Steep: The Precipitous Rise of the Tea Party*, ed. Lawrence Rosenthal and Christine Trost (Berkeley: University of California Press, 2012), 19.

46. Sarah Sobieraj, *Soundbitten: The Perils of Media-Centered Political Activism* (New York: New York University Press, 2011).

47. Ashley Parker, "Yelling and Booing Greet Congressman Back Home, *New York Times*, April 29, 2011; and Jennifer Steinhauer and Carl Hulse, "House G.O.P. Members Face Voter Anger over Budget, *New York Times*, April 26, 2011. See also "Liberals Try to Rekindle Town Hall Fury That Inflamed Health Care Debate, *FoxNews.com*, http://www.foxnews.com/politics/2011/04/26/liberals-try-rekin-dle-town-hall-fury-inflamed-health-care-debate/; Jennifer Haberkorn, "Overflow Crowds for Ryan Town Halls," *Politico* http://www.politico.com/news/stories/ 0411/53759.html; Mark Schlueb, "Florida Congressman Confronted by Angry Town Hall Crowd," *OrlandoSentinel.com*, http://blogs.orlandosentinel.com/news_ politics/2011/04/webster-confronted-by-angry-town-hall-crowd.html; and Anthony Man, "Democratic Protesters Hit GOP Town Hall Meeings,"

SunSentinel.com, http://articles.sun-sentinel.com/2011-04-27/news/fl-republican-town-hall-protests-20110427_1_town-hall-democrats-plan-tea-party. Web references as of May 13, 2011.

48. Seung Min Kim, "Most of House Passes on Town Halls, *Politico*, August 22, 2011, http://dyn.politico.com/printstory.cfm?uuid=4F89D309-0DA8-48E9-910A-EE8DFE95064A, as of August 23, 2011.

49. For locally based interest groups, scaling up can have its disadvantages: Venues can be less hospitable, barriers to entry higher, and resources necessary to compete at a higher level can be beyond the ability of the reorganizing group to acquire. See Lisa L. Miller, "The Representational Biases of Federalism," *Perspectives on Politics* 5 (June 2007): 305–321.

50. Robert G. Boatright, "Getting Primaried: The Growth and Consequences of Ideological Primaries," paper delivered at the State of the Parties Conference, Ray C. Bliss Center, University of Akron, October 14–16, 2009, 30.

51. Boatright, "Getting Primaried," 30. Boatright uses the 75 percent threshold to demarcate serious challenges.

52. Boatright, "Getting Primaried."

53. Based on Robert Boatright's work the number of challengers motivated by ideology also appears to be up sharply from previous elections. See his *Getting Primaried* (Ann Arbor: Univeristy of Michigan Press, 2013), 74. As for 2010, our data on this election and Boatright's own separate data collection on 2010 show relatively similar results. Personal correspondence, August 9, 2010.

54. Stephen Ansolabehere, John Mark Hansen, Shigeo Hirano, and James M. Synder Jr., "The Decline of Competition in U.S. Primary Elections, 1908–2004," in *The Marketplace of Democracy*, ed. Michael P. McDonald and John Curtis Samples (Washington, DC: Brookings Institution Press, 2006), 98.

55. http://www.glennbeck.com/content/articles/article/198/30689/, as of May 23, 2011.

56. http://michellemalkin.com/2009/06/26/the-8-cap-and-tax-republicans/, as of May 23, 2011.

57. http://seeingredaz.wordpress.com/2009/03/08/wheres-jeff-flake-and-why-does-he-want-to-help-turn-more-red-states-blue/, as of May 23, 2011.

58. http://biggovernment.com/sright/2010/06/04/republican-gary-miller-ear-marks-land-deals-and-fbi-investigations/, as of May 23, 2011.

59. http://politicallyfrank.wordpress.com/2009/11/01/r-a-c-e/, as of May 23, 2011.

60. Erick Erickson, "Cleaning Up the GOP Moves to Texas," *RedState*, May 17, 2012, http://www.redstate.com/erick/2012/05/17/cleaning-up-the-gop-moves-to-texas/, as of August 3, 2012.

61. Erick Erickson, "Freedom's Slate," *RedState*, July 5, 2012, http://www.redstate.com/erick/2012/07/05/freedoms-slate/, as of August 3, 2012.

62. *Janine Turner Radio Show*, July 14, 2012, http://www.janineturner.com/blog/category/website_radio_show_podcasts/radio-show-guest-ted-cruz/, as of January 24, 2013.

63. Trip Gabriel, "Clout Diminished, Tea Party Turns to Narrower Issues, *New York Times*, December 25, 2012, http://www.nytimes.com/2012/12/26/us/politics/tea-party-its-clout-diminished-turns-to-fringe-issues.html?hpw; and Jerry Markon, "Tea Party Stays on the Sidelines as Obama, Republicans in Congress Tackle Fiscal Cliff," *Washington Post*, December 23, 2012, http://www.washingtonpost.com/politics/tea-party-stays-on-the-sidelines-as-obama-republicans-in-congress-tackle-fiscal-cliff/2012/12/23/9f82a0d0-4b7e-11e2-a6a6-aabac85e8036_story.html, as of December 26, 2012.

64. Abramowitz, "Grand Old Tea Party," 208.
65. An interesting contrast between the Tea Party and earlier Christian right insurgencies within the Republican Party is offered by Martin Cohen, "The Future of the Tea Party," in *Steep: The Precipitous Rise of the Tea Party,* ed. Lawrence Rosenthal and Christine Trost (Berkeley: University of California Press, 2012), 212–241.
66. Israel Waismel-Manor and Yariv Tsfati, "Why Do Better-Looking Members of Congress Receive More Television Coverage?," *Political Communication* 28 (November 2011): 452. John Geer finds that in presidential elections, the mainstream media are increasingly prone to cover negativity in ads. The result is an incentive for campaigns to go negative. "The News Media and the Rise of Negativity in Presidential Campaigns," *PS: Political Science and Politics* 45 (July 2012): 422–427.
67. See, for example, Aaron Blake, "Republican Rep. Allen West Says Many Congressional Democrats Are Communists," *Washington Post*, April 11, 2012, http://www.washingtonpost.com/blogs/the-fix/post/republican-rep-allen-west-suggests-many-congressional-democrats-are-communists/2012/04/11/gIQApbZiAT_blog.html; and Andrew Rosenthal, "Red Scare," *New York Times*, April 11, 2012, http://loyalopposition.blogs.nytimes.com/2012/04/11/red-scare/, as of April 26, 2012.
68. Gary C. Jacobson, *The Politics of Congressional Elections* (New York: Pearson Longman, 2013), 139.
69. See Gary C. Jacobson, "The Republican Resurgence in 2010," *Political Science Quarterly* 126 (Spring 2011): 27–52. Jacobson credits the Tea Party for strongly influencing Republican perceptions of the election.
70. From *Talkers.com* daily compendium.
71. Kenneth Janda, "How About a Nice Sup of Tea," Northwestern University, n.d.
72. Jacobson, "The Republican Resurgence in 2010," p. 39. This finding was also confirmed by Jon R. Bond, Richard Fleisher, and Nathan A. Ilderton, "Was the Tea Party Responsible for the Republican Victory in the 2010 House Elections?," paper delivered at the annual meeting of the American Political Science Association, Seattle, September, 2011; and Christopher F. Karpowitz, J. Quin Monson, Kelly D. Patterson, and Jeremy C. Pope, "Tea Time in America? The Impact of the Tea Party Movement on the 2010 Midterm Election," *PS: Political Science and Politics* 44 (April 2011): 303–309. A study by Michael A. Bailey, Jonathan Mummolo, and Hans Noel found that the number of Tea Party activists did have an electoral impact at the district level. See "Tea Party Influence: A Story of Activists and Elites," *American Politics Research*, 40 (September 2012): 769–804.

CHAPTER 7

☙

Continuity, Change, Synergy

final step in assessing the Outrage Industry is to examine its impact on public policymaking. Does the vitriol that pours forth daily on TV, on the radio, and in blogs have an impact on decisions made by those in power? Are politicians and policymakers truly influenced by the likes of Rush Limbaugh, Rachel Maddow, and Michelle Malkin?

This is no easy task. Media effects are notoriously difficult to tease out under even the best of circumstances, and myriad forces shape policy outcomes. In light of this, we focus on better understanding the relationship between the Outrage Industry and policymaking rather than on trying to make causal claims. Still, we find evidence that the Outrage Industry has the capacity to influence issue framing, in terms of both affecting perceptions and adding new policy dimensions to issues before the nation. Our data suggest that outrage media have also contributed to the long-term trend toward the increase in polarization between the two parties in Congress. By vilifying compromise and collaboration, key voices from the Outrage Industry have made it more difficult for the parties to work together to address the nation's most pressing problems. While it is not the only force influencing these patterns in American politics, it's clear that the Outrage Industry shapes the terrain in which lawmakers work.

POLARIZATION IN CONGRESS

As the parties have become more ideologically homogeneous, it stands to reason that the candidates it nominates for office will mirror the evolving political dispositions of party voters.[1] Yet candidates may be pulled further to the ideological extremes by the nature of primary electorates. For example, in the Republican Senate primary in Kentucky in 2010 (discussed more fully later), just 33.6 percent of registered Republicans went to the polls. In a choice between a conventional conservative and a hyperconservative, the hyperconservative, Rand Paul, won with 59 percent of the votes cast. But that 59 percent majority represented just one in five Kentucky Republicans. Independents actually form the largest "party" in America, with four in ten identifying this way.[2] If moderates are underrepresented in both parties, the structure of our decentralized party system with its open primaries makes it easier for ideologues to control nominations.

The Push for Orthodoxy

If we look at party-line voting—the measure typically used to assess polarization in Congress—we see that there has always been a substantial level of division in Congress, though it has fluctuated significantly throughout history. There was a high level of polarization at the end of the nineteenth century and the beginning of the twentieth century, while it was relatively low between the 1930s and the 1970s.[3] Since the 1970s there has been a steady rise in rigid partisanship as more and more members of Congress choose to vote with their party or against the other party. McCarty, Poole, and Rosenthal find that in this period, "The positions of the average Democrat and average Republican member of Congress have become more widely separated."[4]

Members of Congress are now strikingly more ideological than the public at large. Bafumi and Herron conclude that "both Senators and House members are politically extreme compared to the voters who put them in office."[5] An increase in the number of representatives at the ends of the spectrum means, conversely, that there are fewer moderates in the House and Senate. Alan Abramowitz finds that the proportion of moderate legislators shrank from 30 percent in the 95th Congress (1977–78) to just 8 percent in the 108th Congress (2003–04). This trend was even sharper among Republicans. The percentage of moderate Republicans shrank from 33 percent in the 95th Congress to just 3 percent in the 104th Congress.[6] This heightened polarization is also manifested in state legislatures.[7]

"Partisanship," despite its pejorative connotation, is fundamental to democracies. Party labels help voters to choose candidates who, if elected as part of a majority, can enact the legislation they favor. Yet partisanship can become so pronounced that it works against compromise and damages the Congress's ability to effectively address the nation's most critical problems. Many Americans would prefer a party system in which moderate legislators of each party held the balance of power and that they constrained the more conflictual instincts of their more ideological brethren.[8] The contemporary Congress appears to moving in the opposite direction.

This rising tide of partisanship in Congress has developed from the convergence of many historical streams. In placing the rise of the Outrage Industry in this historical context, it is particularly significant that the increase in party-line voting in the 1970s begins *before* the sharp upsurge in outrage media. Yet if the Outrage Industry was not "present at the creation," it has surely helped bolster this polarization. The Outrage Industry has helped fuel the trend toward divisiveness in Congress in three ways. In turn we'll consider the evolution of the media, party recruitment, and the monitoring functions of outrage media.

Changing Media Mix

The proliferation of outrage and concurrent atrophy of conventional news has facilitated the deepening congressional divisiveness. In light of declining newspaper readership, the closing of Washington bureaus by midsized news organizations, and decreased budgets for local newspapers, policymakers looking for coverage have to work a bit harder than they did a quarter century ago. But in the contemporary media landscape, legislators and candidates have many ways to reach their target audience. Eager to broaden favorability and awareness in the district, incumbents and their press aides work to create opportunities for press coverage by the local news and opinion media. Bloggers who are sympathetic to the incumbent may be rewarded with posts from the member or his aides. A group of GOP representatives who are strong Tea Party enthusiasts created "Conversations with Conservatives," a media outreach program aimed especially at bloggers. Blog coverage of these comments has stimulated some secondary coverage in the mainstream press.[9] For their part, legislators and candidates relish invitations to be interviewed by sympathetic talk radio hosts, as the interviews are best described as a series of softballs thrown gently down the middle. From a legislator's perspective, sympathetic state and local outrage media are ideal: they are hungry for content, easy to satisfy, and lavish in their praise. It is almost as if outrage media were designed by legislators for their own means. At the same time, legislators are frightened at the prospect of outrage allies turning against them, as such a development can work against their reelection.

Party Recruitment

Although the national political parties do not control party nominations, state or local party organizations will sometimes coalesce behind a particular candidate when a seat opens. Even with an anointed candidate, primaries are often contested by two or more viable contenders. It is not uncommon for someone who has not been particularly active in the party but has a lot of his or her own money to use those resources to compete with a party favorite. Affluence provides an alternative route to nominations. For those without their own riches or party backing, being identified with activists in the district is another potential route. Geoffrey Layman and his colleagues write, "open nomination systems and the ambitious politicians competing within those systems encourage activists with extreme views...to become involved in party politics."[10] As shown in the previous chapter, the 2010 primaries unleashed a torrent of candidates running for both open seats and against incumbents, including the 282 candidates formally endorsed by Tea Party organizations.[11]

Kentucky Senate candidate, Rand Paul, rattled the state's Republican establishment with his insurgent campaign against party favorite Trey Grayson. Grayson, the incumbent secretary of state, was a proven vote getter, and party leaders were unified around his candidacy, including support from the state's senior senator, Mitch McConnell. Grayson was also a proven conservative in a conservative state and could not be called a moderate or dismissed as a RINO (Republican in Name Only). Paul ran as a Tea Party supporter, and although he had done little for the state's Republican Party, he built his candidacy around his appearances throughout the state, his work as chair of the Kentucky Taxpayers Association, his interviews with local talk radio, and his appeal to conservative political blogs. He largely funded his campaign through "money bombs" on the Internet—appeals that yielded a large number of small donations on a single day.

More broadly, the Outrage Industry may be working to shift the fundraising equilibrium within parties. Michele Bachmann used her frequent appearances on programs such as *Hannity* and the *O'Reilly Factor* to raise an astronomical $13.5 million for her 2010 House race in a safe district. Most of this came as donations from individuals over the Internet. After dropping out of the 2012 Republican presidential nomination race, she turned her attention back to her Minnesota district and a more formidable challenge. This time she raised an impressive $15 million, again predominantly from small contributions.[12] South Carolina Republican Representative Joe Wilson, who yelled "You lie" at President Obama during a State of the

Union speech, became a hero on conservative blogs. Immediately after the incident he put advertisements on conservative websites asking for contributions. He was enormously successful, increasing his campaign funding from $1.2 million in 2008 to $4.7 million in 2010.[13]

For more politically extreme candidates who lack years of party networking, the Outrage Industry is particularly attractive. Given the audience they pursue, it is in the business interest of local outrage outlets and interest groups to make orthodoxy a critical factor. This emphasis has consequences. As we saw in the 2010 primaries, outrage media were particularly influential in cueing the most sharply conservative members of their audiences as to who might best push the cause forward. Fans trust their favorite hosts and bloggers and, thus, their cues can be enormously valuable.

Monitoring

Due to its ideological nature, harsh language, and exaggerated predictions about the consequences of policy choices, outrage political talk may not readily come to mind when we consider the accountability of legislators, something of critical democratic importance. In a democracy, voters should be reasonably knowledgeable about the positions of their legislators in order for their participation to be meaningful. Douglas Arnold terms this "traceability"—the capacity of a citizen to track a legislator's connection to a government action.[14] A rich media environment has been shown to be linked to a more informed electorate.[15] When President Obama's stimulus package was poised for passage in the Senate in 2009, Michelle Malkin swung into action using her blog to denounce the Republicans said to be leaning toward legislation that she described as "stealing $1 trillion from future generations for a Crap Sandwich Supreme." She provided links to the contact information for the GOP "wobblers" (Senators Collins, Snowe, and Specter) and implored readers to call or write to them. *Moonbattery* went after the same three, again with contact information, warning they would be held responsible for the "wanton looting of our country's future by voting for the $1+ trillion (with interest) Porkzilla 'stimulus' package." *Twilight's Last Gleaming* attacked them for having "abandoned the Republican party's goal of protecting America from socialism." It warned ominously, "We'll remember these three come reelection time."[16]

Most broadly, this heightened sense of accountability may make it more difficult for legislators to take actions that are unpopular but necessary. In his analysis of political party behavior, David Karol concludes that "the increasing connectedness of people and the greater ease in mobilization via talk radio and the internet...suggest that it may easier for activists to organize party supporters in a way that compels politicians to take notice."[17] In political terms, monitoring appears to be one of the Outrage Industry's greatest strengths.

A Credible Signal? A Credible Threat?

If legislators are to regard a signal as politically meaningful, they must regard the source as credible.[18] The debt ceiling crisis that consumed the country in July of 2011 is a case when the signaling was pronounced. Was it also credible? To avoid default on U.S. securities, Congress needed to raise the country's debt ceiling no later than August 2nd of that year and the Republicans used the deadline as leverage in an effort to force a cut in government spending. The Democrats were on the defensive and President Obama quickly capitulated to the Republicans' demands. Only a week before the national debt limit would be reached, Republican Speaker John Boehner brought forth his own bill to enact the agreement with the Democrats. It not only embodied Republican priorities of budget cuts and no tax increases but also included mechanisms to make sure that cuts would actually be implemented. Surprisingly, though, Boehner found himself without sufficient votes to pass the legislation. In an effort to make it more comfortable for recalcitrant House Republicans to vote for the bill, Boehner called Rush Limbaugh on his radio show to try to sell him and his listeners on the legislation.[19] That apparently wasn't sufficient and Boehner was forced to call off the scheduled vote, an embarrassing public defeat for the Speaker.

Why wouldn't Republican backbenchers accept a bill that was an unequivocal Republican victory, consciously embarrassing their own leader in the process?[20] Although legislators come with their own priorities and sense of just how far they can go in pressing for their own preferences, it's hard to ignore the volcanic response that poured forth from conservative outrage outlets. The Outrage Industry's campaign against various plans in the works began before the Boehner plan was revealed. Various media figures and ideological groups seemed to delight in threatening Republicans. The Tea Party Express warned legislators who got out of line that they would find themselves facing a primary opponent in 2012. Erick Erickson, whose *RedState* blog is widely read by conservatives and who often appears on cable news, posted an entry, "If You Support Mitch McConnell, We Don't Support You." *RedState*, too, threatened incumbents with opposition in upcoming primaries. The popular conservative radio host Mark Levin told his 8.5 million weekly listeners that primary challengers were warranted in 2012 and that a group of Republicans and Democrats working together were a "gang of schmucks." Glenn Beck said there was no default threat, one of many outrage figures who ridiculed the notion that the debt ceiling was a real problem.[21]

Politics is always characterized by inflated rhetoric. Did these threats register as credible? It's one thing for Mark Levin to tell listeners that jihad against incumbent Republican senators is necessary and quite another for someone to actually put together a campaign strong enough to topple an incumbent. Recent Republican primaries suggest these are not empty threats. The 2010 Congressional Primary Database described in Chapter 6 (Table 2) shows that in addition to the four Republican incumbents who were defeated in primaries, many more Republican incumbents received less than 75 percent of the primary vote. At the time of the debt ceiling debate Senator Richard Lugar (R-Ind.) already had an announced primary opponent, and a challenge to Orrin Hatch (R-Utah) was expected. In the wake of the collapse of the Boehner plan the popular inside *Washington Post* column, "The Fix," identified the defeat of South Carolina Representative Bob Inglis in a Republican primary in 2010 as a reason that the state's five Republicans would not support the Speaker.[22]

And what did the Tea Party, emboldened by the firestorm of criticism from conservative outrage media, and Republican backbenchers in the House gain by embarrassing the Speaker? In terms of public policy, they gained nothing of substance. After Boehner pulled his bill, he found that the price of support for a debt ceiling agreement was the inclusion of a provision that required Congress to pass a balanced budget amendment to the Constitution. In other words, with just a few days remaining before a default on the nation's debt, the Congress would have to vote to amend the Constitution of the United States.[23] With this addition, Boehner's second plan was passed and went on to the Senate where it was immediately voted down. The conference committee that reconciled the two bills reported out legislation that merely contained a requirement that a vote on a constitutional amendment be taken. Such a vote was entirely symbolic as Congress was not going to amend the Constitution. The most plausible explanation for why veteran GOP lawmakers who were sympathetic to Boehner failed to fight for his bill (and permitted him to be publicly dressed down by Tea Party sympathizers) was that the high-profile vote had become "traceable." No Republican wanted an unpopular vote on his or her record when the Republican primaries rolled around. Both extensive outrage media coverage and local Tea Party communications networks made the Boehner bill political poison. In the end, Boehner's bill did not differ in any meaningful way from the final bill, but a consensus seemed to emerge among Republicans that the issue had run its course and legislation was finally enacted.[24]

Despite their victory in the congressional budget fight, polls showed that two thirds of Tea Party identifiers voiced opposition to the deal.[25] Tea Party leaders we interviewed were dismissive about the budget agreement. "I don't think it accomplished anything," concluded one Tea Party organizer. "It was spit in the ocean, it did nothing," said a statewide coordinator. Politically, however, the debt crisis fight demonstrates how effective the Outrage Industry has become at enhancing the traceability of actions by legislators. Such monitoring acts to enforce partisanship. Unfortunately for Boehner, the debt ceiling vote was not the only revolt by his conservative colleagues that forced him to retreat openly. After this defeat he became something of a pincushion, humiliated again in December of 2012 as the government faced its so-called fiscal cliff problem. Unable to find a grand bargain of tax increases and budget cuts that could pass the House, Boehner offered a more modest proposal to his caucus. When enough members refused to go along he had to withdraw the bill.

AGENDA SETTING

Leaving aside these dramas involving Speaker Boehner's proposals, the real decisions about legislation are, of course, typically made earlier in the process in committee or in negotiations between the leadership and committee leaders. But why do bills reach the stage of committee action—that is, how do they reach the agenda? If an issue reaches the agenda, how is influence brought to bear to shape the legislation as it is initially formulated? How might outrage influence the content of the issues or the nature of the policy alternatives considered by policymakers?

Issue Focus

During the 2008 campaign and then through the spring of 2011 a story claiming that Barack Obama was not a citizen of the United States continued to circulate. In various accounts he was born in Kenya or born in the United States but not as a legal citizen, or his citizenship was vitiated by subsequently living in Indonesia or by traveling to Pakistan. The story was openly pushed by a cadre of right-wing zealots, notably Orly Taitz, Jerome Corsi, and Phil Berg, who were wildly successful in attracting attention to the story (and to themselves). The accusations were launched in various blogs and then picked up by the mainstream press which, given the controversy, felt obligated to examine the charge. Despite being debunked by every serious investigation, the story would not die. It gave angry conservatives a scandal to stoke and indignant liberals something to mock. In its wake, a few red states even gave serious consideration to bills requiring presidential candidates to show their birth certificates when they filed for the ballot. Arizona actually passed such legislation, although it was ultimately vetoed by the Republican governor, Jan Brewer. And just when it seemed like the story had finally run its course, Donald Trump, exploring a run for the presidency in 2012, generated a great deal of attention by raising the issue anew. Polls taken in April of that year showed that around 45 percent of Republicans believed that Obama was born outside the United States.[26] It was around this time that the White House finally released a copy of Obama's birth certificate. Only then did the issue subside.

What we find striking about this case, beyond the scope of coverage and the thinly veiled racism, is that the Outrage Industry took this fantasy and put it on the agenda of legislatures in Arizona, Oklahoma, South Carolina, and others. Members of these legislatures took time to work on legislation designed to prevent a fictitious perversion of justice from happening again.

The birther story notwithstanding, the Outrage Industry does not appear to be particularly effective at setting the agenda. We examined this question systematically with the data gathered for our content analysis. In the data collected from cable TV shows, talk radio programs, and political blogs (discussed in Chapter 2), we recorded the first issue to be addressed. In Table 7.1 we have categorized all these issues by the general policy area, drawing on a widely utilized coding scheme developed by political scientists Frank Baumgartner and Bryan Jones.[27] Our research was conducted in the spring of 2009, and as the country was in the throes of a serious recession, it was not surprising that the top policy concern involved the economy. Nine of the twenty categories scored no more than 1 percent. These issues areas, such as agriculture or public lands, are hardly sexy topics for newspapers, much less for cable TV or talk radio.

We added "politics, media bias" to the Baumgartner-Jones schema, which has no comparable category. Elections, other political subjects, and the media are popular topics as almost a quarter of all stories fall into this grouping. Still, we find that hosts and bloggers tend to focus on the substantive issues of the day, taking their lead from the conventional news media. Front page stories from the nation's newspapers are likely to be discussed on that day's talk radio shows and on the evening shows on Fox and MSNBC, although they are ideologically selective, lavishing time on those

Table 7.1 ISSUE COVERAGE, SPRING 2009

Issues receiving the most attention from Cable TV, talk radio, political blogs, and op-ed columnists

Macroeconomics	14.8%
Civil Rights, Minority Issues, and Civil Liberties	5.0
Health Care	3.8
Agriculture	.3
Labor, Employment, and Immigration	3.2
Education	1.3
Environment	.8
Energy	1.0
Transportation	1.0
Law, Crime, Family Issues	7.1
Social Welfare	.8
Community Development and Housing	.8
Banking, Financial Regulation	6.1
Defense	12.3
Space, Science, Technology Communications	1.0
Foreign Trade	1.3
International Assistance	3.2
Government Operations	2.2
Public Lands and Water Management	0.0
State and Local Government Administration	.5
Politics, Media Bias*	23.1
Other	<u>10.3</u>
Total	99.9%

The classification of policy areas follows the master schema from the Policy Agendas Project, developed by Frank R. Baumgartner and Bryan D. Jones. Their detailed codebook is available at http://www.policyagen-das.org/page/topic-codebook.
*Under this category we include elections; general assessments of political figures and institutions; political strategy; claims of media bias in political coverage; discussion of political commentators and their various roles.

topics that give their listeners the moral high ground.[28] Another question was whether there were issue differences across the three outrage platforms. Cable TV and talk radio were very similar while blogs demonstrated the most diversity in subject matter. Newspaper columnists were also more varied than commentators on TV and radio. Finally we examined whether there were any differences between left and right. The data indicates that there is little difference in the types of issues addressed by liberal and conservatives.

By and large, the Outrage Industry comments on issues; it doesn't create them. The birther issue is unusual in that it really was created out of whole cloth. When outrage hosts and bloggers bring forth an issue not already on the agendas of government bodies—it usually remains a hobbyhorse, off the agenda.

Reframing

While the Outrage Industry has a limited capacity to place new issues on the agenda, it is more effective at changing the terms of the debate. This in and of itself is no small matter and scholars across several disciplines have paid a great deal of attention to framing and reframing.[29] Political scientists regard this phenomenon as significant because changing the terms of debate can change the outcome of policy decisions. William Riker pioneered work in this area and concluded that attempting to reframe issues is "structuring the world so you can win."[30] Riker concluded that reframing is everyday politics and portrayed the policymaking process as highly amenable to clever politicians and lobbyists who are able to conceive of new arguments that cause others to see the problem at hand in a new light.[31] This is a Madison Avenue view of the political world: If the product doesn't sell, repackage it and call it something else.

Riker and others built their argument around case studies showing that reframing altered the way that an issue was viewed. Perhaps the best illustration of this dynamic involves the success of anti-abortion groups in gaining acceptance of the term "partial birth abortion." Prior to the widespread usage of this term, the actual physical act of aborting a fetus was seen as a medical procedure or, more precisely, "intact dilation and extraction." Such wordsmithing may seem trivial, but it can have a profound impact on how we perceive public issues. If abortion is described as an act of brutality rather than an as a medical procedure, then opinion about the broader issue of the legality of abortion—or certain types of abortion—may change.[32]

A recent study of the role of advocacy groups in reframing by Baumgartner, Berry, Hojnacki, Kimball, and Leech was the first to systematically measure the frequency of reframing. Is it really everyday politics as Riker argued? Baumgartner and his colleagues assembled ninety-eight detailed case studies of Washington policymaking between 1999 and 2002, each of which was followed over time and then coded into one of three categories. Of the ninety-eight issues, only four underwent any kind of reframing. Just one underwent a complete reframing (a rather minor issue involving a telephone tax), while three were characterized by partial reframing.[33]

This evidence from advocacy groups may translate to outrage media. While outrage personalities spin issues in their programs and blogs, reframing issues of the day for their audiences, they may have little success in changing the way issues are discussed in legislative arenas. Our content analysis does not incorporate information that directly sheds light on reframing, but the Outrage Industry played a crucial role in adding a new frame to the mix for at least two important policy issues that emerged during the time of our study. One case involves President Obama's health insurance reforms. Obama's controversial plan touched upon many different policy dimensions, with debate centering on the lack of insurance coverage for many Americans, inequities in private health insurance, health care costs, and the expansion of government authority over health care. But seemingly out of nowhere a charge emerged from outrage outlets that the Obama plan allowed bureaucratic "death panels" to ration care for ailing seniors. The charge was an imaginative, albeit fictitious, extrapolation from a provision that allowed physicians to charge Medicare for an office visit focused on discussing end-of-life options, such as hospice care. This dramatic accusation created an emotional element that sharpened conservative anger toward the president. The "death panel" myth ricocheted around the Internet and on cable and talk radio with impressive velocity.[34] Some Republicans in Congress began to repeat the claim, burnishing its credibility and allowing outrage figures to then cite congresspersons as credible evidence that such measures were on the table. A poll by the Kaiser Family Foundation showed that the cumulative impact of this misinformation was that fully four of ten Americans came to believe that death panels were part of the legislation.[35] Research by Brendan Nyhan and Jason Reifler shows that misinformation easily endures because efforts to correct such public misperceptions are prone to failure.[36]

Conservative outrage media also played a key role in reconfiguring the debt ceiling debate. In recent years the Republicans in Congress had used the need to increase the debt ceiling as entry to a broader debate about the scale of government activity and spending. But the debate in the summer of 2011 moved beyond that, with some conservative outrage figures arguing that it was a good idea to let the United States default on its debt. Their reasoning was that only through such a crisis would the government face up to the need for a balanced budget and would restore integrity to the governmental process. "Defaulting on our debt is a red herring," noted the popular conservative blog, *Townhall*.[37]

How do we reconcile these cases of reframing with the research by Baumgartner and his colleagues? It might be that the Outrage Industry is adept at reframing in ways that make it more prevalent than in the earlier period studied by Baumgartner et al. The Outrage Industry is more robust today than when they collected their data in 1999–2002. At that point, the blogosphere was in its infancy, there were fewer than half the number of talk radio stations than exist today, MSNBC had not adopted its liberal orientation, and Fox was just emerging as a beacon on the right. Clearly, today, there is more outrage infrastructure and more potential for influencing the reframing of issues.

In thinking about how the contemporary Outrage Industry might influence reframing, some intriguing commonalities characterize the death panels and debt ceiling cases as well as the birther issue. First, in all three cases there was enormous coverage by the outrage media and subsequently by mainstream media, which could not ignore the clamor because legislators were amplifying the policy arguments. In all three cases the coverage was sustained over a significant period of time. Exposure for each of the charges was high, feverish in tone, with broad dissemination across many platforms. Not surprisingly, *scale* makes a difference. Next we see that all three issues were treated by the mainstream media as if they were concerns of ordinary people, masking the influence of outrage in exacerbating these worries and, in some cases, spreading misinformation.

In all three cases it served the interests of the Republican Party to have these messages widely perceived as credible. For Republican legislators these arguments worked to discredit the Democrats while stoking the anger of the party faithful. Conservative outrage hosts and bloggers repeated the charges made by Republican legislators, and Republican legislators repeated the charges made by outrage hosts and bloggers. Influence was maximized by the *synergy* produced by common interests. In all three matters, liberal outrage media became highly animated in trying to refute the conservative storylines. Liberal media figures joined the battle, excoriating conservative hosts and bloggers for what they saw as deliberate misstatement of facts. These were royal battles for *both* sides of the Outrage Industry. But if these cases offer us clues to the success of reframing initiatives, it is that sustained outrage, across many platforms, coincident with complementary messaging from legislators, can be a powerful force in issue definition.

PARTY RATIONALITY

The partisan composition of the country typically evolves slowly and we only recognize significant change as we look back at years of party identification and voting data. The focus here is on the interrelationship between the Republican Party and the Outrage Industry on the evolution of party constituencies. This is a rather ambitious undertaking and we limit the analysis here to just one demographic sector, Hispanic Americans. The incorporation of the nation's largest minority group into the political system is significant in and of itself. In recent years conservative outrage personalities have become increasingly vocal on issues that deeply affect Hispanic Americans.

Is Demography Destiny?

Between 2000 and 2010, the Hispanic population in the United States grew at a rate of 43.0 percent while the non-Hispanic white population edged up just 1.2 percent.[38] Hispanics currently constitute about 17 percent of the American population. By 2025, Hispanics will comprise 21 percent of the population and this figure will climb to 30 percent of all Americans by 2050.[39] As a proportion of the electorate, Hispanics lag behind both blacks and non-Hispanic whites, although their voting power is on the rise, growing from 8 percent in 2008 to 10 percent in 2012. Together with African Americans and Asians, minority groups were 28 percent of the total vote in 2012.[40] Roughly 35 percent of Hispanics are under eighteen years of age, compared to 21 percent of non-Hispanic whites and 29 percent of blacks, clearly indicating that the Hispanic vote will continue to grow more important as this younger generation ages.[41]

The implications of this growth for party politics are a source of debate. Historically Hispanics have been relatively loyal to the Democratic Party. Sixty-seven percent of Hispanics voted for Barack Obama in the 2008 election, a very good year for Democrats overall. In 2010, a terrible year for Democrats overall, 60 percent of Hispanics voted Democratic. In 2012 the performance of Republican Mitt Romney with minorities was nothing short of catastrophic. Among Hispanics, Obama won 71 percent to Romney's 27 percent. Obama also won 93 percent of blacks and 73 percent of Asians.[42]

Republicans argue that although the long-term trend has favored Democrats, the Hispanic vote is still very much up for grabs. Republicans believe that their commitment to family values and economic growth will eventually win over more Hispanics.[43] There's scholarly work supporting the notion that Hispanic political allegiances are still in play. Zoltan Hajnal and Takeu Lee's study of race and partisanship shows that both Latinos and Asians enter the electorate with relatively low levels of partisan attachment. Latinos and Asians may initially identify as independents not because they lie ideologically between the left and the right but because they are uncertain in their understanding of the political system. Over time, one of the parties may prove more attractive, and identification and some level of loyalty will follow.[44]

The effects of political socialization on young Latinos may be stronger than Hajnal and Lee allow. Consider the direction of young Hispanics in terms of partisan identification. A research report by CIRCLE at Tufts University shows that 76 percent of young (18–29) Hispanics voted for Barack Obama in 2008, compared to 62 percent of Hispanics aged thirty or older. Of those who voted, 53 percent of eighteen- to twenty-nine-year-old Hispanics said they were Democrats as opposed to just 16 percent who indicated that they identify as Republicans.[45] What's more, although Republicans point to prominent Hispanic Republican officeholders as evidence of the party's effective appeal to Latinos, they fare poorly in placing Hispanics in office. Among all Hispanic officeholders who held partisan positions in 2007, there were nine Democrats for every Republican. Thus, as young Hispanics begin to learn about politics and about party choice, the political leaders they see in their community, at their churches, and at their neighborhood events are very likely to be Democrats.[46]

Immigration

The Republicans' continuing problem recruiting Hispanic voters has many sources, not least among them are policy initiatives that Hispanics regard as hostile if not downright racist. Together with outrage media and advocacy groups, the Republicans have aggressively pushed legislation aimed at identifying undocumented immigrants and making it harder for them to find employment.

These policy initiatives have roots in events and trends that precede the emergence of the Outrage Industry. The campaign against undocumented immigrants began in earnest in California with three state ballot initiatives during the 1990s. All were linked to Republican politicians who provided leadership and articulated the case for aggressive action against the undocumented. Proposition 187 (on the ballot in 1994) denied state services to those in the country illegally. Aimed at both blacks and Hispanics, Proposition 209 (in 1996) prohibited the use of affirmative action by state government. Finally, Proposition 227 (in 1998) ended bilingual education programs, requiring English immersion programs instead.

All three ballot initiatives passed easily. Despite the popularity of these policy prescriptions, the California Republican Party's strong support of them amounted to nothing short of a death wish. As Bowler, Nicholson, and Segura demonstrate in their detailed analysis of long-term public opinion trends in California, the three ballot initiatives shifted additional Hispanic support toward the Democratic Party.[47] Moreover, the initiatives had a galvanizing impact on Hispanics, increasing the overall level of Hispanic turnout in elections. The ballot questions also activated immigrants, with more of them applying for citizenship and, thus, turning themselves into voters.[48] Today California is 38 percent Hispanic and overwhelmingly Democratic; Hispanics there are closely tied to the state Democratic Party.

Other anti-immigration initiatives have come and gone in various states, but in 2010 the Republicans in the Arizona legislature ignited a firestorm when they enacted new legislation requiring police to question anyone who is "reasonably suspect" of being undocumented, mandating that legal immigrants carry documentation with them, and making it a violation of state law for an undocumented person to reside in Arizona.[49] In June 2012, the Supreme Court invalidated most of the significant provisions of the legislation, though it left intact the highly controversial policy that allows police to question those they suspect of being undocumented. The issue remains incendiary in Arizona where Hispanics have grown to fully 30 percent of the population. Although John Kerry in 2004 and Barack Obama in 2008 won 56 percent of Arizona's Hispanic vote, 74 percent of Arizona's Hispanics voted for Obama in 2012.[50]

After the 2010 Republican landslide, many state legislative bodies shifted from Democrat to Republican while in others existing Republican majorities greatly expanded. Inspired by the Arizona law, anti-immigrant proposals poured forth. We analyzed legislative initiatives in the ten states with the largest Hispanic populations as well as those in ten other states where there was significant legislative activity on this issue.[51] In particular, we examined the nature of coalitions of Republican legislators and Tea Party activists.

Strong patterns emerged out of this state-by-state research. Most significantly, the legislative proposals were far-reaching. The most common features were requirements for verification of legal status by employers (through E-Verify and other means), criminalization of employment of undocumented immigrants, prohibitions against local governments for failing to cooperate with federal agencies working on illegal immigration, and requirements for police to ask those they interact with who somehow appear suspicious (or who are arrested) for proof of citizenship or legal residence. The proposals were also controversial. We found considerable debate within the states, and substantial opposition to the bills typically emerged.

Of the ten states with the largest Hispanic populations, only Arizona actually enacted legislation. In eight of the other states, bills moved forward in the legislature but ultimately failed. Of the ten other states we studied, five enacted anti-immigration laws. The new laws in Alabama and Georgia were especially harsh as they criminalized a very extensive range of activity by employers and instituted expanded requirements that residents be able to prove that they are citizens.

The Tea Party's role in pushing for anti-immigration legislation was mixed.[52] In some states these groups were active in lobbying while in others their advocacy was limited to sharp language on websites. On the other side of the equation, liberal coalitions of interest groups such as the American Civil Liberties Union (ACLU), Hispanic groups, and churches organized at the community level and energetically lobbied at the state capitol. In some states business groups were also critics of proposed legislation, recognizing the possible impact on a valuable part of the workforce. In many states, Republicans were split between firebrand conservatives who pushed for anti-immigrant legislation and those who were more pragmatic, presumably recognizing that new laws would likely further alienate Hispanics from the party.

Even though anti-immigration legislation failed in most states, this movement against the undocumented angered Hispanics across the nation, as the hostility toward immigrants has not been indiscriminate but rather has had racist undertones, focusing on Mexican and Central American immigrants. For Hispanics, anti-immigration legislation may be more deeply personal than is generally appreciated. Polling by Latino Decisions in California in 2011 reveals that 53 percent of Hispanic respondents say they "know somebody who is an undocumented immigrant." A quarter of respondents say they know a "person or family who has faced detention or deportation for immigration reasons."[53]

Pulled Off Center

It is axiomatic in political science that a rational party—one that wants to win the most votes—will position itself at the median point in the ideological distribution of the electorate.[54] Immigration, of course, is far from the only issue confronting an electorate and there is no one "median voter." Rather, candidates or parties try to attract a winning coalition of interest groups and issue publics come election day.[55] Given the stark reality of demographic trends, it seems irrational for Republican legislators to push hard for legislation that is likely to broaden and harden Hispanic loyalty to the Democratic Party. On the most obvious level it is sacrificing long-term gain for short-term advantage.

For those Republican leaders who have pushed for legislation aimed at undocumented immigrants, it is easy to rationalize that they are not doing something that will hurt the party, believing instead that they are solving an important problem and that they are standing on principle. In addition, however, they are responding to the Outrage Industry. Both outrage media and advocacy groups push the GOP to sacrifice the long term for the short term as they have little stake in the long-term future of the Republican Party. When we asked the leader of an ideological group fighting against Sonia Sotomayor's nomination to the Supreme Court if his work might be pushing Hispanics away from the Republican Party, he replied tartly, "It's not my job to win elections."

Polling suggests that these Republican initiatives have not been a response to any growth in public antagonism toward immigration. Although voters voice concern about immigration, it is not a priority issue for most Americans. In Gallup's annual question about the most important problem facing the country, immigration garnered only 4 percent in 2011, tied at tenth place with "ethical/moral" decline.[56] And Americans' general views have changed only moderately during the past quarter of a century. The percentage of Americans who think the level of immigration should be increased has risen to 21 percent in 2012 from 7 percent in 1987. Those who want immigration decreased has dropped from a peak of 65 percent in 1993 to 35 percent in 2012.[57] In short, to the degree that there is a trend in public opinion, it has been a movement in *favor* of immigration.

The views of the general public, however, are at odds with those of conservative Republicans. Support for the Tea Party is highly correlated with anti-immigration attitudes.[58] As noted in the previous chapter, those who are favorably disposed toward the Tea Party score very high on racial resentment scales.[59] The conservative wing of the more conservative of our two parties provided a sufficiently large enough audience for outrage outlets and these media formulated provocative content that tapped this resentment.

For Republicans, a turning point came in 2007 when the Senate took up President George W. Bush's immigration reform plan. Supported by the business community, Bush chose a moderate approach, proposing a path to citizenship for those in the country without documentation, a guest worker program, and enhanced border security. Immediately, however, conservative outrage media took up the issue and pounded on the administration's bill with sustained ferocity. For the second quarter of 2007 conservative talk radio hosts devoted 16 percent of their entire airtime to the immigration issue. Republican Senator Trent Lott complained, "Talk radio is running America." In terms of cable TV coverage, the unremitting attack on the Bush legislation by CNN's Lou Dobbs stands out. Dobbs's nightly business show, which was otherwise a conventional news and analysis program, devoted 27 percent of its airtime to immigration during the three-month period when Congress was debating the issue in earnest.[60] Almost all of Dobbs's coverage was negative. Since he was generally viewed as a sober and thoughtful newsman, his ongoing outrage commentary attracted considerable attention as this was a significant departure from CNN's normally staid and middle-of-the-road approach.[61] His decision to emphasize immigration appeared to play well as his ratings climbed skyward, up 46 percent over the same period a year earlier.[62]

As we elaborate in the next section, we interviewed representatives of advocacy groups working on immigration on both the left and right of the political spectrum. Conservative advocacy groups, led by the Federation for American Immigration Reform (FAIR) and NumbersUSA, have been relentless in their attacks on undocumented immigration. These are large organizations with dozens of staff members and mailing lists in the millions. An executive from NumbersUSA told us in an interview that his organization flooded Congress with roughly 6 million faxes during the fight over the Bush plan. There is no way of confirming this number but the *New York Times*, a paper hardly given to hyperbole, concluded that NumbersUSA "doomed" the legislation with its advocacy and that it overwhelmed Congress with its communications.[63] The Bush plan was also a great boost for business at NumbersUSA. It raises virtually all of its money online and its email appeals struck gold by warning recipients of the catastrophe that would befall the country if action wasn't taken against illegal immigration. In the space of just a couple of years its paying membership grew from 12,000 to 180,000. Its spokesman told us that the Bush plan taught the organization how to "surf with the waves."

For all the high-minded talk about principle that we heard from both sides, immigration remains at its core an issue about race, and this is only thinly veiled in outrage venues, as well illustrated by the discourse about "anchor babies." Glenn Beck explained the concept of anchor babies to a TV audience this way: people "come over the border, have a baby here, and then you got a foot in the door."[64] The argument by Beck and others is that children who are born here but whose parents are illegal should not be granted automatic citizenship. One in twelve births in the United States are to offspring of undocumented residents so this is no small population.[65] Overturning birthright citizenship means altering the Fourteenth Amendment, an extremely unlikely development. Nevertheless, Republicans in Congress and outrage media managed to breathe new life into the issue.

In the wake of the Republicans' poor showing with Hispanics in 2012, many party leaders called for a reconsideration of the GOP's position on immigration. Because demographic patterns point toward a larger Hispanic vote in 2016 and a comparable drop in the proportion of non-Hispanic whites, growing its share of the Hispanic vote appears crucial to Republicans' chances of regaining the White House. Supporting immigration reform legislation could aid the party's efforts to build support among Hispanics.

No sooner had the call gone out among Republicans to reconsider their ruinous stand on immigration than the party's defeated candidate, Mitt Romney, said the reason he lost was because Barack Obama had given gifts to various constituencies. Specifically Romney said, "The Obama campaign was following the old playbook of giving a lot of stuff to groups that they hoped they could get to vote for them and be motivated to go out to the polls, specifically the African American community, the Hispanic community and young people."[66] Unlike his observation during the campaign in a private meeting with donors where he said 47 percent of the electorate was already against him, it's inconceivable that Romney could have thought his comments in this post-election phone call to hundreds of top donors would be kept confidential. Indeed, a reporter from the *Los Angeles Times* listened in to the call.

Romney's deliberate insult to black and Hispanic voters might be explained away as a bitter exit by a twice-defeated candidate with no future in the party. But he was repeating a meme that had already circulated widely in conservative outrage media. The day after the election Rush Limbaugh told his listeners that conservatives were beaten because "It's just very difficult to beat Santa Claus. It is practically impossible to beat Santa Claus. People are not going to vote against Santa Claus."[67] Fox's Bill O'Reilly interpreted the election in the same way, concluding: "there are 50 percent of the voting public who want stuff. They want things and who is going to give them things? President Obama. He knows it and he ran on it." As proof of his point, O'Reilly highlighted the huge Hispanic vote for Obama. O'Reilly also observed that the 2012 election marked the end of the "white establishment." "It's not a traditional America anymore," lamented O'Reilly.[68]

Bowing to electoral realities, in the spring of 2013 some leading Republicans in Congress began working with Democrats on immigration reform. Their hope, of course, was that successful bipartisan legislation would help the GOP appear friendly to Hispanics and begin a course by which the party could attract more Latino votes. The turnabout was not driven by Republican grassroots sentiment. Not surprisingly, opposition to a bipartisan accord was led by conservative talk radio hosts who knew their listeners' attitudes differed from the positions of Republicans in Congress calling for reform. The radio hosts did not spend as much time attacking the legislation as they did in 2007 but still devoted significant attention to the issue. Laura Ingraham averaged thirty-five minutes a show on immigration, Mark Levin fourteen, and Rush Limbaugh twelve.[69] Limbaugh frequently ridiculed Republicans for the illogic of helping more Hispanics become citizens—citizens who would then register to vote and cast those votes for Democrats. "It is suicide for the Republican Party to grant amnesty to however millions of illegals are in the country," Limbaugh told listeners. "Why would we agree to something the Democrats are salivating over?"[70]

OUTRAGE AS A LOBBYING STRATEGY

In considering how the Outrage Industry might influence party evolution and public policymaking, we wondered how portable this approach is in terms of actual Washington lobbying. Although the Tea Party has used an outrage strategy with great success, its methods cannot be assumed to be easily transferrable to other ideological organizations. The Tea Party is a unique force in American politics and is too close to the Republican Party to be assessed as strictly an interest group. Here we turn to the broader array of citizen groups organized as lobbies that try to sway policymakers.

The primary question asked here concerns the value of outrage to citizen groups. In terms of interest group behavior, do citizen group lobbyists use rhetoric and appeals designed to provoke anger when dealing with legislators and administrators? For those ideological organizations that employ a professional staff who do organizing, put on events, and directly lobby policymakers in face-to-face meetings, is outrage a viable strategy? Such behavior is clearly out of line with that of the business lobbies and professional associations that dominate the Washington interest group community. Research shows that an outrage approach would also stand apart from the tactics used by citizen groups that have long-term records of success in Washington. The environmental lobbies based there, for example, rely on conventional lobbying and generally avoid outrage.[71] Nevertheless, as we have seen with the Tea Party, violating the norms of convention may have value in galvanizing support and in gaining notoriety and respect from elected officials.

We sought to answer this question about strategy by analyzing the behavior of citizen groups actively working on issues that were being debated in Washington during the time of the 111th Congress (2009–10). We began by identifying issues rather than identifying groups so that we could examine the behavior of all citizen groups working on these matters. The goal was to understand the general pattern in areas where outrage might be used. We chose to examine lobbying around three issues: Sonia Sotomayor's Supreme Court nomination, the White House–backed surge in Afghanistan, and immigration reform. We selected these issues because there were ideological citizen groups actively lobbying policymakers in these areas. These issues evoked great passion in the populace. But inside

Washington, inside the Beltway, did citizen groups sound like Rush Limbaugh, or were they more modulated in tone?

The interviews we conducted along with other data collected indicated that inside the Beltway the approach of ideological lobbies tends to stop short of the kinds of outrage language identified in Chapter 2. We did find exaggeration, but the rhetoric rarely edged into outrage. While Rush Limbaugh called Sonia Sotomayor a "racist," the conservative judicial watch lobbies used more moderate language in describing her decision in an affirmative action case in New Haven.[72]

Among organizations working on immigration, the difference between advocacy organizations inside and outside the Beltway is stark. The goal of the Connecticut-based organization VDARE is reform of the nation's immigration laws. In terms of advocacy, VDARE's primary tactic is online dissemination of diatribes against those who disagree with nativist views. We asked a spokesman about the language VDARE used and he replied, "when the other side tries to make 'anchor babies' not politically correct, we ignore that ...they are trying to pull the wool over our eyes by changing the way we talk about things. Well, we're not going to back down on those things." When asked if VDARE communicates its concerns about immigration to the members of the Connecticut congressional delegation, the spokesman said dismissively, "We don't deal with legislators."

The organizations trying to stop American participation in the war in Afghanistan have also generally avoided outrage rhetoric. An exception is CODEPINK, which is known for heckling politicians and using disruptive tactics that result in the frequent arrest of participants. Other anti-war organizations like Veterans for Peace and Iraq Veterans Against the War have taken a decidedly less combative approach. Both these groups use the stature of their veterans to try to fashion credible anti-war messages. Michael McPherson, the director of Veterans for Peace, told us that as veterans their experiences are critical "in educating people face-to-face. Telling our stories is a huge part of what we do." The Iraq Veterans Against the War's "Winter Soldier Campaign" was designed to increase Americans' understanding of what is really going on in Afghanistan. They had 200 of their members tell firsthand stories of their experiences and then edited and collected them into a book.[73]

The anti-war interviewees all expressed exasperation with the lack of press coverage for their efforts.[74] Michael McPherson spoke of his frustration: "Jon Stewart did an interview on his show with Tea Baggers and a birther [but not us]. They talked about how important Glenn Beck was in making their movement grow. The coverage they've gotten is much more than we got when we had hundreds of thousands protesting in the streets. We got no coverage."

The liberal leaders we spoke to expressed near palpable frustration. Would a greater reliance on outrage have produced more coverage? The experience of CODEPINK suggests otherwise as its press coverage, while more extensive, threw an unfavorable light on the organization. During the first few months of the Occupy movement, the disparate groups across the country garnered enormous press coverage with their unusual tactics. The encampments brought a unique protest strategy to prominent downtown locations. This tactical innovation imbued the encampments with authenticity (in the form of originality), which journalists favor, explaining the difference between coverage of the Occupy encampments and efforts made by CODEPINK. Even with the encampments, coverage was most extensive when conflicts emerged between protesters and the police and/or municipal governments.

In terms of Washington lobbying, an outrage approach seems poorly suited to the needs of citizen groups that interact directly with policymakers. The organizations we observed, which were the citizen groups attracting the most attention from the mainstream press, were sharply ideological in their positions but measured in their rhetoric. The language of outrage could be found in Internet "groups," which were centered around websites with little other organizational presence. In the end, the value of outrage in advocacy is usually best suited for efforts outside the Beltway with tactics aimed at activating ideologues.

SYNERGY

While the Republican Party has been pulled further to the right by the Outrage Industry, the GOP's trajectory is also directly connected to the party's behavior prior to the emergence of a large outrage media sector or the rise of the Tea Party. This path is not a matter of destiny; strategically it makes more sense for the GOP to move more toward the center instead of shifting further right. We cannot predict the direction of the party in the years to come as parties can and do adapt. At some point, the Republicans may become the party of Hispanics just as the Democrats overcame internal division and became the party of civil rights and of African Americans. As it has evolved in recent years, though, the GOP has been influenced by the forceful presence of the Outrage Industry. Building on the ideological sorting that took place in the wake of the civil rights movement, the Outrage Industry has pushed the Republicans toward greater ideological purity, less willingness to compromise over middle ground with the Democrats, and less tolerance toward people from racial and ethnic minority groups.

It is easy to identify structural reasons to explain why conservative outrage sectors and the most conservative members of the GOP have exerted
such great influence. The primary system for nominations, the party's lack
of centralized national control, and the nature of fund-raising have all
worked to the advantage of conservative activists backed by the signaling
and monitoring of outrage media.

Beyond favorable structural conditions, the centrality of outrage in conservative politics is built upon the synergy produced by the interaction of
outrage media, Republican candidates and legislators, and conservative
activists. This collaboration is fueled by clear and powerful incentives to
cooperate. The outrage media need to extend the story of the day in the
Times or *Post* into powerful narratives absent in mainstream outlets. Those
storylines are validated by the actions and words of politicians and pundits. In turn, legislators, activists, ideological citizen groups, and the Tea
Party have an insatiable desire for the visibility offered by the media. At the
heart of this complementary incentive system is profit, broadly defined.
For cable and talk radio, ratings are presumably aided by having dynamic
guests who offer compelling storylines, whereas the guests benefit from
time on the public stage, which can lead to profits such as votes, political
support, job opportunities, and book deals. Former congressman Anthony
Weiner said it all rather succinctly when he would scream at his staff, "Why
the fuck am I not on MSNBC?"[75] This interaction and cooperation, built
around informal norms, has proven to be a powerful business model for
the outrage outlets and good for generating short-term publicity for pundits, candidates, and representatives, if not a healthy force in the longer-
term life of the GOP.

Conservative business lobbies, which avoid an outrage style approach,
benefit from the synergy that links the GOP, conservative media, and strident
advocacy groups. The pro-business, anti-regulatory mantra is interwoven
throughout this constellation of interests and institutions. Although business
is not always on the same page as the Outrage Industry—such as the need to
raise the debt ceiling, for example—it benefits from the provocative and
pointed messaging about the perils of an economy directed by liberals.

What is remarkable about the synergy generated by the Outrage Industry,
conservative interest groups, and the Republican Party is that it is working
against the long-term interest of the party. As the example of Hispanic
voters illustrates, white conservatives in the GOP and outrage media and
advocacy groups have found common cause on issues that push those voters
away. Perversely, short-term incentives produce this result. Candidates need
to win the next election, outrage advocacy groups need to work on what
constituents are currently angry about, and outrage media need to induce

their consumers to come back the next day. Hispanics do not constitute a significant cohort in Republican primaries, nor are they a major portion of conservative outrage media audiences. In the end, their value in the general election is sacrificed for more immediate needs. There is no powerful coordinating body to offset these short-term market forces.

We note that we have emphasized the synergy on the conservative side because these ties are far more extensive than on the left. On the liberal side of the equation, there is little talk radio, no equivalent of the Tea Party, and no media institution that approximates the centrality of Fox Cable News to conservatives. The party is pulled to the left by activists as it always has been, but change brought to the Democrats from outrage institutions appears far less significant. In this sense, it comes down to business. Synergy has developed much more on the right because there are larger audiences for conservative outrage programming on cable and radio.

In the end, the synergy on the conservative side derives from strong business incentives coinciding with political opportunity structures. There are common interests by multiple sectors in promoting the same message, enhancing and validating issues, stories, and candidates.

NOTES

1. See Matthew Levendusky, *The Partisan Sort* (Chicago: University of Chicago Press, 2009).
2. Jeffrey M. Jones, "Record-High 40% of Americans Identify as Independents in '11," Gallup Poll, January 9, 2012, http://www.gallup.com/poll/151943/Record-High-Americans-Identify-Independents.aspx, as of April 4, 2012.
3. Sean Theriault, *Party Polarization in Congress* (New York: Cambridge University Press, 2008), 30.
4. Nolan McCarty, Keith T. Poole, and Howard Rosenthal, *Polarized America* (Cambridge, MA: MIT Press, 2006), 24.
5. Joseph Bafumi and Michael C. Herron, "Leapfrog Representation and Extremism: A Study of American Voters and Their Members of Congress," *American Political Science Review* 104 (August 2010): 519.
6. Alan Abramowitz, *The Disappearing Center* (New Haven, CT: Yale University Press, 2010), 141.
7. See, for example, Seth Masket's analysis of California, *No Middle Ground* (Ann Arbor: University of Michigan Press, 2011).
8. On how polarization influences the actual operation of committees and the process of policy formulation, see Barbara Sinclair, "Spoiling the Sausage? How a Polarized Congress Deliberates and Legislates," in *Red and Blue Nation*, Vol. 2, ed. Pietro Nivola and David W. Brady (Washington, DC: Brookings Institution and the Hoover Institution, 2008), 55–87.
9. Sean Cockerham, "Idaho Rep. Raul Labrador Takes Tea Party Message to the Media," McClatchy Newspapers wire service, April 19, 2012, http://www.mcclatchydc.com/2012/04/18/145801/idaho-rep-raul-labrador-takes.html, as of April 20, 2012.

10. Geoffrey C. Layman, Thomas M. Carsey, John C. Green, Richard Herrera, and Rosalyn Cooperman, "Activists and Conflict Extension in American Party Politics," *American Political Science Review* 104 (May 2010): 324.

11. Kenneth Janda, "How About a Nice Sup of Tea," Northwestern University, n.d.

12. http://www.opensecrets.org/politicians/summary.php?cycle=2010&cid=N0002-7493&type=I; and http://www.opensecrets.org/politicians/summary.php?cid=N00027493&cycle=2012. Despite her enormous fundraising, she won only a narrow victory in 2012 and subsequently chose not to run for her seat in 2014.

13. http://www.opensecrets.org/politicians/summary.php?cycle=2010&type=I&cid=N00024809&newMem=N; and Paul Kane, "South Carolina's Wilson Rakes in $750,000 in Less than 48 Hours," *Washington Post*, September 11, 2009, http://voices.washingtonpost.com/capitol-briefing/2009/09/scs_wilson_rakes_in_750000_in.html, as of July 6, 2012.

14. R. Douglas Arnold, *The Logic of Congressional Action* (New Haven, CT: Yale University Press, 1990), 47.

15. R. Douglas Arnold, *Congress, the Press, and Political Accountability* (New York: Russell Sage Foundation; Princeton, NJ: Princeton University Press, 2004), 247.

16. Michelle Malkin, "Senate Switchboard: All Circuits Are Busy," *Michelle Malkin*, February 6, 2009, http://michellemalkin.com/2009/02/06/senate-switchboard-all-circuits-are-busy/; "Pen Pals," *Moonbattery*, February 7, 2009, http://www.moonbattery.com/archives/2009/02/pen_pals.html; and "Traitors," *Twilight's Last Gleaming*, February 6, 2009, http://www.twilightslastgleaming.com/traitors.htm, all as of January 25, 2013.

17. David Karol, *Party Position Change in American Politics* (New York: Cambridge University Press, 2009), 186–187.

18. James N. Druckman, "On the Limits of Framing Effects," *Journal of Politics* 63 (November 2001), 1041–1044.

19. Robert Draper, *Do Not Ask What Good We Do* (New York: Free Press, 2012), 245.

20. There is not a clear consensus on whether it was the freshmen elected in 2010 who drove the rebuke of Boehner forward. An incisive roll call analysis by the *New York Times* shows that it was the most conservative members of the House who were most likely to vote against the Republican leadership. This does not make the concerns of Tea Partiers back in the districts any less a factor, only that their views are most likely to resonate with those who were already very conservative. Jennifer Steinhauer, "G.O.P. Freshmen Not as Defiant as Reputation Suggests," *New York Times*, March 16, 2012, http://www.nytimes.com/2012/03/17/us/politics/house-freshmen-not-as-defiant-as-their-reputation-suggests.html, as of April 4, 2012. A somewhat different perspective is offered by Robert Draper in *Do Not Ask What Good We Do*. Draper's qualitative study was based on his following the behavior of sixteen members of the House of Representatives during the first year or so of the 112th Congress. In Draper's very close analysis of the votes that bedeviled Boehner, the freshmen appear to play a central role.

21. Associated Press wire copy, "GOP Tactics Draw Lowest Mark in New CBS Poll," July 19, 2011, http://www.vindy.com/news/2011/jul/19/gop-tactics-draw-lowest-mark-new-cbs-poll/?mobile; Erick Erickson, *RedState.com*, July 18, 2011, "If You Support Mitch McConnell, We Don't Support You," http://www.redstate.com/erick/2011/07/18/if-you-support-mitch-mcconnell-we-dont-support-you/; "Audio: Mark Levin Blasts 'Gang of Schmucks' Budget Deal," July 20, 2011, http://www.thehotjoints.com/2011/07/20/audio-mark-levin-blasts-gang-of-schmucks-budget-deal/ (site discontinued); "Beck Again Downplays Debt Crisis: 'There Is No

Default. Default Is a Red Herring,'" *Media Matters*, June 15, 2011, http://media-matters.org/mmtv/201107150005. All Internet entries as of July 30, 2011.

22. Rachel Weiner, "Boehner's South Carolina Problem," *Washington Post*, July 29, 2011, http://www.washingtonpost.com/blogs/the-fix/post/boehners-south-caro-lina-problem/2011/07/29/gIQAaXXHhI_blog.html, as of July 30, 2011.

23. Jake Sherman, John Bresnahan, and Jonathan Allen, "Boehner Builds Momentum," *Politico*, http://www.politico.com/news/stories/0711/60205.html, as of August 3, 2011.

24. What the Tea Party did get from this fight was a lowering in its approval rank-ings in polls. See Kate Zernike, "Poll Shows Negative View of Tea Party Is on the Rise," *New York Times*, August 6, 2011, http://www.nytimes.com/2011/08/05/us/politics/05teaparty.html, as of August 9, 2011.

25. Frank Newport, "Tea Party Supporters Oppose Debt Agreement, 68% to 22%," Gallup Poll, August 4, 2011, http://www.gallup.com/poll/148841/tea-party-sup-porters-oppose-debt-agreement.aspx, as of August 23, 2011.

26. "The Republicans: Many Possible Contenders Are Unknown," http://www.cbsnews.com/htdocs/pdf/poll_GOP_042111.pdf?tag=contentMain;contentBody, as of April 5, 2012.

27. The Baumgartner and Jones master codebook can be found at http://www.policy-agendas.org/page/topic-codebook. A bibliography of the ample literature using the policy agendas coding is located at http://www.policyagendas.org/biblio.

28. In terms of coverage, we wondered whether it might be that the issue of the day, while discussed initially, was not representative of the whole TV or radio show. Blog posts and columns tend to be about only a single subject. As the second issue discussed was also included in the database, it was possible to produce a comparable distribution to that in Table 7.1. The results were close to identical to those for the first issue discussed.

29. For examples from political communication, see Robert M. Entman, "Framing: Toward Clarification of a Fractured Paradigm," *Journal of Communication* 43 (December 1993): 51–58 and Dietram Scheufele, "Framing as a Theory of Media Effects," *Journal of Communication* 49 (March 1999): 103–122. For examples from a sociological perspective, see Todd Gitlin, *The Whole World Is Watching: Mass Media in the Making and Unmaking of the New Left* (Berkeley: University of California Press, 1980) and David A. Snow, R. Burke Rochford Jr., Steven K. Worden, and Robert D. Benford, "Frame Alignment Processes, Micromobilization, and Movement Participation," *American Sociological Review* 51 (August 1986): 464–481.

30. William H. Riker, *The Strategy of Rhetoric* (New Haven, CT: Yale University Press, 1996), 9.

31. William H. Riker, *The Art of Political Manipulation* (New Haven, CT: Yale University Press, 1986), ix.

32. Frank I. Luntz, *Words that Work* (New York: Hyperion, 2007).

33. Frank R. Baumgartner, Jeffrey M. Berry, Marie Hojnacki, David C. Kimball, and Beth L. Leech, *Lobbying and Policy Change* (Chicago: University of Chicago Press, 2009), 166–189.

34. Jim Rutenberg and Jackie Calmes, "False 'Death Panel' Rumor Has Some Familiar Roots," *New York Times*, August 14, 2009, at http://www.nytimes.com/2009/08/14/health/policy/14panel.html, as of August 8, 2011.

35. Kaiser Health Tracking Poll: July 2010, http://kaiserfamilyfoundation.files.word-press.com/2013/02/8084-t.pdf, as of June 4, 2013.

36. Brendan Nyhan and Jason Reifler, "When Corrections Fail: The Persistence of Political Misperceptions," *Political Behavior* 32 (June 2010): 303–330.

37. Rachel Alexander, "Democrats Faking Debt Ceiling Crisis in Order to Continue Irresponsible Spending," July 13, 2011, *Townhall*, July 13, 2011, http://townhall.com/columnists/rachelalexander/2011/07/13/democrats_faking_debt_ceiling_crisis_in_order_to_continue_irresponsible_spending, as of July 6, 2012.

38. "Population by Hispanic or Latino Origin and by Race for the United States: 2000 and 2010," *Overview of Race and Hispanic Origin: 2010*, US Census Bureau, March 2011, 4, http://www.census.gov/prod/cen2010/briefs/c2010br-02.pdf, as of August 10, 2011.

39. Data from US Census Bureau, American Community Survey, in *The New State of America*, Alma DDB, http://www.ddb.com/yellowpapers, as of August 10, 2011 (site discontinued).

40. Paul Taylor, "The Growing Electoral Clout of Blacks Is Driven by Turnout, Not Demographics," Pew Research Center, December 26, 2012, http://www.pewsocial-trends.org/2012/12/26/the-growing-electoral-clout-of-blacks-is-driven-by-turn-out-not-demographics/, as of December 28, 2012.

41. *The Latino Electorate in 2010: More Voters, More Non-Voters*, Pew Hispanic Center, April 26, 2011, 4, http://pewhispanic.org/reports/report.php?ReportID=141, as of August 10, 2011.

42. Taylor, "The Growing Electoral Clout."

43. For an *overview* of Hispanic opinion and partisan choice, see Marisa A. Abrajano and R. Michael Alvarez, *New Faces, New Voices* (Princeton: Princeton University Press, 2010), 35–73. On the values of Hispanics, see Deborah J. Schildkraut, *Americanism in the Twenty-First Century* (New York: Cambridge University Press, 2011).

44. Zoltan L. Hajnal and Taeku Lee, *Why Americans Don't Join the Party* (Princeton, NJ: Princeton University Press, 2011).

45. Surbhi Godsay, Amanda Nover, and Emily Kirby, *The Minority Youth Vote in the 2008 Presidential Election*, CIRCLE, Tisch College of Citizenship, Tufts University, October 2010, http://www.civicyouth.org/wp-content/uploads/2010/10/fs_race_09_final1.pdf, as of July 14, 2011.

46. *Profile of Latino Elected Officials in the United States and Their Progress since 1996*, NALEO Education Fund, n.d., http://www.naleo.org/downloads/NALEOFactSheet07.pdf, as of July 21, 2011.

47. Shaun Bowler, Stephen P. Nicholson, and Gary M. Segura, "Earthquakes and Aftershocks: Race, Direct Democracy, and Partisan Change," *American Journal of Political Science* 50 (January 2006): 146–159.

48. Adrian D. Pantoja, Ricardo Ramirez, and Gary M. Segura, "Citizens by Choice, Voters by Necessity: Patterns in Political Mobilization by Naturalized Latinos," *Political Research Quarterly* 54 (December 2001): 729–750.

49. Anne E. Kornblut and Spencer S.Hsu, "Arizona Governor Signs Immigration Bill, Reopening National Debate," *Washington Post*, April 24, 2010, http://www.washingtonpost.com/wp-dyn/content/article/2010/04/23/AR2010042301441.html, as of April 24, 2010.

50. Mark Hugo Lopez and Paul Taylor, *Latino Voters in the 2012 Election*, Appendix A, November 7, 2012, Pew Hispanic Center, http://www.pewhispanic.org/files/2012/11/2012_Latino_vote_exit_poll_analysis_final_11-09.pdf, as of December 28, 2012.

51. Melissa Weigand, "State by State Analysis," Outrage Industry Project, Tufts University, September, 2011.The states with the largest Hispanic populations (in descending order on the basis of Hispanic population) are New Mexico, Texas,

California, Arizona, Nevada, Florida, Colorado, New Jersey, New York, and Illinois. The ten other states we examined were Alabama, Georgia, Indiana, Kansas, Mississippi, North Carolina, Oklahoma, Oregon, South Carolina, and Utah.

52. This pattern seemed to hold across issue areas. See Louis Jacobson, "Welcome to the Tea Party," *State Legislatures* (September 2011): 12–15.

53. Pilar Marrero, "June Tracking Poll: Immigration Is a Critical Issue for Voters," Latino Decisions, June 10, 2011, http://latinodecisions.wordpress.com/2011/06/10/june-tracking-poll-immigration-is-a-critical-issue-for-voters/, as of August 9, 2011.

54. Anthony Downs, *An Economic Theory of Democracy* (New York: Harper, 1957). See also Jacob S. Hacker and Paul Pierson, *Off Center* (New Haven, CT: Yale University Press, 2005).

55. See Kathleen Bawn, Martin Cohen, David Karol, Seth Masket, Hans Noel, and John Zaller, "A Theory of Political Parties: Groups, Policy Demands and Nominations in American Politics," *Perspectives on Politics* 10 (September 2012): 571–597.

56. "Budget Rises as Most Important Problem to Highest Since '96," Gallup Poll, April 13, 2011, http://www.gallup.com/poll/147086/budget-rises-most-important-problem-highest.aspx, as of August 9, 2011.

57. "Americans More Positive about Immigration," Gallup Poll, June 16, 2012, http://www.gallup.com/poll/155210/Americans-Positive-Immigration.aspx?version=print, as of December 28, 2012. Even among Republicans there is no majority for an anti-illegal immigrant policy response. When offered a choice between allowing those undocumented "a chance to keep their jobs and eventually apply for legal status" or deporting them "back to their native country," Republican respondents are evenly split. *Washington Post*-Kaiser Family Foundation Poll, *Washington Post*, August 19, 2012, http://www.washingtonpost.com/page/2010-2019/WashingtonPost/2012/08/18/National-Politics/Polling/question_6370.xml?uuid=wGKBHumEEeGXOe75nF-yhQ, as of August 21, 2012.

58. Gary C. Jacobson, "The President, the Tea Party, and Voting Behavior in 2010," paper delivered at the annual meeting of the American Political Science Association, Seattle, September, 2011.

59. Jacobson, "The President, the Tea Party, and Voting Behavior in 2010"; Alan I. Abramowitz, "Grand Old Tea Party," in *Steep: The Precipitous Rise of the Tea Party*, ed. Lawrence Rosenthal and Christine Trost (Berkeley: University of California Press, 2012), 195–211; and Christopher Parker, "2010 Multi-state Survey on Race & Politics," University of Washington Institute for the Study of Ethnicity, Race, & Sexuality," http://depts.washington.edu/uwiser/racepolitics.html, as of June 3, 2013.

60. "Immigration: Did Talk Hosts Kill the Bill?," PEW Research Center's Project for Excellence in Journalism, August 20, 2007, http://www.journalism.org/node/7174#1, as of August 16, 2011.

61. Dobbs's continuing campaign against illegal immigration put CNN in an uncomfortable position. He attracted viewers but his one-sided treatment of the issue fit poorly with the network's position in the marketplace. Under pressure from CNN executives Dobbs resigned, apparently with a generous severance package. After a period Dobbs joined the Fox Business network in March, 2011, and was given a 7:00 PM show.

62. Schildkraut, *Americanism in the Twenty-First Century*, 7.

63. Jason DeParle, "The Anti-Immigration Crusader," *New York Times*, April 17, 2011, http://www.nytimes.com/2011/04/17/us/17immig.html?pagewanted=all&_r=0, as of December 28, 2012.

64. http://mediamatters.org/mmtv/201005060042, as of April 5, 2012.

65. Miriam Jordan, "Illegals Estimated to Account for 1 in 12 U.S. Births," *Wall Street Journal*, August 12, 2010, http://online.wsj.com/article/SB10001424052748704216 804575423641955803732.html?mod=WSJEUROPE_hpp_MIDDLESecondNews, as of December 28, 2012.

66. Maeve Reston, "Romney Attributes Loss to 'Gifts' Obama Gave to Minorities," *Los Angeles Times*, November 15, 2012, http://articles.latimes.com/2012/nov/15/nation/la-na-romney-donors-20121115, as of December 28, 2012.

67. *Rush Limbaugh Show*, November 7, 2012.

68. "Bill O'Reilly: 'The White Establishment Is Now the Minority,'" *Fox Nation*, November 7, 2012, http://nation.foxnews.com/bill-oreilly/2012/11/07/bill-o-reilly-white-establishment-now-minority, as of December 28, 2012.

69. Dan Balz, "Rubio's High-Stakes Push for Immigration Reform," *Washington Post*, May 11, 2013, http://articles.washingtonpost.com/2013-05-11/politics/39178917_1_marco-rubio-immigration-reform-rubio-s/2, as of June 4, 2013.

70. *Rush Limbaugh Show*, April 23, 2013.

71. Jeffrey M. Berry, *The New Liberalism* (Washington, DC: Brookings Institution, 1999).

72. Andy Barr, "Rush Limbaugh: Sonia Sotomayor a 'Reverse Racist,' Hack," *Politico*, May 26, 2009, http://www.politico.com/news/stories/0509/22983.html, as of December 31, 2012; and *Ricci v. DeStafano*, 557 U.S.___(2009).

73. Iraq Veterans Against the War and Aaron Glantz, *Winter Soldier* (Chicago: Haymarket Books, 2008).

74. See Sarah Sobieraj, *Soundbitten* (New York: New York University Press, 2011).

75. Draper, *Do Not Ask What Good We Do*, 53.

CHAPTER 8

The Future of Outrage

CONFLICTING METRICS OF SUCCESS

We have shown that outrage-based opinion is abundant because it has proven to be lucrative in a cluttered, competitive, and largely unregulated media space. Virulent, distorted, and demeaning political analysis appears with remarkable regularity in cable news analysis shows and the most widely syndicated political talk radio programs, is common in the most highly trafficked political blogs (although slightly less so than in television and radio), and it is even appearing regularly in the writing of columnists whose work appears in highly regarded conventional newspapers. The genre is successful not only because its dramatic content and charismatic hosts draw us in but also because the dominant format resonates with our contemporary popular and political culture by capitalizing on our interest in celebrities, cynicism, familiarity with reality television, and fear of discussing political issues openly in our communities. It has grown with particular vigor on the right and plays a considerably greater role in conservative politics than on the left where the industry has been slower to develop and has had less consistent success. On the supply side, this is an outgrowth of Rush Limbaugh's early success and producers' tendency to replicate commercially successful formulas. On the demand side, we find conservative audiences hungrier for such programming as they are more distrustful of the news media and perceive the world as hostile to their political views, increasing the value of these like-minded spaces.

Although this new incivility makes many uncomfortable, as social scientists we have more of a mixed response. We conclude the book by reflecting on the social and political implications of the genre's success, examining the public response to outrage, assessing efforts that have been made to curtail this type of speech, and offering a few recommendations to promote healthier political discourse.

The Expansion of the Public Sphere

The contours of the genre have been shaped by economic rather than democratic imperatives, but if democratic health guided our political opinion media, we might very well seek some of the same attributes found in outrage. The expansion of space for political dialogue and the broader range of options contribute to a more robust political public sphere. There are more voices talking in new ways about public issues and these conversations are accessible—unlike the analysis available in monthly news magazines, these blogs and programs are readily available at little or no cost. Freed from the perceived obligation to cover all current events, outrage platforms are also able to give extended attention to topics of interest to their viewers. What's more, they are colorful and entertaining, engaging tens of millions of viewers, listeners, and readers, increasing their interest in politics as well as their likelihood of political involvement (as discussed in Chapter 2).

As a genre, outrage has made forms of political expression, such as emotion, humor, and the sharing of personal narratives commonplace when they have traditionally been unwelcome in the context of news and news analysis. We have always had irreverent political commentary—the *Onion*, political cartoons, *Saturday Night Live*, stand-up comedy, the *Daily Show*, and the *Colbert Report* come immediately to mind—but it has been largely walled off from news networks and newspapers. Network news may include witty banter between hosts during transitions, but political content has traditionally been communicated with staid neutrality, and newspapers relegate more spirited talk and humor to the opinion and comic pages. In contrast, outrage transgresses the lines between fact, analysis, and opinion. There is an integrity to this transgression; conventional news has presented them as divisible, when story selection, sources, photographs, and editing have always (and necessarily) introduced subjectivity and offered views of the world that reflect professional biases and demands of news routines. Related to this, the fact that conventional news outlets work actively to seek neutrality means that it can be difficult for viewers and readers to envision the implications of current events and policy proposals. The impact of immigration reform, a troop surge, or falling off the "fiscal cliff" can be difficult to discern when the focus is on facts and developments. Turning to someone you feel shares your political values for an analysis of a current event can be useful. For democracy to function well, voters need to be relatively abreast of current affairs, understand the implications of their choices, and be motivated to go to the polls. Some might argue that outrage—as an addition to the political media space—may help on all counts.

A diverse political media environment is critical to democratic health. Unfortunately, while the growth of cable news analysis programming and political talk radio have unquestionably provided more choices, until recently outrage (and political opinion more broadly) was almost exclusively the arena of white men, particularly on television. MSNBC has made some noteworthy strides in this regard, bringing on Rachel Maddow in 2008, Al Sharpton in 2011, and Melissa Harris-Perry in 2012. Talk radio has a longer tradition of white women and people of color on air, but the most widely syndicated hosts remain disproportionately white and male. Of the twenty-one top hosts (there is a tie for audience size) with the largest audiences, nineteen are white men and two are white women.[1] We are unable to assess the demographic composition of top political bloggers, but perhaps they represent a greater diversity of voices. Nevertheless, political opinion media using public interest and democratic outcomes as a metric of success rather than advertising revenues would be more inclusive.

Not only would an ideal political opinion media include a broader range of people, it would also include a greater diversity of political perspectives. Public discourse would benefit from the voices of those who are less well represented in our governing bodies, such as those sympathetic to or a part of larger third parties such as the Green Party, the Constitution Party, or the Reform Party. Instead, virtually all top hosts and bloggers share views compatible with those at the margins of the Democratic or (more often) the Republican Party, although there is some representation of Libertarian perspectives (for example, Allahpundit, who blogs at *Hot Air*). Given the economic imperatives that support the industry, these omissions are not at all surprising as the number of potential viewers and listeners for less prominent viewpoints is small. More surprising is the fact that there are no centrist or moderate voices in outrage media, as the potential audience is large, and given the state of bipartisanship and the Republican shift toward greater conservatism, such a host should have plenty to be outraged about.

Beyond the overrepresentation of white men and the narrow range of political perspectives, when we look at outrage media we also see little diversity in communicative style. As we explained in Chapter 1, outrage is a genre with recognizable attributes. It is formulaic from the opening monologue and the segment structure to the forms of critique and limited presence of guests on TV and callers on radio. They are nothing if not predictable. This is something evinced beautifully in political satire programming (discussed later). The distinctions between outrage programs are superficial. Even what Jacobs and Townsley call the "dueling host" format (e.g., *Hannity & Colmes*, *Crossfire*), a former variant of outrage, has become nearly extinct in the interest of sticking to the blueprint for ratings success.[2] There is a bit more internal diversity in style among top blogs—but primarily in volume of outrage and preference for particular variants (e.g., mockery and belittling versus ad hominem attacks and conspiracy theories) rather than in the format.

In essence, these programs and blogs do expand the political public sphere, and many find that they make political information more entertaining than other formats. The playfulness, sense of intimacy between viewer and host, colorful antics, snark, and intensity are engaging in unprecedented ways. If the literature in Chapter 2 on the impact of political incivility extends to outrage, we have reason to believe that outrage audiences may become more eager to participate in political life and vote in elections. They also help some who feel politically isolated find comfortable spaces to hear perspectives on current events that reflect their values. These are positive developments, but the expansion of the public sphere has been uneven and the fact that this particular type of political talk has expanded so dramatically also presents some concerns worth taking seriously.

Outrage and Democratic Life

For many happy producers and devoted fans, outrage is invigorating, but our research suggests it may pose a threat to some of our most vital democratic practices. At the individual level, outrage discourse may undercut our tolerance of other views and promote misunderstandings about public issues. At the institutional level, outrage is working to stigmatize compromise and bipartisanship, and undercutting the political prospects of more moderate voices. We explore these concerns here, and then turn to the anxiety and resistance coming from other quarters.

As audience members, we interact differently with the media we encounter, including outrage. The interpretations we make are shaped and reshaped by our own knowledge and experiences, through discussion with friends and family, and by other sources of information that we find valuable. As part of the cultural landscape, our media diet informs what we see as common sense, what and who we see as important, and the things we consider particularly desirable and objectionable. Mass media make up one of several social forces that shape our worldviews and personal choices. In this context, participation in outrage-based publics, depending on the extent of our involvement and the degree to which our experiences in these publics reflect our experiences in other contexts, may shape the way we see ourselves, other people, and our social institutions.

When outrage hosts vilify and belittle the people with whom we disagree and inflate our own sense of moral righteousness, different perspectives on the role of government in addressing public issues are inflated from policy preferences into litmus tests for human decency. This slippage between the critique of ideas and the critique of those holding the ideas likely limits our openness to other perspectives and the people who hold them. Perceiving others as malicious and inept undoubtedly makes cross-cutting political conversations and collaborations even more difficult than they already are. And fanning the flames of intolerance and distrust is unlikely to lead to social harmony.

We are also concerned that chronic misrepresentative exaggeration and conspiracy theories obscure rather than illuminate political issues (as we saw in the health care debates), as does the focus on unimportant details in the interest of ideological one-upmanship. As entertainers and analysts, outrage personalities have no journalistic obligation to see that pressing issues of the day are addressed thoroughly; that is not their job. But whether or not it is their obligation, a healthy democracy requires an informed citizenry, and their actions may work to misinform rather than illuminate. The combination of ideological emphases, omissions, and exaggerations used for narrative effect, coupled with the relentless and often wholesale condemnation of conventional news media (and often of academic research and scientific studies) is a concerning mix. The outcome, as we see in our respondents, are fans who distrust the *New York Times* but see Glenn Beck as a reliable source of information in a sea of politically motivated bias.

We also have concerns about the impact of outrage media on our political institutions. Although a high level of partisanship can be expected in our system of government, such behavior has typically coexisted with a significant measure of bipartisanship in Congress. But the measures of party unity for Congress suggest that bipartisanship is in decline. More voices of moderation are desperately needed in Congress. With divided control of the federal government common, more moderate voices might help our obstacle-laden legislative process become more responsive to the problems we face as a nation.[3]

Despite the general public's preference for compromise, it has become a dirty word to ideologues on both sides of the political spectrum, fueled by pressure from outrage media. Some candidates even tout their unwillingness to compromise as a badge of honor, as we have seen in several primary campaigns. As noted in Chapter 6 Indiana Republican Richard Mourdock's 2012 campaign against incumbent Senator Richard Lugar was centered around Mourdock's promise not to compromise as Lugar had been doing throughout his career. Pressed by reporters on this seemingly exaggerated promise, Mourdock pushed back, saying: "We are at that point where one side or the other has to win this argument. One side or the other will dominate."[4] The politics of anger feed the belief that someday the American public will come to its senses and move decisively to the correct ideological pole. And it is the Outrage Industry that trumpets this vision.[5]

The nation needs leaders open to bipartisan coalitions comfortable with compromise, understanding that if both sides stand rigidly on principle, government becomes dysfunctional. Compromise is essential to good government. In *The Spirit of Compromise* Gutmann and Thompson write, "Rhetoric makes a difference. How politicians describe the substance of the proposals they oppose and the motives of the colleagues proposing them affects the possibility of mutual respect."[6] The long partnership of Orrin Hatch (R-Utah) and Ted Kennedy (D-Mass.) in the Senate is just one illustration of what is possible. Neither became a moderate in his overall approach to public policy, but both helped to craft moderate legislation nurtured in a bipartisan process. They represented no golden era of moderation in American politics but they created cooperation within the partisan environment of their day.

Today the voices of moderation among legislative leaders are few and far between. As we noted in earlier chapters, the party primary system for legislative nominations created incentives for ideological purity among candidates, and outrage media has exacerbated the pressure. Rush Limbaugh was explicit in telling his listeners to vote as conservatively as possible, suggesting a rule of thumb: "The Limbaugh Rule: You got a liberal or RINO or a conservative, you vote conservative. Per-i-od! Exclamation point. That's the Limbaugh Rule."[7] And RINO is not a difficult label to earn; Rush Limbaugh called Incumbent Senator Bob Bennett, who lost his seat, a RINO despite his 91 percent conservative voting record in 2010.[8]

Some candidates who have dared to work with the opposition (including Orrin Hatch) have survived ideological challenges, but incumbents today can take nothing for granted when it comes to primaries. A few states, notably California, have adopted a blanket or "jungle" primary where the top two candidates (regardless of party) face off in the general election. It's too soon to know if such an electoral system is more likely to produce moderate legislators. One reason to be skeptical is that a blanket primary in a district that leans ideologically one way or the other can simply produce two candidates at one pole who campaign on the basis of who is most pure and uncompromising. What we do know is that ideological purists do not reflect the political preferences of the public.

RESISTANCE, INDUSTRY LIMITS, AND THE FUTURE OF OUTRAGE

For the reasons just described, we find outrage worrisome, and we are not alone. In spite or perhaps because of the large audiences enjoyed by outrage-based programs and blogs, the new incivility has not gone unchallenged. Alongside the enthusiastic fans, outrage has strident opponents, and others with more metered voices express unease with the tenor of American political discourse. Most critics are concerned with political or democratic outcomes, but as we have argued in this book, economic interests, the media landscape, and the regulatory climate are the forces that have driven the industry's growth. Changes in these structures, rather than complaints about discrimination, concerns about civility, or demands for bipartisanship, will most likely dictate the trajectory of the genre. In the sections that follow, we examine pockets of resistance, the limits the industry is facing, and the trends we anticipate in the future.

Not Everyone Loves Outrage

Ideologically driven media watchdog groups offer constant pushback against outrage-based content. Liberal organizations FAIR (Fairness and Accuracy in Reporting) and Media Matters for America monitor news and political opinion media, attempting to catch conservatives making statements that they find offensive, believe to be inaccurate, or consider otherwise incriminating. At the same time, conservative stalwarts AIM (Accuracy in Media) and the Media Research Center hold vigil for the right, combing political media for liberal bias, exaggerations, and missteps. Yet their noble mission statements touting the importance of journalistic integrity downplay the partisan nature of their surveillance, and belie the way their drumbeat of indignation often contributes to rather than cools the heated rhetoric we describe. While these groups identify outrage incidents, extending the discussion and in many cases offering valuable corrections, they regularly present the incidents using the same outrage techniques described in Chapter 2.[9] Their "gotcha" orientation often decontextualizes the excerpts they highlight and wraps them with mockery, name-calling, belittling, and misrepresentative exaggeration. For example, Media Matters welcomed 2013 with a list of the "10 Dumbest Things Fox Said about Climate Change in 2012."[10] More thematically, they create villains in ways quite similar to the outrage hosts themselves. First and foremost, these watchdog organizations function to provide like-minded audiences with the tools they need to discredit the voices they find objectionable. What's more, their selective presentation ignores similar behaviors of their political compadres, ultimately serving less as meaningful democratic correctives than as entities waging and defending ideological assaults. Such efforts are valuable to those looking to fortify their sense that their team is good and the opposing team is misguided, but it does not represent a meaningful effort to resist outrage. Indeed, they create more of it.

There have, however, been more earnest pockets of opposition to outrage rhetoric. Several prominent eruptions of public dismay have emerged in the form of vocal opposition, mediation efforts, and in some cases boycotts against politicians and political media operatives who have been seen as pressing the bounds of social acceptability.

Public Unease

Although the Outrage Industry has been churning out uncivil material for decades, public concern about the tenor of American politics began to swell during the 2008 campaign season when political vitriol became more visible in mainstream politics. There were reports of political T-shirts bearing the slogan "Sarah Palin is a Cunt" and of rowdy McCain supporters shouting insults about Obama from the crowd. Vice-presidential candidate Sarah Palin offered her own brand of outrage from the podium, saying candidate Barack Obama had been "palling around with terrorists." In spring 2009, the news and opinion circuits showcased the acrimonious health care town hall meetings, and 2010 began with Congressman Joe Wilson yelling "You lie!" at President Obama during his State of the Union address.

But anxieties about incivility took a more serious turn in the wake of Jared Loughner's 2010 attempted assassination of Congresswoman Gabrielle Giffords, an act which took the lives of six bystanders and wounded

others, including Giffords herself.[11] Many attributed the violence to the
increase in ugly political rhetoric, and a great deal of speculation ensued
about a graphic on Sarah Palin's website that depicted crosshairs over targeted Democratic districts, including Giffords's. Representative Bill Pascrell
Jr., a Democrat from New Jersey, told one reporter: "There's an aura of
hate, and elected politicians feed it; certain people on Fox News feed it."
Former Democratic Senator Gary Hart also pointed a finger at political
rhetoric, saying that references to political opponents as "enemies" that
need to be "eliminated" leads to the kind of violence that occurred in
Tucson. And President Obama called for "a more civil and honest public
discourse."[12] A causal link between this new incivility and the violence in
Arizona is murky at best and there is certainly no scholarly research that
establishes this connection. Yet the public perception that name-calling
and vilification in political media have gone too far erupted in the aftermath of the shootings. Jon Stewart and Stephen Colbert tapped into the
zeitgeist with their well-attended "Rally to Restore Sanity and/or Fear" on
the National Mall late in 2010.

National figures and laypeople regularly express dismay when outrage-
based remarks that normally go unnoticed trickle into the mainstream
news media (for example, when Ann Coulter called President Obama a
"retard" in late 2012), but the rumblings of discontent usually fail to get
the kind of national attention wrought by the Arizona shootings and diffuse in a matter of days.[13] The fleeting nature of this kind of public condemnation, then, rarely has an impact on revenues for programs, salaries for
hosts, or speaking engagements and book deals for freelance provocateurs.
And unless advertisers are rattled, such shaking heads certainly don't
bother producers or hosts who use controversy by design. Since the incentives for outrage are primarily economic, calls for "more civil and honest
public discourse" fail to chip away at the structural foundations of outrage
we have outlined. Indeed, while they create space for valuable conversations about productive communication, such flare-ups inadvertently
embolden the very types of speech they seek to restrain—as a form of free
advertising and by rallying the fan base.

Ambassadors of Civility

Although incivility was presumed to be at the root of Loughner's attack,
many responded by focusing on promoting more civil dialogue rather than
by trying to stop outrage-based speech. Most visibly, former presidents
George H. W. Bush and Bill Clinton joined forces to launch the National

Institute for Civil Discourse (NICD) at University of Arizona. The nonpartisan center focuses on advocacy and research aimed at policy, with an eye toward improving the "national conversation" in keeping with First Amendment principles. The INSTITUTE has a board of high-profile political leaders, many who speak publicly on this issue. Scholars affiliated with NICD have generated research briefs, reports, and articles on civility and incivility, and in the past the institute has been involved in the community, promoting healthy political discourse, via seminars for Arizona state legislators and for key leaders at the National Press Club.[14] Their work has focused on issues such as negative campaigning, political polarization, and civility online. These efforts do not target outrage purveyors per se but rather focus on elected officials and candidates as well as laypeople, asking them to be more respectful in their communication, particularly with those whose views differ from their own. NICD's newly created website, your-wordscount.org, for example, seeks to channel the feelings of anger, frustration, shame, and worry (the very sentiments articulated and rearticulated in outrage media) visible in public opinion polls into positive civic engagement such as suggesting that readers volunteer with nonpartisan voter turnout groups, gather more facts (via their publications and blog), and seek opportunities to participate in public discussion of political issues.

The same year NICD was formed, the Center for Civil Discourse was founded at the University of Massachusetts at Boston with a grant from the National Endowment for the Humanities. The Center is "organized around the central principle that open, fair and truthful debate, characterized by respect for opposing viewpoints is essential to a healthy democracy. The Center's mission is to advance the values of respectful discourse and to call on Americans to embrace civility and reject demagoguery in government, media and our personal lives."[15] Their work to date has involved hosting a national forum on "Civility and American Democracy" featuring a diverse group of academics and columnists, and future plans include a series of public debates (among public intellectuals, rather than laypeople) designed to focus on substantive richness and the representation of diverse points of view rather than confrontation or winning.

The NICD and Center for Civil Discourse join other entities formed in recent years to promote civility. Kansas State University has an Institute for Civic Discourse and Democracy; Marymount College has a program to nurture "Intentional Conversation;" Johns Hopkins has a Civility Institute; the University of Tennessee-Knoxville has a Civility and Community initiative, and California State-San Marcos has a Civility Campaign. These institutes broaden public discussion about incivility and civility, promote meaningful dialogue in the spaces where they invest their resources, and serve as a telling barometer measuring our comfort with political talk in the United States, but they are not attempting to rein in Rush Limbaugh or Mike Malloy. Even if this were their goal, their efforts do not target the political-economic underpinnings of the industry that we have identified.

The Satire Circuit

The outrage personalities take themselves very seriously. This isn't to say there isn't laughter—most hosts and bloggers love a good laugh at the expense of their nemeses—but at the end of the day these personalities present themselves as valiant patriots for "truth," easily disgusted by those who might trample on the Constitution, civil rights, or the people who are the heart of this great nation. Although political satire is not new, Jon Stewart and Stephen Colbert have made it their bread and butter, drawing devoted fans who also happen to be younger, more affluent, and more highly educated than Comedy Central had ever hoped to attract. The Outrage Industry has provided the *Daily Show with Jon Stewart* and the *Colbert Report* with an endless font of inspiration and fodder for their writers.

In addition to highlighting what he and his writers see as the general buffoonery of politicos and the news media system that they feel enables them, Stewart lampoons outrage. His most famous lash-out was probably his visit to CNN's *Crossfire* in 2004 when he blinded-sided co-hosts Paul Begala and Tucker Carlson by castigating the program as performance-based, ratings-hungry journalism. Stewart repeatedly suggested that the fiery conflict-based program amplified the strategic misinformation proffered by politicos rather than taking advantage of their unique opportunity to "hold their feet to the fire". Stewart called them "disingenuous." Said Stewart, "You're doing theater, when you should be doing debate....What you do is not honest. What you do is partisan hackery...you have a responsibility to the public discourse, and you fail miserably."[16] It was a lengthy and uncomfortable exchange; Carlson was particularly defensive and threw similar accusations back at Stewart, who asked if CNN was looking to Comedy Central as a model for political reportage.

The *Crossfire* episode was unique in that Stewart offered critique with a (mostly) straight face. The *Daily Show* uses humor as its surgical tool. Melding a sharp eye for irony with a pastiche of excerpts from other media, Stewart's satire most frequently targets two types of outrage not addressed in the *Crossfire* visit: misrepresentative exaggeration and conflagration (depicting minor issues as scandals or crises). His predilection for disrobing these techniques was well illustrated during "Rumble 2012," in which he and Bill O'Reilly debated on Pay Per View. Stewart called Fox News an "alternate reality" and suggested that the Fox bubble makes problem solving in the United States difficult. Later, Stewart pronounced, "I have come here tonight to plead to the Mayor of Bullshit Mountain [gesturing toward O'Reilly] ...talk to your people."[17] Stewart had previously referred to Fox News as Bullshit Mountain in a monologue about the network's reframing of candidate Mitt Romney's "47 percent" remark captured by a hidden camera at a fundraising event during the 2012 campaign. The moniker resurfaced in several subsequent episodes of the *Daily Show* and repeatedly in the debate with O'Reilly. During the event, Stewart also leaned into the network for being misinformative saying, "any time you run an organization where more people believe the president is a Muslim than believe in evolution, that's a problem."[18]

Jon Stewart takes pleasure in pointing a finger at outrage, and his protégé Stephen Colbert goes a step further, in character, parodying an outrageous host himself. The Colbert Report turns its namesake into a satirical political opinion host, who conducts interviews (on and off show), with nary a wink. Colbert presents himself as resolutely "independent" (unbiased in his hatred of all things Liberal), narcissistic, jingoistic, and enamored with his own ability to manipulate guests into revealing their true nature through absurd rhetorical gymnastics that make clear the buffoon is the host, not the entrapped respondent. It is the genre-fication of outrage that allows the show to work. The cult of personality, mise-en-scéne, self-aggrandizing certainty bolstered by misinformation, and use of logical fallacies to establish "facts" would not be funny if the template were not so firmly entrenched in cable news analysis programs. The show's most direct jab at this genre emerges in his suspicion of "so-called facts," disgust with the "lamestream" media, and celebration of "truthiness," which he defined in the pilot episode as "the quality by which one purports to know something emotionally or instinctively, without regard to evidence or intellectual examination."[19]

Some might argue that the satire shows are themselves outrageous—mockery, belittling, and the use of insulting language are the mainstay of both programs—and like outrage programming, these shows are personality-centered and engaging. We see them as fundamentally different. These are programs that are deeply engaged with the genre, but not themselves a part of it. They draw on the material produced in the outrage industry to unmask it. What's more, the *Daily Show* and *Colbert Report* are on Comedy Central, not a news network, and don't purport to be journalism. As Jon Stewart reminded Tucker Carlson, "You're on CNN. The show that leads into me is puppets making crank phone calls."[20]

In short, we see that not everyone is as enthusiastic about outrage as the fans and producers. Yet in spite of these various kinds of resistance to outrage discourse—parody, public condemnation of political vitriol, efforts to teach civility, and finger pointing carried out by ideologically based media watchdog groups—the Outrage Industry appears unfazed. Rush Limbaugh claims to be many things, but he does not strike us as someone seeking to please those who dislike what he has to say or how he says it, particularly since outrage hosts present themselves as fighting for the underdogs. The strategies we've described here don't strike at the foundation of the industry.

THE LIMITS OF OUTRAGE

As we showed in Chapter 1, the Outrage Industry and the genre it has established are the products of a media landscape shaped by the heavy hands of regulatory, technological, economic, and cultural conditions rather than a simple reflection of public political opinions and priorities. Shifts in these arrangements are what we would expect to yield shifts in the industry. Indeed, the industry is dependent upon these structural and cultural conditions. But where are the limits? What are the elements with the greatest potential to introduce change? While we have little reason to imagine that there will be regressive regulatory or technological changes, the economic fruits of the industry hinge on keeping advertisers pleased with their ability to attract desirable audiences.

Boycotts and Advertiser Anxieties

As described in earlier chapters, on some occasions advocacy groups have coordinated boycotts in response to outrage rhetoric. Rather than threatening to take their eyes and ears away from the offending host or writer, these boycotts are directed at advertisers. Activists threaten to stop buying their products or services unless they withdraw support from the offending program or publication. This presents a problem for advertisers on two levels. Short term, a boycott can prove costly if consumers stay away. But it is the longer term risk of rebranding that makes advertisers most uneasy. Brands represent marketers' attempt to link their company, product, or service with a specific set of meanings, ideas, people, or values that they feel will attract customers. Savvy activists recognize that these meanings are arbitrarily linked and often only tenuously maintained. As a result, some activism has tried to shift the meaning of various brands. In the late 1990s, for example, global justice activists attempted to associate sweatshops with the Nike swoosh. In the outrage arena, the risk is that an advertiser could be accused, of example, of supporting a racist, or a socialist, or a homophobe. These are undesirable meanings and may lead an advertiser to withdraw from a program.

Whether boycotts are an effective strategy is another question.[21] They are difficult to sustain over time, and maintaining the involvement required to generate meaningful pressure requires more resources than are available to most advocacy groups. The call for radio stations to drop Michael Savage's show after he made a series of egregious racial statements bore fruit in the short run as some outlets dropped him from their programming. Over time the show recovered and prior to his hiatus from radio in 2012, he trailed only Limbaugh and Hannity in the national ratings. On the other hand, as noted in Chapter 4, Color of Change's effort against Glenn Beck was a clear victory for the civil rights group as Fox was left with few sponsors willing to be identified with Beck, ultimately leading the network to part ways with the host.

The campaign against Rush Limbaugh in the wake of the Sandra Fluke controversy also had a considerable impact on the national sponsors of this program, with many quickly dropping their advertisements. Only a couple of stations dropped Limbaugh's program, but as we detail in Chapter 4, the advertising market for the show weakened in the wake of the call to boycott its sponsors. Although some new advertisers were recruited, the price the show commands has softened (at least for the time being) and it is unclear whether all of the advertising slots are filled. The sharp drop in earnings by Dial, Cumulus, and Clear Channel since the Fluke episode are linked at least in part to the advertising climate for talk radio that emerged in the wake of the advertiser boycott. The longer term impact on Limbaugh and talk radio more broadly remains to be seen. The market for conservative talk radio programming may be saturated and the advertising market might not return to its previous health until the number of political talk stations is reduced.

Conservative groups have also occasionally used boycotts. In 2012, the Media Research Center and a handful of bloggers pressured advertisers and executives at Comcast in an effort to get Ed Schultz off the air for referring to conservative talker Laura Ingraham as a slut; the group argued that Schultz was guilty of an offense on par with Limbaugh's against Sandra Fluke and said the two should not be held to a double standard.[22] It is unclear whether this boycott took a toll on ad revenue for the show or contributed to his demotion from primetime in 2013.

Of course, advertiser defection may or may not ultimately limit outrage speech and behavior. Glenn Beck's transition to Internet television and then ultimately to DishTV, may have reduced his audience size, but there is no evidence that his outrage levels have diminished, and they may have increased now that he is freed from the constraints of terrestrial cable. The jury is also still out for Limbaugh. We do not yet know if such losses in revenue will ultimately alter the way Rush Limbaugh speaks on air.

Regulation and the Courts

Regulatory and legal changes have also shaped the Outrage Industry. As we have discussed, deregulation of mass media during the 1980s and 1990s contributed tremendously to the growth of the industry. In terms of the content of political commentary, the elimination of the Fairness Doctrine in 1987 fundamentally altered the media industry. Given that there is more outrage emanating from conservative media than from their liberal counterparts, it is not surprising that some liberal politicians indicate that they would like to reinstate some form of a Fairness Doctrine. In the wake of the Arizona shootings, Representative Jim Clyburn (D-S.C.) said he would welcome a new Fairness Doctrine. Like previous calls for such rules, Clyburn's went nowhere. Relatively few Democrats regard such an effort as realistic. Conservative commentators, however, welcome liberal Democrats' effort to reinstate, as it fits their ongoing narrative of political persecution. When Clyburn made his remarks, conservative talk radio reacted with a fury. Although no legislation was actually introduced, Rush Limbaugh told his listeners that Clyburn's was a "Hush Rush bill."[23]

It might seem that given the ad hominem attack and misrepresentative exaggeration, outrage discourse would be muzzled by the threat of litigation. Not so. Although there are laws against written (libel) and spoken (slander) defamation of character, court cases in the United States have firmly sided with the principle of freedom of expression;[24] judges have clearly articulated a concern that more restrictive standards on what can be said about public figures could have a chilling effect on journalism. We find hosts are often threatened with lawsuits, but they rarely materialize, and the ones that do are almost always dismissed. In effect then, First Amendment protections have allowed outrage outlets to make questionable and often damaging statements about those in government and politics.

Even if plaintiffs are unlikely to win a defamation suit, the threat of litigation looms over parts of the industry. Commentators do worry about being sued, but those with shallow pockets bear the brunt of this anxiety. For this group, having to hire a lawyer can be penalty enough. An editor of a highly trafficked but poorly resourced liberal blog told us, "We are very careful. I have probably studied defamation, libel, slander and the First Amendment as much as any lawyer who works in media. You have to know what is okay, because it's not just a legitimate lawsuit that can cause a small publishing operation all kinds of trouble. A frivolous lawsuit can do the same thing. It's not going to drag on very long, but you are still going to have to stop everything that you're doing and pay someone hundreds of dollars an hour until it's clear.... So, we are careful. We are a political satire operation and political satire is very well protected constitutionally. So, as long as our focus and our targets are public figures in the political arena, we are okay." Those with large media organizations behind them need not have these apprehensions and can instead rely on the moat around the First Amendment to keep them out of trouble.[25] A Supreme Court verdict against an outrage outlet could affect the industry in significant ways, but contemporary jurisprudence offers little reason to expect such a decision in light of our national commitment to free speech. The U.S. case stands in contrast to democratic countries that do have restrictions on hate speech, such as Canada, Australia, Poland, France, and Britain, which went so far as to legally ban Michael Savage from entering the country on the grounds that his intolerance fosters hatred and might promote inter-community conflict.[26]

A Market for Conventional Political Opinion?

One way outrage-based content might be limited is through competition from more conventional political opinion alternatives. There is no shortage of conventional political opinion in the media today—voices that are opinionated and partisan, but which treat their subjects with civility even as they make their arguments. The Internet has vastly expanded the reach of the mainstream news outlets (including websites of the broadcast networks), giving the voices found in their opinion pieces greater reach than the ratings and circulation numbers suggest. Of the 25 most heavily trafficked news sites on the web, all but two are legacies of mainstream sites (such as the *New York Times*) or news aggregators (like *Yahoo*).[27] More political opinion writers have been added to broaden the content of newspaper websites, including such prominent bloggers as Nate Silver of the *New York Times* and Ezra Klein of the *Washington Post*. The content on the television news sites is extensive—and often include opinion pieces. CNN boasts a particularly deep opinion section. Conventional political opinion work can also be found on political websites unaffiliated with newspapers (such as *Politico* and *Salon*) and the tone in the opinion pages and blogs of many newsmagazines (such as *Time*, *National Review*, and *American Prospect*) can usually be described as respectful. In short, cooler debate abounds, but it is deeper in print and online than on television or radio, where outrageous opinion dominates. It is likely that the heavy traffic on traditional news sites affords them the opportunity to avoid using shock tactics. Advertisers come for the newsreaders. Political blogs that are exclusively opinion based, particularly those unaffiliated with legacy media, find themselves scrambling for attention and competing for audiences in ways more similar to cable news and talk radio. We do not mean to suggest that there are not tempered opinions in the blogosphere, but we find the top political blogs are outrageous. What's more, as we have shown, outrage is on the rise even in traditionally stately spaces. Overall, the presence of non-outrageous political opinion alternatives has done little to undercut the success of the Outrage Industry.

THE FUTURE OF OUTRAGE?

While there is concern about the vitriol and misinformation that characterizes outrage, the structural conditions that support the genre have not been significantly transformed by boycotts, regulatory retrenchment, or competition from less hyperbolic peers. This is not to say that the meteoric rise of outrage will continue. On the contrary, there are signs that outrage may have a saturation point. With Al Jazeera's purchase of Current TV in 2013, a second progressively oriented political media network appears to be off the table at this point, as Al Jazeera is using the network for its "real estate" rather than its content; stations that had been broadcasting Current TV began broadcasting Al Jazeera America. Importantly, though, some speculate that Current TV's inability to gain traction is best explained by the fact that it had opted for a softer, less political approach and had not been ideological *enough*.[28] More outrageous content might have been more commercially successful; it is difficult to say, but for the time being there is no analogous network on the horizon. Similarly, RightNetwork, which launched in 2010, stalled before the end of 2011 and went out of business without so much as a whimper. And as we detail in Chapter 4, after a dramatic rise in the number of talk radio stations, it appears as though the industry is undergoing a modest contraction as advertising has softened.

Still, there may be room for growth on the left, where the industry has less maturity. While we may not see another Current TV in the next few years, we would expect to see outrage-based left-leaning content expand on MSNBC, for example, as the network takes cues from its most profitable programming. This seems less likely on radio where trade magazines suggest that liberal talk has flatlined or decreased, in spite of somewhat higher visibility among radio programs such as the *Ed Schultz Show*. Still, hope springs eternal among liberals that left-leaning talk radio will eventually find a larger audience.

In terms of tone, the upper limits of outrage have been tested at various points over the years: by Don Imus's reference to the Rutgers women's basketball team as "nappy headed hos," Michael Savage's anti-Muslim tirades, Glenn Beck's analogies between the Obama administration and the Third Reich and his accusation that Obama is a racist, and Rush Limbaugh's relentless browbeating of Sandra Fluke; but as we have shown, these are not isolated incidents. Outrage is commonplace, and most frequently ignored or enjoyed. What's more, while certain inflammatory cases have captured national attention, there are equally egregious attacks that fly under the radar—for example, when liberal Mike Malloy makes stunningly vitriolic and vicious ad-hominem attacks on Republican leaders. Perhaps lower profile hosts—Malloy, as noted in Chapter 5, is in only thirteen markets—are more likely to escape scrutiny and deemed as less threatening if/when uncovered. But it does seem that there is a threshold for the level of controversy with which advertisers are willing to be associated. "Pop" to break through the clutter is invaluable in a sea of alternatives, but when escalated to an explosion, judicious marketers begin to retreat, some to return but others to opt for hosts who offer more predictability: when in doubt, Bill O'Reilly might contain risk in a way Glenn Beck proved he could not.

We also expect to see a continued hybridization of political and entertainment media—perhaps not in the form of *Sarah Palin's Alaska* or *Bristol Palin: Life's a Tripp*, reality shows which failed miserably, but instead in political satire à la Stephen Colbert and Jon Stewart, whose style already trickles into programs like the Rachel Maddow Show. There may also be more use of humor, drama, and intrigue in outrage venues and in the routine presence of entertainment news and heart-tugging stories as key features on conventional news programs on networks such as CNN, ABC, NBC, and CBS. From Oscar nominations and American Idol winners to Kardashian weddings and Lance Armstrong's doping, the resilience of these stories is assured by advertisers' affinity for light news, the public fascination with celebrity culture, and the benefits of cross-promotion in a world where conventional advertisements are less reliable. Political documentaries are another arena where we see this hybridization, and with the tools of production and distribution largely democratized, we can expect to see more of them. Infotainment isn't necessarily a bad thing for democracy, particularly when such media drive audiences to seek out additional information, and we expect to see it deepen.

SOME PARTING RECOMMENDATIONS

We hope that as the media space continues to grow, new voices and perspectives will join the broader curriculum of political information, analysis, and opinion that already exists. We value free speech and see outrage as having a place in this landscape. But that does not mean that its consequences should be ignored. Despite the pleasure that many derive from outrage-based content and the genre's potential to make people care about politics, the impact on democratic practices such as political discussion in our communities, tolerance, open-mindedness, collaboration, informed decision-making, and bipartisanship is concerning. We offer a few modest recommendations to promote healthy political media and encourage more informed consumption of outrage.

First, whereas we do not think outrage is generally a matter for the courts—controversial political voices are the very reason the First Amendment exists—access to good-quality political information is the foundation of democracy and should be of the utmost importance to Congress. If citizens vote for candidates or ballot measures, sign petitions, wage protests, work on campaigns, or communicate their preferences to elected officials and these actions are informed by inaccurate or deeply distorted information, or by misguided distrust and fear, the legitimacy of these vital civic behaviors is rendered suspect. As Chapter 3 illuminated, early understandings of the role of the market in mass communications were far more skeptical and vigilant, and focused on ensuring that market forces did not encroach on the public interest. Deregulation altered the relationship between mass media and the marketplace in ways that appear to have taken their toll on the public interest. We think it important that Congress reevaluate the current regulatory environment. If ownership patterns and economic imperatives are creating a media space that is detrimental to democratic processes, protections should be put in place to improve that environment. It may again be time to exercise some of the caution present in early regulatory approaches to mass media.

We also support the development of faster, more visible fact checking by independent observers. We are inspired by the work at PolitiFact.com and FactCheck.org, and encourage nonpartisan civic organizations with related concerns to join these efforts. In the interest of consumer protection we hope that other news organizations and voluntary associations increase their support of fact checkers. While these existing sites are reliable and highly respected, neither is able to fully monitor even the top outrage personalities, yet this is an essential step in identifying misinformation. We would recommend that in addition to regular fact checking, watchdog groups create reliability scores (akin to voting records) for key programs and blogs, to offer a comparative tool for evaluating the trustworthiness of different venues.

We encourage the public support of elected and appointed officials who demonstrate flexibility, open-mindedness, and willingness to compromise. Certainly, at times, politicians can and should stand on principle, but we also rely on them to address pressing public issues. In this spirit, it is often preferable to support not our team, but team players. Public preferences in one election will shape future nominees as well as candidates' perceptions of what the public wants. In this vein, we also encourage journalists and news organizations to highlight political collaboration as much as political conflict.

We also call on corporations to be heedful that while advertising is a way to reach consumers, it is also a form of support: a vote for the content of the programs where the ads are placed. This requires a mindfulness that is often left out of the equation in an advertising world where outside agencies seek access to desired demographics at the most advantageous rates. In the wake of the Sandra Fluke episode, Ford's social media director told a reporter from Bloomberg that he was unaware their ads were being placed on Limbaugh, explaining that Ford had purchased time in a particular advertising package, and in the advertising agency's overall allocation of time, some ads ended up on that show. Ford subsequently issued instructions to its media buyers that their ads were not to play on the Limbaugh show any more.[29]

We recommend that businesses include statements on advertising in their codes of ethical behavior and include these principles in future advertising contracts. In placing advertisements, ad agencies present a contract on behalf of their clients containing detailed stipulations and restrictions on placement. For most, these restrictions are to protect the integrity of the brand and to keep adequate distance between their ads and those of competitors. These specifications should be extended to include a statement on advertising. While businesses have varying priorities and will surely create different statements, it seems likely

that some might refuse to place advertisements in venues that deni-
grate their employees and shareholders, such as in media environments
where offensive remarks are made about women; racial, religious, and
ethnic minority groups; members of the LGBT community; and other
vulnerable constituencies.[30] As we have shown, the driving force behind
outrage's new visibility is commercial success; such shifts in advertiser
preferences provide direct and consequential pressure to shift public
discourse.

NOTES

1. It is worth noting that among them is George Noory, who, while white, is Arab-
   American, a rarity in American talk radio. See *Talkers Magazine* for the full list of
   top hosts, the vast majority of whom use an outrage-based format: http://www.
   talkers.com/top-talk-radio-audiences/, as of February 2, 2013.
2. Ronald N. Jacobs and Eleanor Townsley, *The Space of Opinion* (New York: Oxford
   University Press, 2011).
3. As David Mayhew documents, between 1946 and 1990 divided government per se
   did not make a major difference in the ability of the national government to enact
   major legislation. *Divided We Govern* (New Haven, CT: Yale University Press, 1991).
4. "Soledad O'Brien Presses Richard Mourdock over His Refusal to Compromise in
   the Senate," *Mediaite* May 9, 2012, http://www.mediaite.com/tv/soledad-obrien-
   presses-richard-mourdock-over-his-refusal-to-compromise-in-the-senate/, as of
   August 28, 2012.
5. For a more detailed explanation of the relationship of these media to dysfunction
   in Congress, see Thomas E. Mann and Norman J. Ornstein, *It's Even Worse than It
   Looks* (New York: Basic Books, 2012), 31–80.
6. Amy Gutmann and Dennis Thompson, *The Spirit of Compromise* (Princeton, NJ:
   Princeton University Press, 2012), 123.
7. *Rush Limbaugh Show*, September 16, 2010.
8. As determined by Club for Growth: http://www.clubforgrowth.org/.
9. Although it isn't our focal concern here, and we have not analyzed these sites systematically, it is worth noting that the amount of outrage varies among ideological
   watchdog groups. Accuracy in Media, for example, uses far less outrage than does
   the Media Research Center.
10. http://mediamatters.org/blog/2012/12/31/10-dumbest-things-fox-said-about-
    climate-change/191859.
11. The Giffords shooting stands out in this regard because the violence was politically
    motivated. In subsequent mass shootings, such as those in Aurora, Colorado, and
    Newtown, Connecticut, in 2012, public outcry focused more on media violence
    and gun control than on political rhetoric.
12. http://articles.latimes.com/2011/jan/08/nation/la-na-giffords-shooting-
    media-20110109; and "Remarks by the President at a Memorial Service for the
    Victims of the Shooting in Tucson, Arizona," The White House, January 12, 2011,
    http://www.whitehouse.gov/the-press-office/2011/01/12/remarks-president-
    barack-obama-memorial-service-victims-shooting-tucson, as of June 5, 2013.

13. "Ann Coulter vs. Piers Morgan on 'Retard' Comment and Racism," *Real Clear Politics*, October 26, 2012, http://www.realclearpolitics.com/video/2012/10/26/ann_ coulter_vs_piers_morgan_on_retard_comment_and_racism.html, as of June 5, 2013.

14. See, for example, Kate Kenski, Kevin Coe, and Steve Rains, *Patterns and Determinants of Civility in Online Discussions*, National Institute for Civil Discourse, October 13, 2012, http://nicd.arizona.edu/research-report/patterns-and-deter- minants-civility, as of January 11, 2013.

15. "About Us," Center for Civil Discourse, http://www.umb.edu/civil_discourse/ about, as of June 5, 2013.

16. *Crossfire*, October 15, 2004.

17. *The Rumble in the Air-Conditioned Auditorium: O'Reilly vs. Stewart 2012*, October 6, 2012.

18. Ibid.

19. *Colbert Report*, October 17, 2005.

20. *Crossfire*, October 15, 2004.

21. Andrew McFarland documents more success with boycotts sponsored by advocacy groups in Europe, most notably in the Scandinavian countries: *Boycotts and Dixie Chicks: Creative Political Participation at Home and Abroad* (Boulder, CO: Paradigm Publishers, 2011).

22. MRC director Brent Bozell's letter to the chairman of Comcast can be found here: http://newsbusters.org/blogs/brent-bozell/2012/03/15/bozell-comcast-chief- fire-ed-schultz.

23. Keach Hagey, "Fairness Doctrine Fight Goes On," *Politico*, January 16, 2011, http://www.politico.com/news/stories/0111/47669.html, as of January 11, 2013.

24. See *Hustler Magazine v. Falwell*, 485 U.S. 46 (1988); and *New York Times v. Sullivan* 376 U.S. 254 (1964).

25. Interestingly, outrage hosts bring lawsuits against others. Michael Savage, for example, sued the Council on American-Islamic Relations (CAIR), seeking damages for copy- right infringement after the council posted segments of his show to allow its members to hear his anti-Islamic remarks. The case was dismissed, as CAIR's usage qualified as fair use. "Judge Tosses Savage's Suit Against Islamic Group," *USA Today*, July 26, 2008, http://usatoday30.usatoday.com/life/topstories/2008-07-26-1661046984_x.htm, as of June 6, 2013.

26. "Radio's Savage Wants UK to Remove Name from Banned List," *CNN.com*, May 7, 2009, http://www.cnn.com/2009/SHOWBIZ/05/07/us.savage.banned/, as of June 6, 2013.

27. Tom Rosenstiel, "Five Myths about the Future of Journalism," *Washington Post*, April 7, 2011, http://www.washingtonpost.com/opinions/five-myths-about-the- future-of-journalism/2011/04/05/AF5UxiuC_story.html, as of August 29, 2012.

28. Paul Jay, "Failure of Current TV—Gore Wouldn't Take on Bush," *Truthout*, January 9, 2013, http://truth-out.org/news/item/13806-failure-of-current-tv-gore-wouldnt-take- on-bush, as of June 6, 2013.

29. Edmund Lee, "Limbaugh Clash Has Advertisers Recalculating Web's Power: Tech," *Bloomberg*, March 15, 2012, http://www.bloomberg.com/news/2012-03-15/limbaugh- clash-has-advertisers-recalculating-web-s-power-tech.html, as of August 27, 2012.

30. This is not difficult to accommodate. As we noted in Chapter 4, after sponsors began deserting Rush Limbaugh's show, Clear Channel sent a memorandum to its adver- tising staff instructing them to move ad placements away from shows that might offend and to other Clear Channel properties for sponsors who requested it.

APPENDIX

✧✦✧

Methods Appendix

The five data-focused chapters in this book each draw upon a distinct data set. Chapter 2 ("Mapping Outrage") is based upon data acquired in a large-scale quantitative content analysis of outrage programs and blogs. In-depth, semi-structured, qualitative interviews with industry experts in the various media sectors are the heart of Chapter 4 ("It's a Business"), although it also benefits from insights gleaned by monitoring relevant trade publications (e.g., *Talkers* magazine for talk radio). Chapter 5 ("Political Anxiety and Outrage Fandom") is also built around in-depth, semi-structured, qualitative interviews. These interviews were conducted with self-identified fans of outrage-based programming. A second source for Chapter 5 is a database built around qualitative content analytic research on cable television and talk radio hosts. The chapter on the Tea Party (Chapter 6, "Mobilizing Outrage") uses still another set of in-depth interviews, in this case with founders, presidents, and coordinators of various Tea Party chapters around the country. This chapter also draws heavily on an original database on the 2010 congressional elections, a key element of which is the incorporation of blog coverage of House and Senate primary contests. Finally, in Chapter 7 ("Continuity, Change, Synergy") we utilize case studies to draw out the impact of the Outrage Industry. Interviews also inform sections of this chapter. In this Appendix we offer more detail on the methods used.

QUANTITATIVE CONTENT ANALYSIS

In Chapter 2 we report the results of an ambitious content analysis of cable television, talk radio, political blogs, and conventional newspaper columns. Our sampling procedures are detailed here.

Television

For each media sector we closely monitored content and then used statistical analysis to develop a deeper understanding of the extent to which outrage was embedded in the substance of the commentary. For cable news analysis programs, we focused on eight popular offerings. For the purposes of a establishing a baseline, we added two comparisons: a conventional interview program and conventional cable news coverage.

We included the following programs in the analysis:

Program	Network	Show Type
O'Reilly Factor	Fox Cable	News Analysis
Hannity	Fox Cable	News Analysis
Glenn Beck	Fox Cable	News Analysis
Countdown w/ Keith Olbermann	MSNBC	News Analysis
Rachel Maddow Show	MSNBC	News Analysis
Hardball with Chris Matthews	MSNBC	News Analysis
Lou Dobbs Tonight	CNN	News Analysis
Campbell Brown	CNN	News Analysis

Cable News Comparison

Situation Room with Wolf Blitzer	CNN	News (some commentary)

Traditional Interview Comparison

Meet the Press	NBC	Interview

Our primary unit of observation is the *episode* (rather than a single segment with a guest). An episode is a date-specific presentation of a program.

We chose one television hour as the length of observation for each episode (we did not code commercials, meaning that most observations are from 42 to 44 minutes of running time). Because the *Situation Room* is three hours in length, we coded just one hour of each episode, rotating which hour was coded on a weekly basis. Otherwise we coded one episode per week for each program over the course of 10 weeks commencing on February 9, 2009. To avoid systematic irregularities, we used a rotation chart to ensure that episodes airing on all weekdays were included. For example, the first week, we coded the Monday episode of the *O'Reilly Factor*, and the Tuesday episode of *Hannity*. The second week we coded the Tuesday episode of the *O'Reilly Factor* and the Wednesday episode of *Hannity*, and so on.

Talk Radio

We sampled from the list of all-talk radio programs with the largest audiences and used those that had programs available in audio archives (this constrained our options for liberal programming, as described in Chapter 2) and added two comparisons: a conventional news programs and a conventional talk radio interview program:

Program	Syndicator	Show Type
Rush Limbaugh Show	Premiere Radio Networks	Conservative
Savage Nation	Talk Radio Network	Conservative
Hugh Hewitt Show	Salem Radio Network	Conservative
Laura Ingraham Show	Talk Radio Network	Conservative
Mike Gallagher Show	Salem Radio Network	Conservative
Mark Levin Show	Cumulus Media Networks	Conservative
Alan Colmes Show	Fox News Radio	Liberal
Thom Hartmann Program	Air America Radio	Liberal
Diane Rehm Show	NPR	Comparison
Morning Edition	NPR	Comparison

As with television, our unit of observation is the episode and we used one radio hour as the length of observation for each case, rotating which hour was coded on a weekly basis. We coded one hour of an episode per week for each program over the course of 10 weeks commencing on February 9, 2009. To ensure that episodic irregularities were avoided, we used a rotation chart so that episodes airing on all weekdays were included, as we did for television shows.

Political Blogs

We were interested in political speech that circulates widely and, consequently, sought the political blogs that are most heavily trafficked. In light of the varied flaws in different authority and traffic rankings we opted for a muti-layered approach to sampling.[1]

First, we created a combined master list of conservative blogs (1) identified by name on the *Technorati* authority ranking[2] for conservative blogs http://technorati.com/blogs/directory/politics/conservative (top 10 blogs as of 12/16/08), (2) listed as top conservative blogs on blogs.com[3] http://www.blogs.com/topten/10-popular-conservative-blogs/, and (3) provided by blogger Scott Martin[4] at http://www.conservatismtoday.com/my_weblog/2008/08/conservatism-to.html (top 10 listed). We also created a combined master list of (1) liberal blogs identified by name on the *Technorati* authority ranking for liberal blogs http://technorati.com/blogs/directory/politics/liberal (top 10 blogs as of 12/16/08), (2) the top liberal blogs listed on blogs.com http://www.blogs.com/topten/10-popular-liberal-blogs/, and (3) the Top Ten Liberal Blogs published by Heather Pidcock[5] on *Associated Content* http://www.associated-content.com/article/1013308/top_ten_liberal_political_blogs.html?cat=15.

After omitting the blogs on the master list that were either ideological but not explicitly political, or which were political but more often addressed other matters, we utilized Alexa rankings to determine the most heavily trafficked blogs on both the liberal and conservative lists.

Based on these rankings, we examined the top blogs closely, determining which were primarily political (no more than 25% nonpolitical content) and purged from the roster those that failed to meet this threshold. Our final selections were the following:

Liberal Blogs	Conservative Blogs
Huffington Post	Townhall
Daily Kos	Michelle Malkin
Talking Points Memo	Hot Air
Crooks and Liars	Right Pundits
Think Progress	Gateway Pundit
Wonkette	Power Line
Firedoglake	Hit and Run
MyDD	Little Green Footballs
Orcinus	Ace of Spades
Hullabaloo	Moonbattery

Next, we sampled the first post time stamped at or after 12:00 PM on a predetermined weekday during the sampling period (February 9–April 17, 2009), again rotating days to avoid cyclical patterns. The unique composition of some of these blogs required an additional rule to ensure the integrity of the sampling:

- *Huffington Post*: Coders went to "The Blog" (with the megaphone icon), then Politics, then sampled as described above (The *Huffington Post* is obviously a very different type of blog today than it was in 2009.)
- *Townhall*: Coders selected the "Blog" tab (rather than "Your Blogs") from the buttons across the masthead, and sampled as described above.
- *HotAir*: Coders selected "The Blog" and sampled as described above.
- *Michelle Malkin*: Coders sampled from the blog portion of the site (right-hand column) rather than from the syndicated articles.

For each post sampled, researchers coded text, embedded images, and embedded films, but not linked news stories or other blog posts.

Newspaper Columns

We monitored the five most widely syndicated conservative newspaper columnists and the five most widely syndicated liberal newspaper columnists as identified by the *Media Matters Op Ed Report*.[6] We included the following columnists in the study:

Columnist	Syndicator	Political Perspective
George Will	Washington Post	Conservative
Kathleen Parker	Orlando Sentinel	Conservative
Cal Thomas	Tribune Media	Conservative
Charles Krauthammer	Washington Post	Conservative
David Brooks	New York Times	Conservative
Ellen Goodman	Boston Globe	Liberal
Leonard Pitts Jr.	Miami Herald	Liberal
Maureen Dowd	New York Times	Liberal
E. J. Dionne	Washington Post	Liberal
Eugene Robinson	Washington Post	Liberal

We sampled one column per week per columnist for the same number of weeks covered for TV and radio. We used a rotating day schedule, adding an alternative day when necessary (e.g., for columnists who do not write daily). Each column was coded in its entirety.

MEASUREMENT

Following are thumbnail descriptions that focus on the underlying concepts that we attempted to measure. The codebook has fuller definitions along with a range of examples that fall within the boundaries of each variable. For each case, we coded the number of "incidents" of each variable, capping it at six or more. We also included measures for overall tone and overall amount, to allow the coder to give a more qualitative assessment of the tenor of the case. In those variables, coders opted from a range of choices from 0 indicating that the tone was more aptly described as "conventional political discourse" as defined by the study to 4 indicating that this was very intense outrage, rarely found in political media.[7]

Insulting Language

This variable is intended to measure whether the author or speaker uses insulting language in reference to a person, group of people, branch of the government, political party, or other organization (or their behaviors, planned behaviors, policies, or views). For example, "asinine" in reference to a person or group's behavior is insulting language, but if the person or group is *called* "asinine," this falls under the "name-calling" variable.

Name-Calling

A measurement of whether the author or speaker engages in name-calling in reference to a person, group of people, branch of the government, political party, or other organization. Affectionate, light-hearted teasing was weeded out. Rather, name-calling language is characterized by words and context that make the subject look foolish, inept, hypocritical, deceitful, or dangerous.

Emotional Display

This variable is intended to capture audio and/or visual emotional displays in reference to a person, group of people, branch of the government, political party, or other organization (or their behaviors, planned behaviors, policies, or views). In printed text, such as that in blog posts or on web pages, it is unlikely to appear often but is most likely be communicated through "shouting" via the deliberate use of all caps, multiple exclamation points, enlarged text, and so on. Emotional display is about the *form* of expression. See "emotional language" for emotional *content*, although the two will often present concurrently and in such cases each is to be noted.

Emotional Language

This variable measures instances when the author or speaker engages in verbal or written expressions of emotion in reference to a person, group of people, branch of the government, political party, or other organization (or their behaviors, planned behaviors, policies, or views). Emotion words related to anger, fear, and sadness are key indicators. Emotional language is about the literal content of what is said or written rather than how it is communicated.

Verbal Fighting/Sparring

This variable is for aggressive jousting between speakers. In radio and television it may take the form of dismissive interruptions or rude exchanges between guests/callers or between hosts and guests/callers characterized by a lack of civility.

Character Assassination

Does the author or speaker attempt to damage the reputation of a person, group of people, branch of the government, political party, or other organization by attacking their character? In politics, questioning the veracity of a statement is common and should not be confused with character assassination, which is more extreme. Saying someone was not honest in a reply to a journalist is not character assassination, but saying that someone is a liar who cannot be trusted does constitute character assassination. These are ad hominem attacks.

Misrepresentative Exaggeration

This variable measures whether the author or speaker engages in very dramatic negative exaggeration in reference to the behaviors, planned behaviors, policies, or views of a person, group of people, branch of the government, political party, or other organization, such that it significantly misrepresents or obscures the truth.

Mockery

This variable was designed to measure whether the author or speaker makes fun of the behaviors, planned behaviors, policies, or views of a person, group of people, branch of the government, political party, or other organization (or their behaviors, planned behaviors, policies, or views) to make the subject look bad or to rally others in criticism of the subject. Affectionate, light-hearted teasing should be weeded out. Instead, look for humor that is used to make the subject look foolish, inept, hypocritical, deceitful, or dangerous. It might also come in the form of a physical impersonation intended to make others laugh at the expense of the subject (e.g., Tina Fey as Sarah Palin).

Conflagration

This variable is intended to capture attempts to escalate non-scandals into scandals. The key trait is speech that overstates or dramatizes the importance or implications of minor gaffes, oversights, or improprieties. By non-scandal we refer to an episode, event, or trend that a learned, dispassionate observer would not consider significant or scandalous.

Ideologically Extremizing Language

This variable is intended to capture extremizing language used to critically describe a person, group of people, branch of the government, political party, or other organization (or their behaviors, planned behaviors, policies, or views). Usually the descriptive language will be used as an implicit slur rather than as simple description (e.g., "right-wing" or "far left").

Slippery Slope

This is intended to capture fatalistic arguments, which suggest that some behavior, policy, or decision is a small step that will inevitably pave the way for much more extreme behaviors, policies, or decisions.

Belittling

When an author or speaker belittles or demeans a person, group of people, branch of the government, political party, or other organization (or their behaviors, planned behaviors, policies, or views), the appropriate coding category is "belittling." This may be done in the context of mockery or exaggeration.

Obscene Language

This gauges use of obscene language in reference to a person, group of people, branch of the government, political party, or other organization (or their behaviors, planned behaviors, policies, or views). Here we mean *words that are not used on network television* (as a general rule), not simply insulting words. If the obscene language is used concretely to name-call, code under "name-calling."

QUALITATIVE CONTENT ANALYSIS

In Chapter 5 we report on a qualitative content analysis conducted of 10 outrage-based radio and television programs. The five radio programs used in this study were selected using Arbitron audience estimates for talk radio programs for fall 2009 (and updated in March 2010) and included, from highest to lowest, Rush Limbaugh, Sean Hannity, Glenn Beck, Michael Savage, and Mark Levin. Although Dr. Laura Schlessinger was rated higher than Mark Levin, she was omitted because the earlier quantitative content analysis determined that her program was not sufficiently political in nature. Nielsen Media Cable News Ratings for Spring 2010 were used to select the top five most-watched programs from television, which were the *O'Reilly Factor,* the *Sean Hannity Show,* and the *Glenn Beck Program* on Fox Cable News; and for MSNBC, *Countdown with Keith Olbermann* and the *Rachel Maddow Show,* as they were the most highly rated liberal programs. As described in Chapter 5, there were no liberal radio hosts popular enough to warrant inclusion in this study.

We sampled episodes over an eight-week period beginning June 7, 2010, and ending July 30, 2010. We sampled one episode of each program per week. For hosts with both radio and TV programs, we sampled from each format. Three of the radio programs, those of Limbaugh, Hannity, and Beck, were recorded from live radio broadcast on Rush Radio 1200 using Audacity. *Savage Nation* was downloaded via podcast and the audio for the *Mark Levin* show was downloaded from his website. For cable TV programs, Beck,

Hannity, and O'Reilly were recorded via a DVR. Maddow and Olbermann's shows were downloaded via podcast. To correspond with the hour-length of television programs, only one randomly selected hour of each three-hour radio show was included in each week's sample. As with the sampling for television and radio for the quantitative content analysis, we used a rotation chart to ensure that episodes airing on all weekdays were included. For the radio shows, we again used one-hour segments, rotating which hour was sampled. A handful of technical and other unforeseen complications (vacationing hosts, for example) emerged and required substitutions of alternate episodes.

We used observations made by the coding team that gathered the quantitative content analysis data from Chapter 2 as a jumping-off point to generate a series of themes, which we used to focus our analysis of this new data set. We set out to observe how hosts relate to their audience by focusing on key dimensions, including the following:

Building a sense of Community:

Researchers noted hosts' attempts to create a sense of community among the host and members of the audience. This can be accomplished in any number of ways, including, but not limited to:

- The host using words such as "we" and "us" to articulate shared values, beliefs, demands, or norms, if she or he seems to refer to the audience specifically, rather than the American people or the general public more broadly.
- Overtly or subtly suggesting that the host and audience are "in this together."
- By emphasizing the continuity of the link between host and audience, such as referring to previous shows and taking for granted that the audience member would understand the reference.
- Argot in the form of shared jargon likely to be understood only by repeat vewers/listeners. For example, recurring nicknames for fans or references to loyal viewers/listeners (e.g., "dittoheads"), political figures, historical events).
- Overt references to the audience being "members" of something (e.g., the viewing family, the movement, the fan site).
- The host indicating that he or she "understands" the audience members or their desires, concerns, etc. (especially as a result of past communication or a byproduct of reading fan emails or really listening to on-air callers).

By showing the audience that they have Relatability:

Researchers recorded hosts' attempts to create the sense that they are easy to relate to. This can be accomplished in any number of ways, such as:

- Personal disclosures such as confessions, personal anecdotes, or self-depre-cating humor, in which the overarching message is one that humanizes the host and creates an impression of the host as a typical or fallible person.
- Statements or biographical disclosures that intimate the host is middle or working class, or assertions that they should not be considered elite.
- References to being an "average guy" or to having plebian tastes/interests/hobbies or which create distance between the host and elite tastes/interests/hobbies.
- Colloquialisms, slang, and other devices that separate the host's speech from that of elites.
- Nonverbal behaviors such as directly gesturing to the audience (pointing at the screen while saying, "take a look") help to construct a scene in which the host is communicating one-to-one with the viewer.

By demonstrating his or her Authenticity:

Researchers monitored hosts' attempts to present themselves as sincere or honest. This can be accomplished in any number of ways, such as:

- The host citing sacrifices he or she has made for the job and other examples that demonstrate his or her dedication.
- Emotional displays, such as passionate or angry outbreaks intended to signal that the host is genuinely invested in the issue without having to say so overtly.
- Explicit references to being completely honest/truthful/trustworthy. In a milder form, references to freely speaking his or her mind, such as, "I'm just calling it like I see it" or "I'm not out to win a popularity contest," which conveys that the commentary is rooted in genuine, unfiltered testimony.

By Flattering the audience:

Researchers took note of hosts' attempts to flatter the audience. This can be accomplished in any number of ways, such as:

- Praising or otherwise expressing a positive evaluation of the audience (e.g., reference to the audience being smart, hard-working, principled, moral, benevolent, determined, strong).
- Suggesting that the audience will not be duped by the tricks of opponents (e.g., can see right through A, B, C or is not foolish enough to fall for X, Y, Z).
- Expressing their appreciation of or devotion to the audience.
- Assertions about the power of the audience to change or resist change (e.g., being able to do anything, being unwilling to take it any more, challenges such as I'd like to see them try…if in reference to the audience's inevitable and effective response).

By establishing his/her Credibility/Authority:

Researchers logged hosts' attempts to demonstrate that their perspectives are reliable. This can be accomplished in any number of ways, such as:

- Claiming to be an expert or "the best" source of information, for example, having written a book on the subject or having personally interviewed a political figure.
- Providing evidence, such as citing documents or public figures who support an argument.
- References to their credentials (e.g., professional, military, or academic).

By identifying Heroes and/or Anti-Heroes:

Researchers recorded hosts' attempts to position themselves (with or without the audience) as heroes and those who disagree with them as threatening/dangerous anti-heroes. This can be accomplished in any number of ways, such as:

- The host presenting him or herself as a representative for or crusader fighting on behalf of the audience.
- The host identifying "bad guys," implicitly placing the audience/host together in the role of innocents or "good guys." For example, designating an individual, party, business, or other group as an antagonist that in some way threatens or does harm to the host/audience. The focus is on the malicious intent of the villain.
- Talking tough by directly or indirectly addressing and berating the culprit (e.g., talking to the camera, "You listen to me, President Obama ...").
- The use of symbolic pollution. For example, linking a political figure to Hitler.

By creating a distinction between In-Groups and Out-Groups:

Researchers followed hosts' attempts to create a sense of cohesion among audience members and the host by contrasting this group with groups of people who do not share the audience's values, beliefs, norms, experiences, and so on. This can be accomplished in any number of ways, such as:

- Pointing to groups (e.g., the upper class, immigrants, progressives, Republicans, journalists, religious fundamentalists) who have opposing goals or who just don't get it and can't be counted on to be in step with the desires of the audience/host (in-group).
- When hosts remind the audience of their personal responsibility as members of the ("good") group.

As the episodes were reviewed, segments relevant to the research question were transcribed, along with the time that they occurred. They were organized by themes, and in cases where they fit multiple categories, the segments were cross-listed under all applicable themes. Notes were made to highlight specific phrases or lines, to include context, to indicate connections to quotes from other shows and/or hosts, and to make side-notes on the segments for use during the final analysis.

Please note that the methods involved with the fan interviews are not discussed here, as they are described in detail in Chapter 5.

INTERVIEWS WITH INDUSTRY EXPERTS

In many sections of the book we quote various experts on the topics at hand. Respondents for these "elite interviews" were selected via purposive sampling based on the knowledge they could share by virtue of their background, specific expertise, or position. We used these interviews to familiarize ourselves with the inner workings of the three media sectors. For example, for all the reading we did on the talk radio industry, the reasons for the rapid increase in the number of all talk stations was not entirely clear to us until we started to talk to people working in the industry. Much of what we read suggested a real renaissance for talk radio—that's certainly what radio companies and the trade press supported by radio industry advertising seemed to want to convey. The interviews made it clear that the surge in talk was born out of economic necessity because it had become increasingly difficult for radio stations to make money by playing music. Several helpful respondents took the time to walk us through the finances of running a radio station and instructed us on the broader financial structure of talk syndication.

Our subjects included those associated with cable television (including pundits), talk radio, and political blogs—the three industries we focus on in this book. In addition, we interviewed those who work in advertising as they furthered our understanding of the financial underpinnings of the Outrage Industry. By looking at advertising patterns, we were able to understand the relationships between audience demographics and outrage content. Most experts were interviewed just once but a small number acted as informants who allowed us to come back to them after the initial interview. We also interviewed select citizen group leaders working the issues we use as case studies in Chapter 7. In particular, we spoke with advocacy group leaders addressing immigration, the war in Afghanistan, and the nomination of Sonia Sotomayor to the Supreme Court.

We recruited respondents by introductions from a handful of informants who got us started with some key figures in their field, and then relied heavily on referrals. In other cases we sent introductory emails to those who worked in a given area, and culled interviewees from among the responses.

We used semi-structured in-depth questioning for all our interviews.[8] In such interviews, respondents answer in their own words and interviewers follow up to elicit richer detail. As Berry notes, this method carries some risk: "Open-ended questioning—the riskiest but potentially most valuable type of elite interviewing—requires interviewers to know when to probe and how to formulate follow-up questions on the fly. It's a high-wire act."[9]

With our elite respondents, we conducted the interviews "on background" and we told them they would not be quoted by name. Many said the confidentiality was not necessary and, for that reason, some interviewees are named in the text. Almost all of the elite interviews were done over the phone. Notes were taken contemporaneously and then filled in immediately afterward. In some instances we asked permission to record the interviews. In the end we amassed hundreds of pages of richly detailed interview data.

TEA PARTY INTERVIEWS

The largest set of interviews conducted for *The Outrage Industry* were with leaders of local Tea Parties around the country. These were elite interviews— the interview subjects were chosen based on their leadership positions—and followed the general methodology outlined earlier. We used purposive sampling to capture different regions of the country, including the affiliates of the different national Tea Party organizations. The respondents all held leadership positions in their local or state Tea Party and were generally either the founder, president, or coordinator. The names of those we approached were derived from lists of Tea Party leaders published by national coordinating bodies, from newspaper articles quoting individual leaders, and from utilizing various Internet search procedures. Subjects were initially approached by email and, as with most subjects for other topics in the book, the interviews were conducted over the phone.

In comparison to other interview cohorts, Tea Party activists were less open to being interviewed. Of those approached, including those contacted a second time if they didn't initially respond, only about a third agreed to be interviewed. We suspect this reflects an inclination to equate eastern academe with liberal elitism, as often heard in outrage venues. Still, those who did agree to be interviewed spoke openly, at length, and were unfailingly helpful.

One difference between the Tea Party interviews and the larger set of elite interviews is that some questions were asked of all respondents. For example, we asked each person about racial minorities and the Tea Party. A pattern in the answers quickly emerged and Chapter 6 includes our findings on this topic. These interviews, overall, were still flexible, allowing us to explore the many different areas to which the subjects led us.

Between industry experts, fans, Tea Party leaders, and advocacy group representatives, we completed interviews with 115 respondents.

CONGRESSIONAL PRIMARY DATABASE

Around mid 2009, we began to wonder whether the conservative mobilization at the congressional town hall meetings might expand into something broader and more substantive. Thus we began planning to monitor the congressional primaries in 2010. With the rising force of the Tea Party movement, we came to believe that any influence it might have would be easier to detect in the primaries as the national tide in November 2010 might make it difficult to discern any independent Tea Party effect.[10]

Our instincts certainly proved to be on target—so much so that this research module grew beyond our initial expectations. We developed a media profile of almost every House and Senate primary where there was an open seat or a viable challenge to an incumbent. We use the qualifier "viable" as there were some candidates who managed to get themselves on the ballot but whose campaign never became successful enough to warrant any meaningful press coverage. If all challengers fell into this category, we excluded such cases. Our principal goal was to obtain samples of the media coverage of each race. More specifically, for each race we read and inventoried a selection of stories from both conventional newspapers and political blog postings.

On the surface this might be seem straightforward, but as we point out in Chapter 6, conventional newspapers do not devote much space to primaries for the House of Representatives. (The Senate primaries were much easier to cover as they attracted national press in addition to coverage within the state.) Due to the light coverage we were not able to sample stories at random. For most House races we captured most of what we could find online from local papers. For those races where there was more plentiful coverage, our goal was to inventory a fair representation of the stories we came across.

Blog posts were an even greater challenge. Finding posts on a single congressional race within the larger political blogosphere is not quite like searching for a needle in a haystack but it does take some patience. Searches utilizing the key words that should work do not always succeed. Another problem is that while we could find some stories, we could never be sure of those we missed. We also used political round-up sites, which would summarize the daily postings for a particular race or set of races in a state, and then independently search for the larger stories to gain a broader set of perspectives. It is likely that our search procedures led us to the most widely visited sites but we acknowledge that trying to gain a representative set of blog posts for a congressional race is less than a perfect science.

In light of the difficulties of determining what was a representative sample of blog postings about individual races, we adopted the following strategies: First, we searched periodically rather than undertaking just one large-scale effort. Newly discovered blogs were then incorporated into the set of sites we reviewed at various intervals. Second, we followed up on cross-listed sites. Third, we continually looked for the names of activists mentioned in articles on a race in conventional newspaper or local TV websites. These names sometimes led us to sites of their own that we had not discovered before.

Despite the challenge, we are confident that we captured an important phenomenon described in the text: how blogs "signal" who is the purest of the pure in terms of ideological steadfastness. We included data from posts only, excluding material from the comments section.

NOTES

1. For an overview of such problems, see Eszter Hargittai, "The Population of Political Blogs," *Out of the Crooked Timber*, May 25, 2004, http://crookedtimber.org/2004/05/25/the-population-of-political-blogs/, as of January 4, 2013.
2. Technorati authority ratings reflect the number of other blogs which have linked to the blog in question in the last 90 days.
3. Blogs.com lists are based on editorial selection.
4. This is one informed lay reader's opinion.
5. This is one informed lay reader's opinion.
6. http://mediamatters.org/reports/oped/report, as of October 15, 2010.
7. The codebook defines conventional political discussion in the following way: Conventional argument, where disagreements are sharp and feelings are strong, is not outrage when discussion remains within the bounds of civility. In civil discussion, those on the other side are still regarded as worthy opponents whose ideas are legitimate and must be engaged. Humor is light-hearted and not aimed at diminishing the subject. Argument is aimed at convincing others based on the intellectual qualities of one's position, and not on the personal, deficient qualities of those espousing a contrary view.
8. Beth L. Leech, "Asking Questions: Techniques for Semistructured Interviews," *PS: Political Science and Politics* 35 (December 2002): 665–668.
9. Jeffrey M. Berry, "Validity and Reliability Issues in Elite Interviewing," *PS: Political Science and Politics* 35 (December 2002): 679.
10. See the discussion of the 2010 general election in Chapter 6 and in footnote 72.

INDEX

Figures, notes, and tables are indicated by "f," "n," and "t" following page numbers.

CPSIA information can be obtained
at www.ICGtesting.com
Printed in the USA
BVOW03s0428180817
492353BV00002B/8/P